CENTRES AND PERIPHERIES
OF PSYCHOANALYSIS

CENTRES AND PERIPHERIES OF PSYCHOANALYSIS

An Introduction to Psychoanalytic Studies

Edited by

Richard Ekins

and

Ruth Freeman

Foreword by

Joseph Sandler

London
KARNAC BOOKS

First published in 1994 by
H. Karnac (Books) Ltd.
58 Gloucester Road
London SW7 4QY

British Library Cataloguing in Publication Data

Centres and Peripheries of Psychoanalysis:
An Introduction to Psychoanalytic Studies
   I. Ekins, Richard II. Freeman, Ruth
   150.195

   ISBN 1 85575 091 0

Printed in Great Britain by BPC Wheatons Ltd, Exeter

ACKNOWLEDGEMENTS

Thanks are due to Cesare Sacerdoti of Karnac Books, to Wendy Saunderson of the University of Ulster, and to Klara Majthényi King of Communication Crafts for bringing this project to final fruition.

CONTENTS

NOTES ON CONTRIBUTORS   xi

FOREWORD

     Joseph Sandler   xiii

Introduction

     Richard Ekins   1

PART ONE
Centres of psychoanalysis

1. Anna Freud:

     a beacon at the centre of psychoanalysis

     Jean Murray   15

2. Melanie Klein and W. R. D. Fairbairn:

     the clinical foundations and explanatory concepts

     of their theories

     Thomas Freeman   54

3. The concept of transference:
   an introduction to its role
   in the psychoanalytic process
   Ruth Freeman 74

4. Countertransference:
   some clinical aspects
   Siobhan O'Connor 94

PART TWO
Peripheries of psychoanalysis

Psychoanalysis
and psychoanalytic psychotherapy

5. A psychoanalytic approach to the treatment
   of the schizophrenias in hospital practice
   Thomas Freeman 115

6. A psychotherapeutic approach
   to the understanding and treatment
   of a psychosomatic disorder:
   the case of burning mouth syndrome
   Ruth Freeman 129

Psychoanalysis
and the study of culture and society

7. Freud, religion, and the Oedipus complex:
   some reflections on the infantile origins
   of religious experience
   Peter Torney 143

8. Psychoanalysis and literature:
   a psychoanalytic reading of *The Turn of the Screw*
   Ronnie Bailie 169

9. Psychoanalysis, cinema, and the role of film
    in the psychoanalytic process
    Richard Ekins   193

APPENDIX:
A NOTE ON FREUD'S THEORY OF THE DREAM   215

REFERENCES   217

INDEX   235

NOTES ON CONTRIBUTORS

The Editors

DR RICHARD EKINS has been a Senior Lecturer in Sociology and Psychoanalysis at the University of Ulster since 1984. Since 1986 he has directed the Trans-Gender Archive at the University of Ulster at Coleraine. He is Honorary Secretary of the Northern Ireland Association for the Study of Psychoanalysis (NIASP) and a Candidate of the British Psychoanalytical Society. He has a private practice in psychoanalytic psychotherapy. He has published numerous papers and is the author of *Male Femaling* and co-author of *Gender Blenders*, both to be published by Routledge.

DR RUTH FREEMAN is a Senior Lecturer in Paediatric and Preventive Dentistry, Queen's University of Belfast. She is an Associate Member of NIASP and an Associate Member of the Association for Psychoanalytic Psychotherapy in the N.H.S. She has a private practice in psychoanalytic psychotherapy. She has published several articles that apply psychoanalytic theory and practice to various aspects of dentistry.

Additional authors

DR RONNIE BAILIE has been Lecturer in English Literature at the University of Ulster at Jordanstown since 1972. He is an Associate Member of NIASP and has a private psychoanalytic psychotherapy practice. He is the author of *The Fantastic Anatomist: A Psychoanalytic Study of Henry James.*

DR THOMAS FREEMAN was formerly Consultant Psychiatrist at the Anna Freud Centre, London. He is President of NIASP and is a Member of the British Psychoanalytical Society. He has published seven books and over 70 papers on aspects of psychoanalysis and psychiatry. His books include *The Psychoanalyst in Psychiatry* (Karnac Books, 1988) and *Development and Psychopathology* (Yale University Press, 1989).

MRS JEAN MURRAY is Senior Lecturer in Psychology at St. Mary's College, Belfast. She is Honorary Treasurer of NIASP and a Candidate of the British Psychoanalytical Society. She is a psychoanalytic psychotherapist in private practice with a special interest in child analysis.

DR SIOBHAN O'CONNOR is a Consultant Psychiatrist with Special Responsibility for Psychotherapy at Downshire Hospital, Northern Ireland. She is Chairperson of NIASP and a Candidate of the British Psychoanalytical Society. She has a private practice in psychoanalytic psychotherapy.

DR PETER TORNEY has been Lecturer in Sociology at the University of Ulster at Jordanstown since 1984. He is an Associate Member of NIASP and a Candidate of the British Psychoanalytical Society. He has a private practice in psychoanalytic psychotherapy.

FOREWORD

Joseph Sandler

Past President, International Psychoanalytical Association;
Emeritus Professor of Psychoanalysis, University College, London

A s Richard Ekins points out in his Introduction to this book, the field of "psychoanalytic studies" is undergoing a period of rapid growth. It is increasingly understood that psychoanalysis is not only a method of therapy, but a theory of mind, a theory of development and behaviour that can be applied in many areas. This book provides an excellent introduction to the broad field of applied psychoanalysis.

The origins of psychoanalytic theory lie in the clinical application of the psychoanalytic method, and a great part of the theory is based on observations made in the classical psychoanalytic setting. Yet it is an all-too-common mistake to equate present-day psychoanalysis with the work of Freud. There have been substantial developments in psychoanalytic thinking over the years, and the editors and authors of this book have clearly taken these into account.

The first part of the volume deals appropriately with clinical psychoanalytic concepts capable of being transferred from the analyst's consulting-room. Jean Murray shows clearly how Anna Freud, with her special interest in children, expanded the developmental point of view in psychoanalysis, tackling the issues of what constitutes normality and the relation between the child's innate potential and external environmental influences. All Anna Freud's work, including her study of mechanisms of defence and her elaboration of "developmental lines", is capable of wide application in the fields of child-rearing and education. Thomas Freeman reviews cogently the significant work of Melanie Klein and Ronald Fairbairn, and here again the potential applications of their work are evident.

The concept of transference is dealt with in a most interesting way by Ruth Freeman, who provides convincing examples of the different forms of transference seen during psychoanalytically orientated psychotherapy. As a final contribution to the first section, Siobhan O'Connor, in addition to a useful review of the countertransference concept, illustrates the way countertransference works through a variety of examples and clinical vignettes. She goes on to discuss the application of a knowledge of countertransference to the problems arising in the general psychiatric ward.

The special applications of psychoanalysis are considered in the second part of the book. Thomas Freeman provides us with a lucid explanation of a field in which he is an acknowledged expert—i.e. the psychoanalytic approach to treatment of schizophrenia in psychiatric practice. This is followed by Ruth Freeman's account of the "burning mouth syndrome". She draws on her experience as a psychotherapist and as a dental surgeon in applying psychoanalytic concepts to dentistry, in particular to psychosomatic problems in that field. She illustrates the psychogenic factor in "burning mouth syndrome" by a clear and convincing account of the psychotherapy of a woman with this condition.

The book concludes with three chapters on "applied" psychoanalysis. Peter Torney discusses early developmental factors entering into forms of religious experience. His chapter amply demonstrates that "the psychoanalytic exploration of the infantile origins of religion, far from disenchanting religion, issues a challenge also to theologians to be more adventurous in their thinking". Ronnie Bailie applies psychoanalytic concepts to literature through a consideration of Henry James' *The Turn of the Screw*, and concludes that its meaning may be most fully understood by examining James' early and unsatisfactory identifications.

The last chapter, by Richard Ekins, has the intriguing title of "Psychoanalysis, Cinema, and the Role of Film in the Psychoanalytic Process". Starting from the point of view that psychoanalysts need to be trained within a broad cultural and intellectual climate, he goes on to develop a comprehensive review of the literature on psychoanalysis and the cinema. This is followed by a discussion of the role of film in the psycho-analytic process, exemplified by detailed illustration of the role played by film in a patient's treatment. The chapter ends with a description of a dream of the author that appropriately demonstrates the interaction between cinema and psycho-analytic thought.

Although this book has been written by a number of authors, the editors have skilfully combined the chapters into a coherent whole. They and the other contributors are to be congratulated on a work of substance and importance—a testimony to the skill of a group of devoted psychoanalytically orientated psychotherapists in Northern Ireland. This group has developed under the influence of Thomas Freeman, and he deserves special praise for the level of the work he has fostered.

London
April 1994

CENTRES AND PERIPHERIES
OF PSYCHOANALYSIS

Introduction

Richard Ekins

The field of "psychoanalytic studies" is a rapidly growing area of study for students in higher education. Courses in psychoanalytic studies aim to provide a thorough grounding in psychoanalytic theory, as a basis for the application of psychoanalytic concepts to various fields in the humanities and social sciences, including literature, religion, social theory, and media studies. While such courses do not offer a vocational training in psychotherapy, they do examine the relations between psychoanalytic theory and clinical practice.

The field of psychoanalytic studies was formally institutionalized in the United Kingdom in 1988 (THERIP, 1994, p. 1), through *The Higher Education Network for Research and Information in Psychoanalysis* and its house journal, *The Psychoanalysis Newsletter*. The field has yet to be formalized in student textbooks. At present, students are directed to a sizeable and diverse range of books and papers, providing variously demanding treatments of theoretical and applied psychoanalysis. As such, the available literature remains scattered and difficult to assimilate. This book is designed to

1

meet the needs of students who seek, in one volume, a text that places emphasis upon core concepts and clinical material but reflects at the same time the range of applications in therapy and in the psychoanalytic study of culture and society. It is instructive to consider these two dimensions in terms of "centres" and "peripheries" of psychoanalysis. This introductory chapter unpacks the various interrelations between the centres and peripheries considered, with reference both to the overall standpoint of the book and its individual chapters.

Centres and peripheries in psychoanalytic theory

Psychoanalysis is many things to many people. To Freud, its founder, it was a science of unconscious mental processes, a study of the instinctual life, a developmental theory of psychosexual development and personality, a structural theory of personality, a therapy, a research method, a framework for applied studies, and a social movement.

Soon after publishing *The Ego and the Id* (1923b), his last major theoretical work, Freud (1924f [1923], pp. 197–198) enumerated the factors that he saw as making up the theory of psychoanalysis. In quick succession, he listed "emphasis on instinctual life (affectivity), on mental dynamics, on the fact that even the apparently most obscure and arbitrary mental phenomena invariably have a meaning and causation"; "the theory of psychical conflict and of the pathogenic nature of repression"; "the view that symptoms are substitutive satisfactions"; "the recognition of the aetiological importance of sexual life, and in particular of the beginnings of infantile sexuality"; and "the view that the mental does not coincide with the conscious, that mental processes are themselves unconscious and are only made conscious by the functioning of special organs (agencies or systems)". He completes the list by adding that "among the affective attitudes of childhood the complicated emotional relation of children to their parents— what is known as the Oedipus complex—came into prominence. It became even clearer that this was the nucleus of every case of neurosis, and in the patient's behaviour towards his analyst certain phenomena of his emotional transference emerged which came to be of great importance for theory and technique alike".

In the initial phases of the development of psychoanalysis, Freud was determined to see that his followers maintained their allegiance to these fundamentals. Those who did not were not welcome in the psychoanalytic movement. Dissenters either remained silent within psychoanalysis, or were vocal and left. Typically, they either fell into obscurity or formulated alternative systems that fared variously. This history of dissent has been well documented (Ellenberger, 1970; Kaufmann, 1980; Roazen, 1976).

However, even during Freud's lifetime this situation began to change. As Wallerstein adeptly puts it:

> For already in Freud's lifetime there arose the alternative Kleinian metapsychology with its focus shifted on to the centrality of the earliest life experiences within the matrix of the dyadic attachment between mother and child, and the dominance within that arena of the vicissitudes of the aggressive (or death) drives. Within this enlarged (as well as shifted) psychological focus onto the experiences of preoedipal life, the Kleinians felt enabled to deal therapeutically with patients suffering more severe pathology than did the close followers of Freud's metapsychology, with its focus on the centrality of the oedipal phase and the resolution of oedipally based conflict to which only the psychoneurotic patients who could develop so-called transference neuroses were felt to be amenable. [Wallerstein, 1990, p. ix]

Wallerstein continues:

> The history since then is a familiar one. Next came the development of the British object relational perspective with its wholly new metapsychology of an ego dedicated not to drive discharge but to object seeking, as a new independent or middle group between the Freudian and the Kleinian. Then, in subsequent years, came the Bionian

perspective as an extension from the Kleinian, and the Lacanian as a distinctively French and linguistically centred psychoanalysis. And in America—until that point the one region in the world where Freud's vision of a unified psychoanalysis had persisted through the hegemony of the ego psychological paradigm articulated in claimed descent from Freud's own late developing ego psychology—the rise and challenge of Heinz Kohut and his self psychology focused around the centrality of narcissism. [Wallerstein, 1990, pp. ix–x]

Contemporary psychoanalytic writers and practitioners face the daunting task of situating themselves within this very complex analytic scene. There are four major creative possibilities. Writers and practitioners can keep the original centre of psychoanalysis and return, again and again, to the fundamentals as set forth in Freud's writings, with a view to re-working the various contributions of contemporary psychoanalysis in their terms. They can consider the contributions of the alternative perspectives to be so great, or potentially so, that they warrant a shift in the theoretical centre of psychoanalysis to the favoured approach. They can revel in the diversity of approaches available and draw upon them, or extend them, depending on the purposes at hand. Psychoanalysis is a multi-centred thing. Finally, they can seek integrations at various levels.

In a book that focuses on clinical and applied studies, as this one does, it is particularly important to be clear about theoretical centres. So it should be pointed out at the outset that all the writings in this volume are centred in the first of the four approaches. That is to say, their theory, practice, and application are all rooted in Freud's own writings. This does not, of course, entail a mere biblical exegesis of Freud's work or its slavish following or application. That would be to curtail creative work. It would also be to ignore the very considerable developments that have taken place in psychoanalysis since Freud's death in 1939. Rather, the approach used here means utilizing a framework that incorporates all of Freud's "factors that go to make up this theory" in a way that can develop psychoanalysis within the framework but can, at the same time, confront the formulations and "findings" put forward by the various alternative centres within psychoanalysis.

Freud's approach is rooted in what might be termed "the developmental principle". Few in the psychoanalytic movement have taken Freud's developmental point of view more seriously than did Freud's daughter, Anna. Freud had recognized that psychoanalytic investigations of adults needed to be supplemented by the psychoanalytic study of the child (Freud, 1909b). Anna Freud pursued this line of research by combining systematic and prolonged direct observation of young children with child analysis. It was a direction she followed from the mid-1920s until her death in 1982, always situating her work within her father's developmental view of the fundamentals of psychoanalysis (Young-Bruehl, 1988). In chapter one, Jean Murray outlines the contributions of Miss Freud, demonstrating how she was able to incorporate new knowledge into the body of psychoanalytic theory through her multi-causal and anti-reductionist "assessments of development" (A. Freud, 1965a) in the normal and pathological child. Perhaps Anna Freud's greatest gift, says Murray, was "her ability to make the most difficult concepts clear and simple and to demystify the excessively academic and often dense language of psychoanalysis". Murray displays this ability in the handling of her chapter, which provides a fitting theoretical and clinical starting point for the volume.

It must be recognized that alternative theoretical frameworks do provide major alternative centres within the world-wide psychoanalytic movement (Fine, 1987). The contributors to this book, all of whom have worked under the aegis of members of the British Psychoanalytical Society, must, perforce, be sensitive to this fact. The unique feature of the British Society is its tripartite social structure, housing its separate "Kleinian", "Independent", and "Contemporary Freudian" groups (King & Steiner, 1991; Rayner, 1987). Melanie Klein's influence has been immense. Her work has led to a re-centring of psychoanalysis for many. Fairbairn (an Independent), on the other hand, has remained a more peripheral figure (Sutherland, 1989). However, he did provide us with the most coherent and systematic object relations theory that we have. In chapter two, Thomas Freeman addresses key aspects of these alternative centres in a considered treatment of the clinical foundations and explanatory concepts of the theories of both Klein and Fairbairn from the standpoint of the Freudian centre of this book.

Freud was led to replace his topographical model of the mind with the structural concepts of ego, superego, and id, as a result of his observation of the clinical manifestations of "resistance" (Freud, 1923b). Resistance arises whenever unacceptable ideas come near to consciousness.

In chapter three, Ruth Freeman links this line of thought with the central clinical concept of "transference". She notes how a resistance occurs when a memory of a past event involving shame or embarrassment is remembered, and how thoughts about the therapist arise but are frequently blocked from consciousness. These transferences arise in the course of treatment, when the patient "displaces" onto the therapist thoughts, feelings, attitudes, and attributes that properly belong to significant people in his past and then responds to the therapist accordingly. As Freeman demonstrates, clinical treatment proceeds very largely by the analysis of resistance and transference phenomena. Indeed, Freud (1914d) had asserted that the theory of psychoanalysis was an attempt to account for the clinical "facts" of transference and resistance. It is particularly appropriate, therefore, that Ruth Freeman should trace the development of the concept of transference in Freud's writings, before providing a series of clinical vignettes to illustrate the major aspects of the transference—the floating transference; the positive transference as resistance; the negative transference as resistance; and transferences in terms of psychic structures of superego, id, and ego.

Dream analysis remains pivotal to the Freudian centre of psychoanalysis, and Freeman illustrates a number of her vignettes with examples of dreams. This theme is returned to in subsequent chapters and, again, in the Appendix, which provides an important supplementary "Note on Freud's Theory of the Dream".

Freud first used the term "countertransference" in 1910 (1910d), remarking that the analyst can go no further in his treatment of patients than his own complexes and internal resistances permit. In chapter four, Siobhan O'Connor provides a fitting conclusion to part one in her consideration of this clinical concept, which has become increasingly central to contemporary psychoanalytic discourse. Noting both the broadening of the term in the literature after Freud and its increasing use as a therapeutic tool, O'Connor focuses on a range of clinical examples to illustrate the link between the emotions of the therapist and the therapist's experience with patients. The chapter shows how a sensitivity to the countertransference can illuminate both the therapist's self-understanding and his interactions with patients.

Centres and peripheries
in psychoanalysis
and psychoanalytic psychotherapy

Psychoanalysis is an intensive and specialist form of psychological treatment. In most places throughout the world it has come to entail 45- to 50-minute sessions, four to five times a week, for several years (Sandler, 1988). Inevitably, very soon after the establishment of psychoanalysis, attempts were made to provide a modified form of treatment based on less frequent sessions, or for shorter periods (Roazen, 1976).

Freud himself used to compare "the pure gold of analysis" with "the copper of suggestion", recognizing that an alloy would have to be struck if psychoanalytically inspired therapy were to be applied on a large scale (Freud, 1919a [1918]). It should not be forgotten, too, that psychoanalysis had its origins in the treatment of the neuroses, and only later came to be applied with varying success to the treatment of other disorders. Freud considered psychoanalysis to be quite inappropriate in the treatment of the psychoses, although essential for their understanding. With each application of psychoanalysis to different diagnostic categories—the perversions; character disorders; and the variously termed borderline, narcissistic, non-neurotic developmental disorders (Yorke, Wiseberg, & Freeman, 1989)—there were many who argued for adaptations of analytic technique, or in the frequency of sessions, to meet the particular problems confronted.

Furthermore, issues very soon emerged that had nothing to do with either diagnostic category or therapy. Psychoanalysis came to achieve a status that was frequently aspired to by modified or alternative therapies. In large measure, this explains the energy invested in the somewhat arcane recurring debates over nomenclature, so confusing to the uninitiated (Abram, 1992; Sandler, 1988).

We find it uncontentious that psychoanalysis has its centre in intensive trainings and in intensive treatments—those recognized by the International Psychoanalytical Association (IPA). We also find it useful to distinguish psychoanalysis from psychoanalytic psychotherapy and from analytical psychotherapy. We see psychoanalysis as being located at the centre of trainings, theories, and practices and, as such, holding the high ground that extends through the middle ground of psychoanalytic psychotherapies (entailing trainings and practice centred around two- to three-times-weekly treatment), through to the peripheries of analytical psychotherapy. Here, psychoanalytically informed treatment will be less intensive, even though the therapist's training may well be embedded in more intensive centres. Ideally, it will be so embedded.

Viewed in this light, the significant centre–periphery question then becomes: How might the findings of psychoanalysis be utilized in different peripheral settings? We take up this issue in the first two chapters of part two, where Thomas Freeman and Ruth Freeman consider central issues of therapy on the peripheries of psychoanalysis.

The schizophrenias are generally thought to be outside the remit of psychoanalytic treatment. Nevertheless, for the psychologically minded, the insights of psychoanalysis can prove of inestimable value in the understanding of the schizophrenic's world. The same insights may also be very useful in the management of such patients, as Thomas Freeman demonstrates in chapter five. Here, Freeman introduces the significance of the psychoanalytic approach to the treatment of the schizophrenias, with particular reference to the advantages and disadvantages of chemotherapeutic agents.

Psychoanalytic theory may, of course, be used to understand illness, or to treat it, or both. In chapter six, Ruth Freeman illustrates how psychoanalytic theory can be used to understand psychosomatic disorders, with particular reference to the case of burning mouth syndrome. At the same time, she demonstrates how analytical therapy based on psychoanalytic principles can also be helpful in the treatment of this condition.

Centres and peripheries
in applied psychoanalysis

Not so long ago, the meaning of applied psychoanalysis was relatively straightforward. It referred to the use of insights and concepts gained from clinical psychoanalysis to the study of various aspects of human nature, culture, and society. Studies in history, biography, literature, art, religion, mythology, and anthropology have been particularly prominent. More recently, the boundaries between so-called "pure psychoanalysis" and "applied psychoanalysis" have become increasingly blurred (Chasseguet-Smirgel, 1992; Schwartz, 1992; Wallerstein, 1992). The last three chapters of part two reflect both traditions. Chapters seven and eight, by Peter Torney and Ronnie Bailie, respectively, are illustrative of the mainstream tradition of applied psychoanalytic studies; whereas chapter nine, by Richard Ekins, is a deliberate exploration of the interrelations between so-called "pure psychoanalysis" and "applied psychoanalysis".

Returning to Freud's corpus, it must be said that clinicians frequently show little interest in his cultural and social works (Freud, 1907a, 1910c, 1912–1913, 1927c, 1930a, 1939a). On the other hand, psychoanalysis attracts a more intense interest than ever before amongst scholars in the humanities and social sciences. For the most part, however, the studies produced by such scholars are university-based and often politically motivated applications of psychoanalysis. From the standpoint of this book, an increasing number are so far removed from the clinical centre of psychoanalysis as to be almost beyond its peripheries (Wright, 1986).

Chronological study of Freud's work as a whole shows that from the outset Freud was interested in the interrelations between cultural life and the clinical situation (Paul, 1991). This is sometimes forgotten by those who associate Freud's cultural writings with his later work (Berliner, 1983). The last three chapters of part two return to this original Freudian tradition. In chapter seven, Peter Torney demonstrates the importance of Freud's central focus on the Oedipus complex for an understanding of his theories of the infantile origins of religious experience. Torney demonstrates how Freud's scattered comments on matters as seemingly diverse as religious scepticism, religious delusions, representations of the Devil, and religious conversion are unified, once they are rooted in the Oedipal constellation of early development. Torney concludes that the psychoanalytic exploration of the origins of religion, far from disenchanting religion, issues a challenge to theologians to be more adventurous in their thinking.

The psychoanalytic study of art and literature has a history almost as long as psychoanalysis itself. "The mechanism of poetry [creative writing] is the same as that of hysterical phantasies", wrote Freud in 1897 (Freud, 1950 [1892–1899]). Bailie notes, however, that the original and instinctual sources of art tend to be so heavily disguised that re-establishing the lost links by means of the application of psychoanalysis frequently appears both reductionist and implausible. In Henry James' *The Turn of the Screw*, however, the manifest topics and persons are so close to their latent sources that the text "reads like the relatively undistorted communication that it actually is". Bailie's treatment of James' classic in chapter eight provides, therefore, a particularly accessible study in the psychoanalytic reading of a literary text from the standpoint of a psychoanalytic criticism that remains wedded to the application of Freud's central insights.

The coming together of psychoanalysis, cinema, and film studies goes back as far as Freud's unwillingness to co-operate in G. W. Pabst's *Secrets of a Soul* (1926), the first film about psychoanalysis. In the final chapter, Ekins considers this confluence in terms of psychoanalysis *in* the cinema, the psychoanalytic study *of* the cinema, and the role of film in the teaching of psychoanalysis. He points to the widespread tendency in the literature to divorce theoretical studies from clinical material, and he addresses this gap in the literature by presenting material from a clinical case in which one film played a significant part in a patient's associations and treatment.

Freud, writing in the context of his ideal psychoanalytic training (Freud, 1926e, pp. 252–253), recommended that "peripheral" studies in culture and society should supplement its "centre"—in "depth psychology". Moreover, he considered that while psychoanalysts had nothing to lose by not being associated with the universities, the universities had everything to gain by incorporating psychoanalysis in their curriculum (Freud, 1919j [1918]). This book adopts Freud's views, so frequently honoured in the breach. It is the result of many years of collaboration between a number of specialists in a range of disciplines—all practising therapists, and all committed to the belief that psychoanalysis, therapy, and the university curriculum are best fostered in confluence.

PART ONE

CENTRES
OF PSYCHOANALYSIS

CHAPTER ONE

Anna Freud:
a beacon at the centre
of psychoanalysis

Jean Murray

Introduction

For the student intent on acquiring sound technique in psychoanalytic psychotherapy, there exists a wide range of competing theoretical schools. These schools range from those that claim to foster Freud's original formulations and his adherence to a drive structural model of psychic functioning, to those that replace the drive model with a quite different conceptual framework, in which relations with others (or "object relations") form the basis of all aspects of mental life. Within each of these two broad strands there are further differences of approach and related technical modifications—so much so that the beginning psychotherapist often finds it difficult to find a coherent conceptual framework in which to operate at a clinical level. Greenberg and Mitchell (1983) maintain that the various schools of psychoanalytic thought represent quite different visions of reality and, as such, cannot be integrated or combined. They attempt to clarify the clinician's dilemma by saying that "a theorist's attitude towards the drives determines his place in psychoanalytical circles" (p.

15

304). But is this really true? With the creation and elaboration of the structural model, Freud developed the concept of the ego. This heralded the development within classical psychoanalysis of a movement towards recognition of the ego as a powerful organizing aspect of the personality, which is in contact with external reality. This was coupled with discoveries within child analysis that demonstrated the importance of the external world on the development of the child and emphasized the importance of real experiences. Melanie Klein's entire motivational system remains within the drive structural model; and it was this very adherence to the drives that she used to justify her link with Freud. Finally, within the drive approach, there are theorists such as Mahler, Jacobson, Kohut, and even Kernberg, who purport to espouse the principles of drive theory but use a very different language and propose considerable modifications in technique.

In contrast to Greenberg and Mitchell, Tyson and Tyson (1990) claim that an integration of theories and models is essential in formulating a comprehensive view of how the personality is formed. I believe that an integration of theories is simply an unrealistic expectation of a beginning therapist. The consequence of this is that the beginning therapist faces a dilemma when seeking a theoretical framework within which to work. Such a theoretical framework cannot be imparted through teaching or instruction. It evolves slowly out of the experience of the training analysis, the supervision of work with patients, and the therapist's own continual struggle in trying to understand patients in analysis. Hill (1993), in outlining the experience of his own three Kleinian analyses, shows how different therapists within any one tradition proceed very differently with the analytic task. One way out of this dilemma is to set oneself within a developmentally oriented psychoanalysis. This developmental orientation has the outstanding merit that it gets one straight to the heart of Freud's own approach.

Development refers to something coming into its own, achieving its own potential. It involves growth, i.e. changes in size and shape and the unfolding of structures and properties that are innate. Time is a necessary ingredient for development to take place. The extent to which the developmental stages required for normal, healthy development are satisfactorily achieved will depend on constitutional and environmental factors. It is important to realize, however, that the child at any given stage is structurally different from how s/he is at any other. Nowhere is this more convincingly demonstrated than in the theory of cognitive development proposed and elaborated by Piaget. In this sense, development is not only about change and growth, but about structural transformation. The developing child is not so much like a tree that grows bigger and stronger, but more like the developmental sequence in which the caterpillar becomes a butterfly.

Freud's theory and the technique of psychoanalysis derived therefrom places enormous emphasis on reconstruction of the drive development, childhood traumas and internalized conflict, and the infantile neurosis. In the course of the adult analysis, the goal is to attempt to understand the developmental impact of childhood experiences and in so doing help the person seeking treatment to transform the ordinary neurosis into the transference neurosis that is then amenable to the psychotherapeutic cure (Freud, 1914g, p. 154). More than anyone else, it was Anna Freud who expanded the developmental approach within psychoanalysis through her extensive observations of children, her work in child analysis, and her attempts to establish some sense of what constitutes normality in childhood. It is, therefore, to her writings that we must turn in order to distil the essence of a developmental perspective and establish a coherent conceptual framework within which the beginning therapist can work clinically. Anna Freud's developmental perspective is chosen in preference to Melanie Klein's because Klein's developmental concepts are based on reconstructed abnormal mental states (Freeman, 1987, p. 289), whereas Anna Freud's developmental theories are firmly rooted in her observations of normal as well as disturbed children over many years. In presenting the psychoanalytic theories of Anna Freud, this chapter offers beginning psychotherapists a theoretical centre from which to view and assess the plethora of theories and techniques that abound in the psychoanalytic literature.

The early years

Anna Freud was born on 3 December 1895, the sixth and last child of Martha and Sigmund Freud. Despite the presence of Martha and her sister Minna, Anna was cared for by Josephine Cihlarz, a Catholic nursemaid, until she had completed her first year at school. Freud never encouraged any of his daughters to study medicine; he did, however, encourage them, and his friends' daughters, to study psychoanalysis. Anna had her first lesson when she was 14, and they were passing some beautiful houses in Vienna. Freud pointed out that "things were not necessarily so lovely behind the façades. And so it is with human beings too" (Young-Bruehl, 1988, p. 52). In addition, she used to sit in on the Wednesday evening meetings of the Vienna Psychoanalytical Society and listen to her father and his colleagues discuss their clinical presentations. In 1912, she completed her *Matura*—high-school diploma—and by 1914 she was ready to take her teaching apprenticeship examinations. She taught for a total of six years. Her teaching career was obviously successful; she was offered a four-year contract in 1918. Testimonials from former pupils portray her as a warm but firm teacher who was sympathetic to the needs of those in her charge (see Young-Bruehl, 1988, p. 77). In addition, she experimented with Dewey's progressive educational ideas and introduced project work into her class. One such project was a school trip to Hungary, organized with the help of her father's disciple, Sandor Ferenczi. (For Anna Freud's own reminiscences on her years as a teacher, see Coles, 1992, pp. 4–5.)

Upon her return to Vienna after this trip, she decided to go into analysis with her father. She continued to teach. However, her health deteriorated, and she resigned her teaching post in 1920, shortly after the death of her sister Sophie. She began to translate work for the psychoanalytic journals, and also Varendonck's *The Psychology of Daydreams* (1921). Her entry into the psychoanalytic world was ensured in May 1920, when Freud presented her with one of the gold rings worn by all the members of his circle as a sign of their commitment to psychoanalysis. She began to work with Siegfried Bernfeld, who established the Baumgarten Children's Home to provide food and shelter for Jewish orphans and homeless children. One of the volunteers in this project was Willi Hoffer; and, together with an older and more experienced man, August Aichhorn, the four used to meet at Berggasse 19, the Freuds' home, for an informal study circle. It was at these meetings that Aichhorn first presented the content of what was to become a classic study of adolescence—his book, *Wayward Youth* (1935). It was as a result of her associations with these three men, especially Aichhorn, that Anna Freud's special interest in children and psychoanalytic pedagogy blossomed. By this stage, she was conversant with the pioneering work of Hermine Hug-Hellmuth and had attended the Sixth Congress of the International Psychoanalytical Association in The Hague in 1920, where she heard Hug-Hellmuth read her paper on the technique of child analysis, which was subsequently published in 1921 (MacLean & Rappen, 1991, p. 30). She was also aware of the seminal significance of Freud's 1909 publication on the case of Little Hans, the first child analytic case—albeit treated by Freud by proxy.

Anna Freud's first analysis spanned the years between 1918 and 1922. In 1922, she wrote to Max Eitingon, head of the Berlin Society, to ask for his advice: she wanted to become a member of a psychoanalytical society. She was asked to prepare a lecture for delivery to the Vienna Society in six weeks' time. The ensuing paper, "Beating Fantasies and Daydreams" (1922), describes the three stages in the development and eventual sublimation of a patient's phantasies of being beaten. In the first stage, the patient created a beating phantasy, culminating in masturbation, as a substitute for an incestuous father/daughter wish. When the patient reached her tenth year, these beating phantasies were replaced by what she called "nice stories", which seemed on the surface to have no connection with the beating phantasy. The "nice stories" were interpreted as an advance, an attempt at sublimation. Eventually, the patient began to write short stories, which Anna Freud interpreted as still further progress towards a social pleasure in communicating with an audience. This was an important developmental step, as it involved "the transformation of an autistic [activity] into a social activity" (p. 157). Young-Bruehl makes a convincing case that this is an autobiographical paper, tracing the essence of what Anna Freud worked through in her own personal analysis.

Her acceptance by the Vienna Society, subsequent to the presentation of her paper, heralded the beginning of her career as an analyst. She immediately began to attend Wagner-Jauregg's ward rounds at the psychiatric clinic of the Vienna General Hospital, under the wing of Paul Schilder and Heinz Hartmann. Years later she wrote of the importance of this training: "for you understand the neuroses entirely differently when you consider them against the background of the psychoses" (Anna Freud to Eva Landauer, 15 March 1946 and 5 November 1948, quoted in Young-Bruehl, 1988, p. 122).

In 1924, after a two-year interval, Freud suggested that they resume their analytic work. In this renewed analysis, which lasted nine months, she took up the problem of her "extra-analytical closeness" to her father (Anna Freud to Lou Andreas-Salomé, 15 May 1924, quoted in Young-Bruehl, 1988, p. 123), her masculinity complex, her jealousy of her mother and sister, and what she was later to describe as "altruistic surrender" (A. Freud, 1936). In 1925, she met Dorothy Burlingham and took two of her children, Bob and Mabbie, and their two friends, Adelaide and Harold Sweetzer, into analysis. She became aware that she not only wanted to make them well, but to have them, or something of them, for herself. She felt the same way about Dorothy Burlingham, whose estranged husband had remained in the United States. Her emotional attachment to the Burlingham children and their mother imposed a limitation on her analytic relationship with her father, since she was "too ashamed" to tell him of this great need. She began, instead, to confide in Max Eitingon and wrote to him of her "wanting to have something" for herself (Young-Bruehl, 1988, p. 133). Freud came to hear about the relationship between the two women, not from his daughter, but from Dorothy Burlingham, whom he had taken into analysis after she had terminated with Reik. Eventually, the Burlinghams moved into the apartment above the Freuds in Berggasse 19 and had a summer house next-door to them; and then, in 1930, the two women jointly bought a cottage in the Semmering.

The 1920s were characterized for Anna Freud by her career move from teaching to psychoanalysis and her acceptance into the inner circle; her collaboration with Hoffer, Bernfeld, and Aichhorn in courses for teachers and school administrators on psychoanalytic pedagogy and the founding of the journal of that name, the forerunner of *The Psychoanalytic Study of the Child*; her personal friendships with Lou Andreas-Salomé, Max Eitingon, Eva Rosenfeld, and especially Dorothy Burlingham; her work with patients, especially children; and, finally, her differences with Melanie Klein.

Anna Freud's first book, *Four Lectures on Child Analysis* (1927), crystallized her theoretical differences with Melanie Klein. This book was based on her lectures to the newly formed Training Institute of the Vienna Psychoanalytical Society in the winter of 1926. Unlike Klein, Anna Freud believed that children's difficulties were often due to external sources, and that in seeking psychoanalysis, the parents were seeking relief for themselves as much as for the child. For Anna Freud, this was a most important difference between child analysis and adult analysis, since adults refer themselves for treatment. Because of this, she felt that the analyst had to initiate the child into the analytic process. She suggested a preparatory period (a suggestion later retracted), during which the child could be inducted into the analytic method (p. 7). She felt that the analyst had to win the child's confidence and questioned whether a transference neurosis would ever develop in a child, because his actual parents continue to exert a predominant influence on the child's life. She questioned how a child can produce a "new edition of his love relationships because, as one might say, the old edition is not yet exhausted. His original objects, the parents, are still real and present as love objects, not only in fantasy as with the adult neurotic" (p. 44).

In addition, she felt that Klein was mistaken in maintaining that the child's superego developed early on into an "immutable structure" and that it derived from the child's cannibalistic and sadistic impulses rather than from identification with the parents. More crucially, she was critical of Klein's challenge to Freud's timing of the Oedipus complex and her view that it reached a peak two years earlier than Freud had stipulated. The consequence of this was a major theoretical dispute between the two women. Klein held that since there was no essential difference between child and adult analysis, deep interpretations should be made to the child from the start. She assumed that both positive and negative transferences are established immediately by child patients as well as adults. In addition, she held that since play is to the child what free association is to the adult, it can be interpreted in the same way. Anna Freud criticized Klein's interpretation of the symbolic content of play on the grounds that the nature of a child's play can be occasioned by actual events in the child's life. She also questioned the therapeutic effect of making deep interpretations. Furthermore, she stressed the importance of working from a detailed developmental history of the child and insisted on taking reality factors into account in the child's analysis. I recently assessed a seven-year-old girl, who had been extensively burned in a house fire when she was left unattended. In the early sessions, she behaved violently and aggressively towards the toys in the room, sticking scissors into them, breaking them, or ripping them apart. It would be a mistake to interpret such aggression as unrelated to the traumatic experience that this child had suffered and to see this behaviour only in terms of internal pathology.

Anna Freud's first book was "deliberately provocative" (Grosskurth, 1985, p. 166). She made it clear in this publication what constituted the Vienna school of child analysis, and she distanced herself from what was beginning to emerge as the Kleinian approach. In her reminiscences to Coles on the subject of her differences with Klein, all Anna Freud would say was:

> I was more cautious than Mrs Klein—and we disagreed on that basis. . . . She had enormous energy, and she was— how should I say it?—more imaginative than I was willing to be in my daily analytic work with children, more imaginative, maybe, about what takes place in the minds of young children! [Coles, 1992, p. 123]

This caution remains the hallmark of the Classical or Vienna school of psychoanalysis. In addition, Anna Freud had an enduring belief that improving the external environment of children will have a beneficial effect on their psychic functioning. This view grew out of Aichhorn's work with juvenile delinquents, Bernfeld's Baumgarten Children's Home, which attempted to educate orphaned and homeless children, and the Vienna Psychoanalytical Society's centre for young children run by Editha Sterba, together with Anna Freud's own experience of teaching children. Within the Vienna group, there was a definite sense that the real world has a part to play in the internal life of the child.

Anna Freud and Melanie Klein finally spoke on the one platform at the International Psychoanalytic Congress in 1929, in Oxford—the first congress to be held in England. Anna Freud read a paper entitled, "A Counterpart to the Animal Phobias of Children". In this paper, which was never published in English, but which is discussed in Chapter 6 of *The Ego and the Mechanisms of Defence* (1936), she addressed a conclusion reached by her father in the "Little Hans" case study, in which he interpreted Little Hans's fear of the horse as his fear of being castrated by his father. She presented two of her patients, both boys, who, instead of developing a phobia to disguise their unacceptable feelings towards their father, developed a phantasy to alleviate their anxiety. If phantasies are successful in denying reality, Anna Freud argued, "the ego is saved anxiety and has no need to resort to defensive measures against its instinctual impulses and to the formation of a neurosis" (1936, p. 80). This paved the way for what were to become two of Anna Freud's most important contributions to psychoanalytic theory: the defensive function of the ego, and the difference between normality and pathology. Why did one child (Little Hans) develop a phobia, while others developed phantasies? This led her to conclude that all children, not just neurotic ones, need to find some ways of dealing with their smallness and their vulnerability. Any nursery teacher will attest to the fact that children resolve difficult or traumatic experiences through phantasy play. Nowhere is this more compellingly seen than in the phantasy play of the Oedipal male child who can drive a truck, or build a house, "just like daddy", thereby minimizing his inadequacy in the face of a strong rival. Anna Freud's insight into the importance of phantasy no doubt reflected her own inner life, as she had been a day-dreamer who had sublimated her unacceptable wishes through various forms of phantasy.

Psychoanalytic pedagogy

In her second book, *Four Lectures on Psychoanalysis for Teachers and Parents* (1930), Anna Freud underlined the importance of observation in understanding why children behave as they do. Equally important was the view that what weighs most heavily on the minds of children is not accessible to conscious memory:

> Children give no information about the past: they willingly talk about the events of the last few days or weeks, about holidays spent elsewhere, about a previous birthday, perhaps even about Christmas of last year. But there their recollections stop, or at any rate they lack the ability to tell about them. [A. Freud, 1930, pp. 78–79]

* * *

Matthew, a four-year-old boy, was referred to me by his nursery-school teacher because of his aggressiveness towards other children and his extreme sleepiness during the day. Consultation with the mother confirmed these concerns, together with a concern because of Matthew's inability to sleep in his own bed, or even to go to bed, until his mother, a single parent, was going to bed herself. In addition, it came to light that Matthew had no problem in sleeping on his own when in his maternal grandmother's house. During the course of Matthew's twice-weekly therapy, he told me of his deep sense of shame at not being able to sleep in his own bed, and he said it was because he saw "circles" in the window. He was also able to tell me that he didn't see circles in his granny's house because the window was behind his head. This led to his re-enactment of a traumatic incident that had occurred when Matthew was two, when the wheel of a car was thrown through the window of his home. He was playing under the window at the time and suffered scratches from the glass. Within days of this traumatic incident, Matthew's parents split up, and his paternal grandmother, to whom he was very attached, died in his home. Matthew was unable to remember this incident consciously, but his irrational fears bore all the signs of the memory of it.

Through the medium of play, he was eventually able to remember this incident and to understand its significance.

Also in this book, Anna Freud sets the scene for two of her most pressing theoretical issues. What constitutes normality? And what environmental influences interfere with the normal development of the child? She addresses the enormous scepticism with which most teachers, in my own experience, initially greet a psychoanalytic view of the child. She differentiates child education from child care on the basis that "education . . . always demands something of the child" (A. Freud, 1930, p. 94). She goes on: "The universal tendency of education is always to turn the child into a grown-up person not very different from the adult world around him" (p. 94). This highlights how education "struggles with the child's demeanour, or as the adults see it: his misdemeanours".

She goes on to describe the types of habits and forms of behaviour that young children exhibit, much to the chagrin of parents. She claims that psychoanalysis can help explain why children behave in such ways; and that such habits are not deplorable indicators of abnormal development, but links in a pre-determined chain of normal development. She addresses the tactic frequently deployed by parents of threatening children with violence, or actually using violence, if they do not stop behaving in an undesirable way. Alternatively, parents may threaten to withdraw their love from the child. Both threats are effective, because the child, under the pressure of such impending dangers, abandons his primitive desires, initially by pretending that he has changed his attitudes, but eventually by denying that he has ever felt otherwise. The renunciation of this pleasure has two possible effects: (1) he now applies this adult standard, which was imposed upon him, to the rest of the world and treats with intolerance any infringement of these values by others; or (2) he represses from memory any of the pleasure associated with his early primitive desires which he can now only see as repulsive.

In her third lecture, Anna Freud attempts to unravel the intricacies of the unconscious. She points to the strange paradox whereby an event that has been repressed continues to exert an influence upon the child's mind. She explains the operating of the defences of reaction formation and sublimation, before going on to talk about transference and the teacher (A. Freud, 1930, p. 109). She then discusses what, in 1930, must have taken her audience by storm—namely, the basis of the psycho-sexual stages and the concept of libido—and she lists the emotional experiences that the child has undergone before he comes to school.

> He has suffered a curtailment of his original egoism through love for the parents; he has experienced a violent desire for the possession of the beloved mother; and he has defended his rights by death-wishes directed against others and by outbreaks of jealousy. In relation to the father he has developed feelings of respect and admiration, tormenting feelings of competition with a stronger rival, the sense of impotence, and the depressing impact of a disappointment in love. He has, moreover, already passed through a complicated instinctual development and has learned how hard it is to be compelled to repudiate a part of one's own personality. . . . The school-child who enters the classroom is prepared to find that there he is only one among many, and he cannot count on any privileged position. He has learnt something of social adaptation. Instead of constantly seeking to gratify his desires, as he did formerly, he is now prepared to do what is required of him and to confine his pleasures to the times allotted for this purpose. His interest in uncovering the intimate secrets of his environment has now been transformed into a thirst for knowledge and a love of learning. In place of the revelations and explanations which he longed for earlier he is now willing to obtain knowledge of letters and numbers.
> [A. Freud, 1930, pp. 110–111]

She spells out the characteristics of the latency period, which arises around the age of 6 and is characterized by a kind of peace; it is a "quiet phase" (p. 115). However, she adds, though instinctual development seems to have come to a standstill, the instinctual drives "are latent, dormant and wake up again with renewed vigour after a period of time" (pp. 114–115). The period of adolescence is thus a reawakening of all the old difficulties that have lain dormant in latency and now burst forth for a second time in an attempt at resolution. This re-awakening of the sexual drives in puberty frequently overwhelms the child and marks the end of his educability. This is more normally expressed in the typical "adolescent protest", but it may find expression in symptoms.

Brian, a 15-year-old only child, was referred to me for treatment because of his refusal to go to school. When Brian did go to school, he felt sick, claustrophobic, and had to leave. His fears reached such a pitch that he tried to stick a knife in himself. The only thing that stopped him was his concern for his horses, and his fears of reincarnation, about which he had seen a television programme: he did not want to "come back" (from the dead) and have to live in a different family, with other siblings. In addition, Brian was unable to sleep and would bang his head on the wall separating his bedroom from his parents', until his mother would come in to talk to him. This happened so frequently that his mother had put a spare bed into his room so that when he banged, she could go in and sleep in the room with him, until he was calm and had fallen asleep. When Brian was a child, his mother had had 18 major operations, and she was close to death on a few occasions. Through the course of his twice-weekly therapy, Brian came to see that his refusal to go to school represented his fears about what might happen at home when he was absent. He was also able to understand that his banging his head on the bedroom wall was a way of depriving his father of his mother's company in bed. He realized, too, how jealous he would feel if he had any other siblings (the basis of his reincarnation fears) and how much he wanted to possess his mother. Interpretation of these fears led to a complete cessation of the wall banging and the disappearance of his suicidal thoughts and reincarnation fears. He still is unable to go to school, but this is because of his shame about having missed so much school-work. With the help of home tuition, arranged since he came into therapy, Brian plans to take his GCSE examinations next year.

Anna Freud discusses the difficulties the mother and father transferences pose for the teacher: the teacher's difficulty in dealing with all children individually without incurring jealousy on all sides; not to mention the difficulty in being both an object of fear (the father transference) and a personal friend to each child. The teacher's task, she says, is aided by the development in the child of detachment from the original love objects (the parents) and an increased independence of them. The child now acts on the basis of inner controls, or conscience; and this is a

continuation of the voice of the parents which is now operative from within instead of, as formerly, from without. The child has absorbed, as it were, a part of his father or mother, or rather the commands and prohibitions which he has constantly received from them, and made them an essential part of his being. [A. Freud, 1930, p. 118]

The child who is thus independent of his parents gives a special place of honour to them in his own ego and regards this as an ideal. The child is inclined to submit more slavishly to this ideal than he did to his actual parents in the past. In this way, Anna Freud introduces the superego as "the successor of the parents" (p. 119). The mildness or severity of the parental attitudes will be reflected in the attitude of the child's ego to his superego. The teacher's task is to win the superego to his/her side and make an ally out of it. In so doing, "the battle for drive control and social adaptation will be won", because two are working against one (p. 120). If this happens, the teacher will have no difficulty in influencing the child in whatever way s/he wishes.

In the final lecture, Anna Freud considers the relationship between psychoanalysis and pedagogy. She outlines three basic principles. The first is the notion of three major epochs in the development of the child: pre-latency, latency, and adolescence. In each period, the child's reaction to those around him is different and dependent upon his instinctual development. Because of this, a child's reaction to any given event cannot be considered perverse or abnormal until the criterion of age-appropriateness is applied (A. Freud, 1930, p. 122). The second principle is based on the tripartite division of the personality: id, ego, and superego. Contradictions in a child's behaviour can only be understood in terms of the predominance of one or other of these parts of the personality at any particular time. The third basic principle stresses the conflictual nature of the relationship between the instinctual drives (id), and the ego, and the superego. She goes on to point out how psychoanalysis has always expressed the wish to limit the force of education and to highlight the real dangers arising from "shooting at sparrows with cannonballs" (A. Freud, 1931, p. 97). She provides clinical examples of disturbed children and concludes that the task of a psychoanalytically orientated pedagogy is "to find for each stage in the child's life the right proportion between drive gratification and drive control" (A. Freud, 1930, p. 128).

For Anna Freud, psychoanalysis enriches teaching in three ways: (1) it provides a perspective from which to criticize existing educational practice; (2) in focusing on the theory of instinctual drives, the libido, and the unconscious, it extends the teacher's knowledge of the complicated relations between the child and the teacher; (3) it offers a treatment method whereby children can attempt to repair the injuries incurred during the process of socialization. She points to the dangers of teachers identifying with their pupils because of their own unresolved conflicts; and to the dangers of ignoring those children whose life experiences are different from the teacher's. Though directed at an audience of teachers, this book is an invaluable aid to any psychotherapist. As well as outlining the essence of Freud's developmental theory, it shows clearly that the therapist, like the teacher, faces the same difficulties with the transference and encounters the same difficulties with the ego and the superego. Anna Freud's next book would take many of the insights gleaned from this work and apply them directly to the clinical situation.

The analysis of defence

The increasing scope of her analytic practice led Anna Freud to change some of the technical positions she had taken up in her first book. Due to the influence of Berta Bornstein, she began to work with patients as young as 2 years, and she retracted her notion of a preparatory non-analytic phase in child analysis in which the child's trust is won. In addition, she now claimed that the analyst does not have to perform pedagogical functions for the child, which, she now felt, stood in the way of the manifestation and analysis of the child's aggression and the negative transference. As she and her co-workers in Vienna began to work with defence analysis, she formulated her own ideas on what was to become a major contribution to the theory of psychoanalysis: the mechanisms of defence.

In 1936, on her father's 80th birthday, Anna Freud presented him with a copy of what was to become a most influential book—*The Ego and the Mechanisms of Defence*. In the first chapters of this book, she surveys the ego's activity, drawing attention to its functions of synthesis, observation, and defence. She highlights as the analyst's main task the analysis of the ego (1936, p. 14), especially the recognition of the ego's defence mechanisms. The analyst is "a disturber of the peace", whose work is seen by the ego as a menace (p. 29). She describes the ego's work in analysis as threefold. Firstly, it transmits to the analyst a picture of the other institutions (id and superego) because of its capacity for self-observation. In so doing, the ego is an effective ally of the analyst. Secondly, the ego is an enemy of the analysis, because in its self-observation it is biased and often falsifies facts or rejects them. Finally, the ego is itself the object of analysis, in so far as it is engaged in defensive operations that are carried on unconsciously but can be made conscious through the analytic work. Anna Freud cautions against child analyses that "yield a wealth of information about the id but a meagre knowledge of the infantile ego" (p. 38). She reiterates her reservations about translating the child's play into the equivalent of free association, insisting that we must substitute some new technical method to assist us in our analysis of the child's ego. She claims that analysis of the child's defences is the key. The more successful we are in bringing defences into consciousness, the more impotent they become and, consequently, the more our understanding of the id progresses.

These technical recommendations are valid for the adult patient as well as for the child.

A 25-year-old married man, who had been seduced by a brother when he was ten years old, came into therapy because of his obsessions. These involved washing and decontamination rituals that had a crippling effect on the patient's life. The patient's home was divided into three areas: a clean area, a semi-clean one, and a dirty one. In order to move from one part of the house to the other, the patient had to decontaminate himself by washing and changing his clothes en route. These rituals were so extensive and so time-consuming that the patient almost never managed to get himself clean enough to sleep in the marital bed, designated as being located in the clean part of the house. The consequence of this was that, although a married man, the patient lived the life of a celibate.

This case shows clearly how the pleasure experienced in the childhood sexual experiences fell victim to the patient's defences. All that this man could experience as an adult was a sense of shame and disgust at any sexual contact, which found expression in his fears of being made dirty, or of being contaminated. The patient's disgust and fears were so extreme, because so great was the childhood pleasure, that he had to protect himself from ever experiencing it again. The patient's obsessions were a defence; they were his "security blanket" or "comforter". So long as his mind was consumed with trying to avoid dirt, he never had to deal with the force of his own sexual drive.

The case of Joey, a 9-year-old boy, illustrates the power of defensive operations in a child.

Joey was brought for therapy because his parents were very worried about his aggressiveness towards other children, especially his only sibling, Roy, who was three years younger. In the beginning phase of Joey's therapy, he was an ideal patient who used the time well. He played imaginatively and had to be dragged away from the play when time was up. He made models, drew many pictures, had a vivid phantasy life, and was keen to involve me in it. There was not a thing in the consulting-room that, at some time or other, Joey didn't use in a play sequence. We even added new toys to the toy box to give expression to aspects of his inner life that he wanted to express in play. In addition, he had a strong ego that enabled him to observe himself, from a distance, so to speak, and which enabled him to interpret his own play with a maturity far beyond his years. I looked forward to seeing the child, and he loved to come for his therapy sessions. But things were going too well. At this point Joey became concerned about our time together. Despite the real clock sitting on the play table, Joey made clocks out of Plasticine and on sheets of paper, all of them set to the time that he was due to leave the session. He stuck these on the walls of the consulting-room so that he could be constantly reminded of the time that he had to leave. I interpreted his fear about leaving me and the eventual ending of the therapy, but the clock-making persisted. There were times when we had six or seven clocks up on the walls, all showing the time of his departure, which was always the same time.

Eventually, Joey expressed his fears about things creeping up on him; he liked to be prepared. His play sequence and drawings of sharks biting the legs off children led to the expression of his fears that we were getting into "deep water". This unleashed a series of concerns about "the complicated nature of the human life cycle". He charted the life cycle of a "boy baby", showing with arrows how it became a toddler, child, teenager, man, husband, and daddy; he then made Plasticine models of this developmental life cycle. But he couldn't figure out how the daddy was connected to the baby. He knew the daddy put the "sperm" into the mother but he couldn't understand "how he made the connection". He thought this was where "making love" came in, but he had no idea what that meant, except that on television people making love seemed to make grunting noises. As he was explaining this, he grunted and pushed his pelvis out to demonstrate how these noises were made. At this point he told me that his daddy had had an operation, so he didn't have any more sperm to make babies. Joey then told me in graphic language the details of daddy's vasectomy, and his own circumcision because of a tight foreskin. Both the

father's vasectomy and Joey's circumcision were
performed when Joey was 3 (i.e. when Roy was born), and
they were done "in the same hospital at the same time, on
the same day". The historical truth of this is not
important. What is important is that for Joey these two
surgical interventions were inextricably linked. Joey was
concerned that he was "peeing all his babies down the
toilet"; he was worried about "using them all up".

Joey's case highlights how it is only by getting behind the
defence that we can really understand a child's (or an adult's)
fears. We must remember that Joey was referred because of his
aggressiveness. The therapy uncovered that what lay behind
this aggression was a very, very frightened little boy, who
feared that his development had been interfered with.

Anna Freud next outlines three types of transference phenomena. The first type is transference of libidinal impulses,
which the patient experiences as "an intrusive foreign body"
(1936, p. 19) and which provide the analyst with an insight into
the patient's id. The second type is transference of the patient's
defences, which confronts the analyst with a major technical
challenge, because "the form in which they emerge in [the
patient's] consciousness is ego-syntonic"—or, so to speak, ego-
friendly. Furthermore, the patient is inclined to rationalize this
type of transference reaction, because "whenever the interpretation touches on the unknown elements of the ego, its
activities in the past, that ego is wholly opposed to the work of
the analysis" (p. 21). Finally, there is "acting in the transference". This occurs when the patient begins to act out in his
relations with other people the contents of the instinctual impulses and the defensive reactions that belong in the patient's
relationship with the analyst. This is the most difficult type of
transference to deal with. Anna Freud cautions against concentrating too much on the interpretation of the transference, on
the grounds that the ego can too easily become overwhelmed
and become involved in acting rather than analysing (p. 27).

In Chapter 4, Anna Freud (1936) reviews Freud's work on
defence and his view that there may be a connection between
types of illness and specific defences. She lists ten defences—
regression, repression, reaction formation, isolation, undoing,

projection, introjection, turning against the self, reversal, and sublimation—and then considers a developmental chronology of them. However, she concludes that the question of chronology has to be left unanswered, because her camp and "the English School" (the Kleinians) are so deeply at odds on this issue. A more productive line of research is the study of those situations that instigate defensive reactions. She approaches this task by considering the defences in terms of the three types of anxiety outlined by Freud in *Inhibitions, Symptoms and Anxiety* (1926d [1925]), viz., objective anxiety, instinctual anxiety, and superego anxiety. Prognostically speaking, those defences that are the result of superego anxiety are likely to have a favourable outcome. Similarly, defences against objective anxiety also have a good prospect of success. The only states that fail to respond favourably to analysis are those defences against the strength of the instincts. In such cases, there is a danger that in rendering the defensive processes inoperative, the ego is further weakened, and the morbid process is advanced.

In the second part of the book, Anna Freud presents clinical material and attempts to show how different defences are bound up with different symptoms and illnesses. In particular, she considers the extent to which the neuroses first described by Freud—the hysterias and the obsessional neuroses—can be explained from the point of view of the activities of the ego, not just the id.

The third part of the book is the most original and most powerful section. In these two chapters, she writes about two new defences: identification with the aggressor, and altruistic surrender. One of the most powerful ways the ego has of dealing with an external threat is to imitate that threat and, in doing so, become like the aggressor. A child who was accidentally knocked on the head by one of his teachers came to his next session armed with a toy pistol and a wooden sword. In this way, he made himself powerful and big and capable of doing to others what had been done to him. In this defensive operation, according to Anna Freud, we see a normal stage in the development of the superego. It is equivalent to internalizing criticism from parents or other authorities and then, through projection, turning this criticism onto others, thereby preventing it from being experienced as self-criticism. A child who is beaten both internalizes the beating and beats someone else—usually someone smaller. This stage in the development of the superego is a preliminary stage of morality. True morality begins when the internalized criticism or punishment coincides with the ego's acceptance of blame. From that time on, the severity of the superego is turned inwards not outwards, and the person is more tolerant of others. Some people never develop to this more advanced stage and remain aggressive in their dealings with others, while others, like the melancholic, become ruthlessly aggressive towards themselves. Identification with the aggressor (and its accompanying processes of introjection and projection) was seen by Anna Freud to be a normal and innocuous process in situations of real aggression. It can, however, become pathological when it is carried over into a person's close relationships, as is the case in morbid jealousy or persecutory delusions. From a clinical point of view, analysis of identification with the aggressor enables the therapist to differentiate in the transference between attacks that emanate from aggression and those that emanate from anxiety.

Miss W was referred for psychoanalytic treatment because of her depression. Her therapy was being paid for by her employer. She was the second-youngest child in a family of four. Her parents had been very strict and rigid in her upbringing, had lacked feeling, and had found her a difficult child. Her father, especially, had been domineering and very demanding, and used to "push her around a lot". In addition, he never spoke to her. In the transference, Miss W experienced me in the same way and treated me the way she had been treated. She arrived late, or didn't come at all, without sending any message. She was gruff, she never greeted me, and she never closed the door behind her. She treated all my interpretations with total disdain: I was being paid to listen to her, I had to do it whether I liked it or not. She demanded answers to her questions, and she was fed up being treated like a "nit-wit". Parents never answered children's questions, they just told them to go away and be quiet. She constantly abused me verbally and accused me of "dragging her down". In reality, she was determined to push me down, to deprive me of any satisfaction, and to make me as miserable as she was: in short, to behave towards me just as her parents had behaved towards her. The patient re-enacted in the transference the defence of identification with the aggressor. At times, she was the parent who pushed me around; at others, she was the child being pushed around by me. She played out both parts. Klein would explain this phenomenon in terms of projective identification, rather than identification with the aggressor. According to Klein, the patient is aggressive, domineering, and demanding in order to rid herself of an unacceptable part of herself; so she projects it into others. However, explaining this patient's defensive constellation in this light roots her aggressiveness in her own internal pathology and ignores the very real experiences that this woman had had to contend with when she was a child.

"A Form of Altruism" (in A. Freud, 1936) contains what has become accepted as an autobiographical study of a govern-ess who practised the defence of altruistic surrender. In this defence, the mechanism of projection leads to the surrendering of one's own instinctual impulses in favour of others. This defensive process serves two purposes: (1) it facilitates the development of a healthy interest in the needs of others, thereby by-passing the severity of the individual's own super-ego, because the gratification is obtained indirectly through others' gratifications; (2) it liberates vicariously the aggression designed to secure the fulfilment of one's own wishes. Analysis of this defence traces its origin to some infantile conflict with parental authority over instinctual gratification. The factors that determine the selection of the person better qualified to fulfil the instinctual gratification are based upon how best to overcome "narcissistic mortification" (p. 131). In this way the life of the other person becomes more precious than one's own, and fears about one's own death are consequently kept at bay.

In the final part of the book, the author addresses the relationship between the ego and the id in puberty, and she goes on to describe two defences associated with puberty: asceticism and intellectualization. Her growing interest in this stage of development was partly motivated by the neglect of it in the psychoanalytic literature, but also by the progress of the Burlingham children into this developmental stage. This section highlights Anna Freud's perceptiveness and powers of observation. She attributes the particular anxieties of puberty to the intensification of libidinal impulses. This aspect of development was almost ignored by Klein because of her emphasis on anxiety rather than libidinal development; furthermore, puberty is a stage of development of which she had no knowledge or expertise. According to Grosskurth (1985), while *The Ego and the Mechanisms of Defence* was not an outright attack on Klein, it was "an oblique criticism of Klein's premises, aims, and methodology" (p. 225). There is no doubt that Anna Freud's concept of identification with the aggressor was a counter to Mrs Klein's emphasis on aggression as a manifestation of the death instinct and consequently an internally arising force. Anna Freud argued that children's real experience of aggression cannot be ignored. In addition, this way of conceptualizing the development of the superego raised questions regarding Klein's timing of the superego and the Oedipus complex.

Observational studies

After the publication of her 1936 book, Anna Freud threw herself into a new project. Edith Jackson, an American psychiatrist who had been in analysis with Freud and had trained in Anna Freud's child analysis seminar, donated a substantial sum of money to set up a nursery for children under the age of 2, which would serve as a research tool to highlight developmental information about the infancy period in a child's life. This became known as the Jackson Nursery and opened in February 1937, with a roll of 11 children. Other American benefactors were sought, and the project encompassed a wide range of experienced key workers, including Anna Freud, Edith Jackson, Dorothy Burlingham, Dr Julia Deming ("Auntie Porridge"—who was responsible for the feeding arrangements in the nursery and for keeping a record of the food choices of all the children), and Dr Josefine Stross, a paediatrician, who was responsible for the medical examination of all the children.

The children were bathed and changed each morning when they arrived. During the rest of the day, the adults took notes on small cards about their behaviour. These notes were copied and filed thematically in a wooden file box at the end of each day and formed the basis for later discussions. This simple indexing system was later elaborated into the Hampstead Index. These records highlighted how some children were unable to pass a stool until after they had been in the nursery for one week, and the weight gain in children when they were allowed to choose their own food from a tray. Some of the children did show crazes for certain foods that lasted quite a few days, but over the course of the week they selected food that provided a nutritional balance. Finally, the records showed the strength of the pleasure derived from playing, which sometimes distracted the children from eating. However, as their desire to eat increased, this ceased to be a problem. The Jackson Nursery remained open for only one year, owing to the rising political turmoil that culminated in the Freuds' departure from Vienna in June 1938; but it established the model for what later became the Hampstead War Nurseries after the Freuds had settled in London.

In the autumn of 1938, Anna Freud, now living in London, was invited by J. C. Hill, a London Schools Inspector, to deliver a series of lectures on psychoanalysis. These lectures were simply called "Psychology by Miss A. Freud" (Dyer, 1983, p. 139) and were significant because they were her first public lectures in England. These lectures extended into 1939 and were well attended and enthusiastically received. In September 1939, Sigmund Freud died. The 1940s saw the development of the Hampstead War Nurseries, which continued the work of Anna Freud and Dorothy Burlingham in the Jackson Nursery. The first of these, a children's rest centre, opened in January 1941, at 13 Wedderburn Road, and housed between 10 and 12 children. The furniture and toys had been shipped by Dorothy Burlingham from the Jackson Nursery. By the summer of 1941, two other houses were equipped and opened, a babies' rest centre at 5 Netherhall Gardens in Hampstead, and a country house in Essex, called New Barn, for older children. When the three buildings were working to full capacity there were 120 children being cared for. Dorothy Burlingham and Anna Freud ran the London houses, and New Barn was run by Alice Goldberger. Unlike other British residential wartime nurseries, the Hampstead Nurseries made a point of involving parents as much as possible. Consequently, the houses were open to visiting at all hours.

In 1944, Anna Freud published *Infants Without Families*, with Dorothy Burlingham. This was the culmination of the insights gleaned from their experiences in the Hampstead Nurseries, and it noted the effects of residential care at each developmental level. It pointed to how language and toilet training are disadvantaged by residential care, because these depend totally on the ongoing emotional bond with a mothering figure. Regarding eating, the Jackson Nursery experience was borne out.

> But the experiences of the first year, when love for food and love for mother were identical, leave their imprint on the reaction to food throughout life. The child from his side shows every inclination to treat food given by the mother as he treats the mother, which means that all the possible disturbances of the mother–child relationship turn easily into eating disturbances. [A. Freud & Burlingham, 1944, p. 556]

Anna Freud returns to this issue in "The Psychoanalytic Study of Infantile Feeding Disturbances" (1946). This paper built on her observations in the Jackson Nursery and the Hampstead War Nursery of how children do, or do not, take pleasure in eating. Because the primary purpose of eating is a biological one based on the body's need for nourishment, one would expect a harmony of id and ego forces united in the self-preservation of the individual. However, "eating may, on the other hand become invested with sexual and aggressive meaning and thereby, secondarily, become the symbolic representative of id forces which are opposed by the ego" (p. 41). Such occurrences will result in eating disturbances. She concludes: "Considerate handling of the child's feeding, with a reasonable amount of self-determination, to safeguard the child's appetite, makes the function of eating less vulnerable and less favorable ground for neurotic superstructures" (p. 59). This subject was to be given an even fuller discussion in her concept of developmental lines (A. Freud, 1965a).

After the Hampstead Nurseries had been open for one year, the children were organized into artificial families of about four/five children plus a surrogate mother. These groups were formed in accordance with the preferences of the children and the staff. Attachments formed within a week, but these attachments brought anxieties about loss and sibling rivalry. Anna Freud concluded that it was not the separation itself, but the manner of the separation that traumatized the child. Billie abandoned his compulsive symptom of putting on his coat and zipping it up when his mother returned (A. Freud, 1941, p. 21). When the mother was persuaded to visit the nursery as often as she could, Billie became a member of the nursery like all the other children. At the end of the war, all but 16 children were returned to their parents. Some of the children had been in the Nursery for five years. Anna Freud looked upon these long-timers, together with the six concentration-camp children rescued from Theresienstadt in 1945 and housed at Bulldogs Bank in Sussex, as her own children (A. Freud, 1951a). She corresponded with them, and she sent them gifts on birthdays and at Christmas.

In addition to her commitment to the Hampstead Nursery, during the war years Anna Freud ran a Wednesday seminar, modelled on the famous Wednesday evenings of the Vienna Psychoanalytical Society. Eva Rosenfeld, Kate Friedlander, and Barbara Lantos all attended and pressed for the establishment of the Hampstead Child Therapy Clinic (now the Anna Freud Centre) and a training course. The training course began in 1947, and the Clinic opened in 1952. Within a few years the Clinic purchased two more houses (21 and 14 Maresfield Gardens) and housed a well-baby clinic under Dr Josephine Stross and a nursery school under Manna Friedmann. In addition, a number of research groups were set up: the group for the study of borderline children, under Sara Kut-Rosenfeld; an adolescent project under Ilse Hellman; and the Motherless Children Project, the Blind Study Group, and the Identical Twins Study Group, all under Dorothy Burlingham. The Clinic had four aims: "to learn, to treat, to teach and to apply psychoanalytic knowledge to educational and preventative purposes" (A. Freud, 1975, p. ix).

There were two areas of research that were especially important to the Hampstead Group. One was the Index and the other the assessment of childhood pathology. Dorothy Burlingham, drawing on the practice in the Jackson Nursery, instigated the Index in 1954 to provide a means of assessing the expanding case material of the Clinic. In preparation for it, 50 case reports were catalogued, and from this a set of common categories was extracted for subsequent use on a wider scale. The Index thus offers a set of categories—for example, defences, anxieties, object relationships, transference manifestations—under which cards are filed, indicating how any particular phenomenon is illustrated by a particular case. It received its public debut in 1958, at the Psychiatry Section of the Royal Society of Medicine, and was referred to as the "Hampstead Index". Anna Freud described it as a "collective analytic memory" (1965b, p. 484), which remains at the disposal of any individual researcher or therapist. (For a full description of the Index, see Dyer, 1983, pp. 196–203.)

All this work at the Hampstead Clinic was set against the backdrop of the profound differences of opinion that existed within the British Psychoanalytical Society between Anna Freud and Melanie Klein. These differences of opinion eventually came to a head in 1942, in a series of Controversial Discussions, but this provided no respite, since the differences were irreconcilable. This raised serious problems for the British Society concerning what constituted an acceptable training in psychoanalysis. Finally, this matter was put to rest when Anna Freud proposed her "separate but equal" principle. Henceforward, students would elect to train either in Course A, which had two possible tracks, one Kleinian and the other taught by analysts of all persuasions (the so-called Middle Group), or, alternatively, in Course B, which was taught by adherents of the Vienna group. After the harrowing Controversial Discussions, Ernst Kris sketched the way forward for the classical group and tried to galvanize its members into making writing and the training of new candidates, many of them army psychiatrists, their top priorities.

Professional interests after the war

After these personally difficult times, Anna Freud developed pneumonia in January 1946 and was close to death. During her illness she learnt of Otto Fenichel's death at the age of 48. A few days later, she learnt of the mysterious death of Ruth Mack Brunswick. There were other losses, too: the death of her niece, Eva, and the news in 1946 that her four aunts, Freud's sisters, had all been killed in 1942 in the concentration camps. These losses, together with her illness, made her resolve to make writing a priority, as Kris had urged in his Memorandum. She embarked upon what was by far the most prolific period in her life. All her papers from this period are collected in Volumes 4 and 5 of her *Writings*. Volume 4, entitled *Indications for Child Analysis and Other Papers* (1968a), contains an extensive selection of papers spanning the decade between 1945 and 1956. It includes papers on her teaching activities, both in London and the United States, and papers on her clinical work at the Hampstead Clinic. The fifth volume, *Research at the Hampstead Child-Therapy Clinic and Other Papers* (A. Freud, 1969), covers a further decade, 1956–1965. It highlights once again Anna Freud's never-ending concern with the development and assessment of the child, and her growing interest in psychoanalysis and the law, the upbringing of children, and the provision of services for them. The majority of these papers were first published in *The Psychoanalytic Study of the Child*, which first appeared in the Winter of 1946. Many of them paved the way for her major study of normality and pathology, which was to be the subject of her next book. Two of these papers, however, are particularly appealing and deserve special mention.

The background to these papers dates back to the death of Aichhorn in 1949. His death seemed the most important milestone in the history of psychoanalysis since the death of her father. She and Aichhorn had a lot in common. In her obituary for Aichhorn, she pointed to his work with adolescents, his distinction between neurotic symptoms and delinquent behaviour, and his pioneering work in developing therapy for delinquents (A. Freud, 1951b, pp. 625–638; see also Coles, 1992, pp. 58–59). Equally significant was the death of her mother in 1951. Though mourning this loss, she was liberated by it, as Dorothy Burlingham moved into Anna Freud's home at 20 Maresfield Gardens. These losses, and her ambivalence towards her mother, were to form the basis of two elegantly written papers, one about loss and the other about the rejecting mother. In preparation for these papers, she kept notes of her dreams and self-analysis and her correspondence with Aichhorn, in a file entitled "About Losing and Being Lost". These notes formed the basis for an essay with the same title, which she published in 1967.

In the first part of "About Losing and Being Lost", she examines the dynamic interpretations of losing that Freud and others had proposed—i.e. that it originated in the conflict between unconscious and conscious desire. Next she considers losing from an economic point of view, highlighting how losing, misplacing, or finding objects or people is related to whether they are invested with libido or aggression. She stresses that losers become identified with the thing or person that they have lost by means of projection, and she cites the "lost" children during the war who imagined that their mothers were lonely, distressed, and unhappy: "I have to telephone my Mummy, she will feel so lonely." She comments that this plea was a frequent wish, especially in the evenings (p. 310). It is not difficult to understand such displacements, because

> when traced back to their source, they reveal themselves as based on early childhood events when the loser was himself "lost", that is, felt deserted, rejected, alone, and experienced in full force as his own all the painful emotions which he later ascribes to the objects lost by him. [A. Freud, 1967, p. 310]

Children who have experienced difficulty in the capacity to love and form object ties very often get lost or become chronic losers.

> By being chronic losers, they live out a double identification, passively with the lost objects which symbolize themselves, actively with the parents whom they experience to be as neglectful, indifferent, and unconcerned towards them as they themselves are toward their possessions. [p. 313]

This is bound up, too, with the observation that children never blame themselves for getting lost but instead blame the mother who lost them. "'You losted me!" (not "I lost you"). In the final section of the paper, Anna Freud compares experiences of losing and being lost to mourning. She refers to dreams, myths, folk stories, and ghost stories where images of the dead come back to haunt the living and challenge their loyalty. She notes, too, how the concept of the lost or wandering soul, who is aimlessly searching to find rest, symbolizes "the emotional impoverishment felt by the survivor" (p. 316), who, deprived of the former object, can find no substitute for their libidinal strivings. Eternal rest only comes to such "lost souls" when the living successfully detach themselves from the lost object.

A 29-year-old professional man came for treatment because he was unable to form relationships with anyone. The patient's mother had died when he was eight, leaving him and a brother, one-and-a-half years younger, to be brought up by his father. In the beginning phase of this intensive therapy, this man exhibited all the signs of a "chronic loser". This behaviour was so pronounced that the patient used to refer to himself jokingly as "the man who was not all there!" Never a day passed—the patient came five times weekly—that he did not leave one of his possessions behind him in the consulting-room. Scarves, gloves, sweaters, briefcases, suitcases, car keys, and his glasses were all left with me. Interpretation of the dynamic and economic aspects of his forgetting led to the cessation of this behaviour, except at times of stress, when he would revert to the same pattern again. Anna Freud's insight into this behaviour was invaluable in helping this man to see his double identification with his possessions. They represented the parts of himself that he wanted to leave with me, and also highlighted his neglectful indifference to himself, which was an active identification with the dead mother who had abandoned him.

In "The Concept of the Rejecting Mother" (1955), Anna Freud outlines the inequalities in the mother–child relationship. "The demands are all on one side (the infant's), while all the obligations are on the other side (the mother's)" (p. 589). Consequently, rejection is impossible to avoid. This rejection may be due to external factors, like death or hospitalization, or to internal factors involving the psychopathology of the mother and her unresolved childhood conflicts. Either way, the child experiences separations as rejections and is unable to differentiate between a long and a short one. Such separations may be expressed in a disturbance of the body's functions such as sleep or feeding, or in increased susceptibility to infection. Alternatively, such separations may be accompanied by regressions, or falling back to earlier forms of behaviour—an issue that Anna Freud develops in depth in her next book. Even the most devoted mother will inadvertently reject the child, because "no degree of devotion on the part of the mother can successfully cope with the boundless demands made on her by the child" (p. 601).

Assessments of development

In 1965, Anna Freud published *Normality and Pathology in Childhood: Assessments of Development* (1965a). This book, which charts the insights gleaned from the reconstruction of adult analyses, highlights how the emergence of child analysis necessitated alternative hypotheses and altered perspectives. A major contribution to this advance was the direct observation of children and the resultant importance that had to be given to the surface of the mind, taking its place alongside the reconstruction of the hidden depths. Instrumental in this change of direction was Anna Freud's focus on the work of the ego, which is accessible to observation. She maintains that problems of prediction and prevention "lead inevitably to a study of the normal, as opposed to the study of pathological mental processes" (p. 55). This was her overture to the notion of developmental lines (p. 62), which offer the clinician "deceptively simple" developmental scales (Edgcumbe, 1983, p. 431), integrating id and ego development and thereby presenting the child's personality in total. Developmental assessments that separate the libidinal sequence (oral, anal, phallic, latency, adolescent genitality) from the corresponding developments in the ego are of limited benefit.

> We need more from our assessments than these selected developmental scales which are valid for isolated parts of the child's personality only, not for its totality. What we are looking for are the basic interactions between id and ego and their various developmental levels, and also age-related sequences of them, which, in importance, frequency, and regularity, are comparable to the maturational sequence of libidinal stages or the gradual unfolding of the ego functions. [A. Freud, 1965a, p. 63]

Developmental lines constructed on this basis take account of the libidinal phases on the id side, as well as the corresponding object-related attitudes on the ego side. As a result, they trace the child's maturation from a state of dependence, irrationality, and id dominance, to increasing ego mastery of the internal and external world. The developmental lines are not intended as theoretical constructs, but as a way of representing real events in the life of the child and highlighting personal achievements, failures, harmonies, or conflicts in development. Consequently, the lines can be used to ascertain whether a child has matured sufficiently to be able to deal with separations, go to school, cope with the birth of a sibling, or even go on holiday. Anna Freud lists a number of developmental lines:

1. from dependency to emotional self-reliance and adult object relationships;
2. from sucking to rational eating;
3. from wetting and soiling to bladder and bowel control;
4. from irresponsibility to responsibility in body management;
5. from egocentricity to companionship;
6. from the body to the toy and from play to work.

Each of these lines is influenced by instinctual drives, the ego, and the superego, as well as by the external social reality.

At the end of this chapter, she examines regression within the context of normal development. She discusses types of regression and the difference between temporary and permanent regressions, drawing attention to the fact that a child's attainment of a high level of functioning is no guarantee that this performance will be stable and continuous. On the contrary, returns to infantile behaviour must be seen as a normal part of psychic functioning rather than as evidence of pathology. She identifies those conditions—like tiredness or frustration—where children's behaviour regresses rapidly to previously achieved levels of functioning; and she maintains that such regressions are part of "the immature individual's flexibility" (A. Freud, 1965a, p. 105). They are normal responses to strain and serve the purpose of adaptation and defence. Unlike drive regressions that involve a falling-back to a point of fixation, regressions on the side of the ego follow the line pursued during ego development. Consequently, in the falling back, the most recent achievements are lost first. Thus permanent drive regressions lead to neurotic conflict disorders, the infantile neuroses, and character disorders, whereas drive regressions when accompanied by ego and superego regressions lead to infantilisms, borderline pathology, or delinquent or psychotic disturbances (p. 147).

A 29-year old, highly intelligent woman was referred for treatment because of her depression. In the developmental history, the patient disclosed that she had been encopretic (soiled) until she was 11 years of age. This soiling had begun with the birth of her younger brother, who was born when she was 3 years old. In the transference, the patient was very attached to me and was sure that she was the most important person in my life. Despite improvements in her mood and her relationships in work and at home, she could not bear to tell me that she was feeling an improvement. She noticed, too, that she went to enormous lengths to worry me about how badly she felt, especially over the weekend breaks, and that this was the only way she knew how to get my attention. It became clear that the depression represented the heir to the soiling. It offered her, as an adult, a way to get the full and undivided attention of the people she loved, just as the soiling had guaranteed her her mother's undivided attention when she was a child.

In the second part of this book, Anna Freud addresses the assessment of pathology and introduces the Metapsychological or Diagnostic Profile. What inspired the Profile was a research group at the Hampstead Clinic on diagnosis and Anna Freud's view that the descriptive classification of disorders derived from adult psychopathology was not applicable to the child. She claimed that a list of symptoms was uninformative because the same symptom can have very different meanings at different developmental stages, while the same basic disturbance may seek expression in a range of diverse symptomatology. She felt that attention had to be redirected away from the presenting symptomatology and should focus instead on the patient's position on the developmental scale of drives, ego, and superego development. The Diagnostic Profile, therefore, is a practical instrument for formulating a diagnosis on the basis of information gathered at the initial interview stage (the diagnostic interview). It provides a scaffolding for organizing and eliciting the patient's material. "All good diagnosticians have some such framework and the Profile is Anna Freud's" (Edgcumbe, 1983, p. 431). Using this approach, Anna Freud was attempting to see whether preliminary diagnosis can get behind the manifest symptoms and assess the basic psychopathology, before the analytic work begins. As the analysis of the child unfolds, the results are compared with the original diagnosis for confirmation or otherwise. This instrument enables the therapist to assess a patient over time, to compile similar cases, and to compare differing clinical presentations. In this way, it can form the basis for research and training.

The Diagnostic Profile has thus led to a new classification of childhood phenomena: one that takes account of normal developmental processes, the typical developmental difficulties, and the various manifestations of childhood pathology. These, in turn, have opened up a new approach to the relationship between childhood and adult disturbances, as well as emphasizing variations of normality. The Profile has since been extended for use with adults (A. Freud, Nagera, & Freud, 1965), adolescents (Laufer, 1965), babies (W. E. Freud, 1967), handicapped children (Burlingham, 1975; Edgcumbe & Baldwin, 1986), psychotic children (Thomas et al., 1966), and psychotic adults (Freeman, 1973).

Developmental psychoanalysis:
theoretical and applied

Normality and Pathology in Childhood (A. Freud, 1965a) represented Anna Freud's break with her father. Freud had written: "symptoms . . . give us our bearings when we make our diagnosis" (1916–17, p. 271). Anna Freud was claiming, however, that the symptoms, inhibitions, and anxieties of children are produced by processes that have more to do with the strains and stresses of development than with pathology. Consequently, they cannot be relied upon in assessment and diagnosis (A. Freud, 1965a, p. 120). To mark this theoretical advance, she wrote a paper entitled "Beyond the Infantile Neurosis" (1982a). She had discussed the infantile neurosis in her 1965 book and had pointed to the fact that, contrary to what had been originally thought in the early years, one cannot assume adult pathology from childhood manifestations. "Beyond the Infantile Neurosis" echoed her father's paper, *Beyond the Pleasure Principle* (1920g), but only in its title, not in its content. For Freud, what lay beyond the pleasure principle was the death instinct and its manifestation in the repetition compulsion; but for Anna Freud, what lay beyond the infantile neurosis was a developmental psychopathology. Freud had worked from pathology and drawn conclusions about normality. Anna Freud, on the other hand, worked from detailed descriptions of normality to assessments of pathology.

The 1960s proved to be one of Anna Freud's most creative periods. As she entered the 1970s, she was intent upon making child analysis an activity of equal status with adult analysis. To this end, she returned to Vienna after 30 years of exile in order to urge the International Psychoanalytical Association to accredit the child analysis training course run at the Hampstead Clinic. This petition was unsuccessful; however, a compromise was reached with the British Society, who agreed to accept the Hampstead Training Course as an official training in child analysis, but only for those who were already adult analysts. After the Vienna Congress of 1971, she declared that the great unknown of psychoanalytic theory and practice was normal development. In this she was echoing Kris's contention that knowledge of the normal was an "underdeveloped" or "distressed" area in psychoanalysis (Kris, 1951, p. 15). This was the field in which child analysis, and the name of Anna Freud, was going to leave its mark for posterity. In 1978, she asserted that child analysis would contribute "the vicissitudes of forward development and exploration of the ego's synthetic function" to psychoanalysis (A. Freud, 1978, p. 99). She set about pursuing the research direction taken in *Normality and Pathology in Childhood* (1965a) and began to study child cases where normal development was hindered by environmental circumstances of deprivation, developmental delay, or deviation. These papers are collected in Volume 7 of her *Writings*, entitled *Problems of Psychoanalytic Training, Diagnosis, and the Technique of Therapy* (1971a), and in Volume 8, entitled *Psychoanalytic Psychology of Normal Development* (1982b). They include the only paper in the literature on termination in child analysis (1971b), a developmental metapsychological attempt at the classification of childhood symptomatology (1970), indications and contraindications for child analysis (1968b, 1982c), and a psychoanalytic view of developmental psychopathology (1974, 1976, 1982a).

Her most innovative contribution in this period of her work was her twofold classification of infantile psychopathology: one based on conflict and responsible for the anxiety states, and phobic, obsessional, and hysterical manifestations, i.e. the infantile neuroses, the other based on developmental defects in the personality as a result of developmental irregularities and failures, and responsible for psychosomatic symptomatology, backwardness, and the atypical and borderline states (A. Freud, p. 70). She spelt out the implications of these two psychopathologies and cautioned against the failure to recognize the distinction between them. Errors in assessing psychopathology can lead the clinician to link neurotic symptoms in either children or adults to events in the first year of life. "Whatever clashes occur at that time proceed externally between the infant and his environment, not internally within a not yet existing structure. Where deprivation and frustration are excessive, this leads not to symptom formation but to developmental setbacks" (1974, p. 71). This notion of developmental psychopathology was an attempt to offer an alternative to the reconstructive approach of Klein (who had died in 1960).

Anna Freud's guiding principle was to focus on the many types of observable milestones in the child's life, especially in the first year, and to make assessments from these, rather than focusing on what can never be reconstructed with certainty.

Anna Freud went on to apply the results of this work in three areas: child-rearing practices, training for child-care workers and child and adult analysts, and child and family law. Her interest in the latter had been awakened by an invitation in 1968 to teach in the Law School at Yale University and at the Yale Child Study Centre. This brought her into contact with Joseph Goldstein, a Professor of Law, and Albert J. Solnit, an analyst and professor of paediatrics and psychiatry. The initial fruits of this collaboration were published in 1973 as *Beyond the Best Interests of the Child* (Goldstein, Freud, & Solnit, 1973). This book attempted "to translate what we know from psychoanalysis about growth and development into procedural and substantive guidelines for deciding a child's placement" (p. 7). Concepts introduced in this book such as "the psychological parent" and "the least detrimental alternative" (pp. 53–64) have become part and parcel of legal proceedings involving children all over the world. The aim of the book was legal reform, so that the best interests of the child would be paramount in courts of law where cases involving divorces, foster-care placements, and adoptions were being heard. It was universally hailed as a milestone in the psycho-legal field.

In the two succeeding volumes, *Before the Best Interests of the Child* (Goldstein, Freud, & Solnit, 1979), and *In the Best Interests of the Child* (Goldstein, Freud, & Solnit, 1986), the authors discuss the question of the removal of children from their parents. Such an action should only be contemplated when parental care has been a complete failure. The authors specify the kinds of neglect, violence, or insanity that are grounds for removal of children from their parents, as well as indicating the kinds of parental behaviour that, though alarming, are not grounds for state intervention. What is required of the adjudicators is an empathic understanding of how children, with differing histories, feel at the different developmental stages. The third volume in this trilogy is directed at the decision-makers. It cautions professionals against overestimating their skills and expertise because of their unconscious rescue phantasies and urges them to be vigilant to ensure that personal views do not form the basis of professional judgements. It attempts to highlight the limits of knowledge, training, and authority with which professionals working in child placement have to contend.

Conclusion

Anna Freud died on 9 October 1982. The trilogy that culminated in *In the Best Interests of the Child* (Goldstein et al., 1986) proved to be one of the joys of her later life, as it gave her a platform from which to make meaningful recommendations that would directly affect the lives of many thousands of children. Another great joy was the launching in 1978 of the *Bulletin of the Hampstead Clinic*, now the *Bulletin of the Anna Freud Centre*. Despite these joys, however, she had outlived many of her family and friends, including her closest companion, Dorothy Burlingham, who died in 1979. Anna Freud mourned these losses, but she remained active up until her own death. Memorial tributes abound: they hail her as a child expert (Solnit, 1983; Solnit & Newman, 1984), as a radical innovator and staunch conservative (Wallerstein, 1984), as a child analyst (Edgcumbe, 1983); for her contribution to psychiatry (Freeman, 1983), and to the psychoanalytic study and treatment of adults (Yorke, 1983); for her contribution to the work of the International Psychoanalytical Association (Limentani, 1983); and, finally, for her contribution to the technique of child analysis (Edgcumbe, 1985). In addition, the Anna Freud Memorial Issue of the *Bulletin of the Hampstead Clinic* (1983) contains tributes from over 30 colleagues and friends that attest to her breadth of interests, her expertise, and her humanity.

Beginning psychotherapists, whether working with adults or with children, have much to learn from a study of her life and work. Perhaps her greatest gift was her ability to make the most difficult concepts clear and simple and to demystify the excessively academic and often dense language of psychoanalysis. When one sets out to write in simple and elegant language, one always runs the risk of having one's work considered an over-simplification of complex topics; but as any good teacher knows, the ability to express difficult concepts simply is the mark of a knowledgeable mind. Anna Freud was first and foremost a teacher. In her reminiscences to Coles, she says: "What you were early in your career, you'll probably find a way of being again. That's the way it's been for me, at least. When I write, I think the teacher in me comes out" (Coles, 1992, p. 174). I think it does; and I hope that this chapter has captured her clarity of style and ease of expression. It is this quality, together with her faithful adherence to the fundamental tenets of Freud's drive structural theory and her own elaborations of it, that render her work a singularly appropriate starting point for any student of psychoanalysis.

CHAPTER TWO

Melanie Klein and W. R. D. Fairbairn: the clinical foundations and explanatory concepts of their theories

Thomas Freeman

Melanie Klein and Fairbairn have introduced new concepts that are at variance with Freud's theories of normal and abnormal mental life. Klein postulated that the Oedipus complex has its beginnings in the fifth month of life, while Freud hypothesized that it emerged between the third and fourth year. Fairbairn proposed that the decisive influence in mental development and in mental pathology consists of the child's endopsychic relationship to the mother. The psychic manifestations of instinct and the conflicts to which they give rise—whether in the spheres of anality or genitality—are secondary to these endopsychic object relations. This is again in direct opposition to Freud who theorized that it is the psychic representations of the instincts (wishes, needs) that drive endopsychic object relations, and not the other way round, as Fairbairn believed. Despite these and other fundamental differences, Klein and Fairbairn did not follow Jung and Adler and break away from the mainstream of psychoanalysis. In fact, both these innovators claim that their additions, emendations, and deletions are a development of Freud's basic assumptions about mental life. All these changes, claimed as advances in the understanding of healthy and pathological mental life, have had an inevitable influence on the technique of treatment. This led to significant differences in technique of psychoanalytic treatment. In this chapter an account is given of the theories of Klein and Fairbairn, the clinical phenomena on which they are based, and the principal features of their therapeutic methods.

The work of Melanie Klein

[I]

There is general agreement that the source of Melanie Klein's theoretical concepts of healthy and pathological mental life is the work of Karl Abraham with whom she was in analysis in Berlin in the 1920s. Attributable to Abraham (1924) are the concepts of oral incorporation (introjection), oral-sadism, anal expulsion of the damaged or dangerous internal object, the part object, and the protection of the "good" or satisfying object from attack. Abraham (1924) had formulated these concepts on the basis of his psychoanalytic work with patients suffering from manic-depressive psychoses. He confirmed Freud's (1917e [1915]) theory that the depressed patient whose illness followed loss of a loved one—albeit ambivalently—incorporates (introjects) this lost object. Abraham postulated that this incorporation takes place orally. In doing so, the patient regains the lost object by psychically becoming the object himself. However, the hate engendered in the patient by being abandoned can now only be directed against the self identified with the lost object. The self-criticisms and self-hatred of the depressed patient are, in fact, expressions of hatred of the lost object. Abraham (1924) hypothesized that when the lost object is incorporated it is psychically attacked. This was suggested by the oral-sadistic phantasies of biting and incorporating the object expressed by the depressed patients. The guilt that is such a striking feature of manic-depressive depressions is thus caused by the psychic fact that they have murdered the lost love object.

Further observations on obsessional neuroses and the schizophrenias led Abraham (1924) to put forward a developmental schema the essential element of which was the concept of a gradual recognition, by the infants, of the mother as a whole-object representation, who had to be protected from a violence and sadism which accompanied the need for satisfaction at the breast. This violent acquisitiveness begins with the appearance of the teeth (Freeman & Freeman, 1992). The infant, at this stage, is absolutely egocentric and without thought or feeling for the mother. Abraham theorized that the breast–mother is psychically incorporated with the milk and is subject to oral–sadistic attacks. As mental development proceeds through the oral phase, a trend towards the preservation of the love object (the mother) makes its appearance. The sadistic attacks are confined to a part of the love object. Thus a part object (the breast) is sacrificed to save the mother as a whole. With further development the destructive attacks against the internalized mother are reduced in frequency and intensity as the mother becomes recognized as a separate individual, with her own sensitiveness and limitations.

Klein, like Abraham, attributes great importance to the role of the mother in the child's mental development, and to that extent the influence of the father is diminished. For the first time in psychoanalytic theorizing derivatives of the aggressive instinct—destructiveness, hatred, and acquisitiveness—are given a greater prominence than expressions of the libido. Klein's developmental scheme is an extensive elaboration of that described by Abraham. Much greater emphasis is laid on unconscious phantasies, many new contents are described, and their constitutional determinants are underlined. There is, however, one significant difference between Abraham and Klein which claims attention. This is the concept of the part object. As described above, for Abraham (1924) this hypothesized mental representation only comes to the fore with the slackening of the attacks on the whole "good" internal object. It is not present from the beginning of mental life. Klein's (1932) hypothesis is that the part object (the breast) is the infant's first object relationship and precedes the appearance of the mother as a whole-object representation.

[II]

Melanie Klein's theories are derived from her psychoanalytic work with young children who suffered from night terrors, phobias, obsessive–compulsive symptoms, and disturbances of sleep and excretion (Klein, 1932). These children were over-dependent on their mothers and suffered separation anxiety. In play they were destructive and cruel. Klein based her therapeutic (play) technique on the theory, in part derived from dream analysis, that the children's play gave symbolic expression to the unconscious conflicts which led to the symptomatology. Interpretations of the symbolic content of play were not to be made indiscriminately. Interpretation was called for when the child's play was disturbed by anxiety. This affect could be discerned when changes and interruptions occurred in the flow of the play. Using this method of symbolic interpretation, Klein (1932), following Abraham, was able to identify a number of unconscious phantasies that she believed to be ultimately responsible for the children's anxiety and the resulting symptoms and abnormal behaviour. The contents of these unconscious phantasies were of a cruel, vicious, and destructive nature—phantasies of biting and cutting up the breast, greedily devouring the contents of the breast, attacks on the contents of the mother's body, robbing the mother of the father's penis believed to be in her body. These phantasized attacks were carried out with the teeth, with urine, and with faeces. The mother was the object.

Klein (1932) explained the children's terrors, their separation anxiety, and their destructive and cruel play in the following manner. The imaginary figures who terrified the children were the result of the projection of the sadistic phantasies. This projection, creating "bad" (unsatisfying) objects, spared the mother, who could remain a "good" (satisfying) intrapsychic object. The mother had now been split into a protecting, "good" object and a "bad" frightening (persecuting) object. The mother's presence protected the children from the feared attacks by the imaginary figures representing the "bad" mother seeking retaliation for the damage done to her. Klein observed that she was immediately drawn in to this series of mental events. She was split into "good" and "bad" objects. She was needed for protection but was also feared. Klein concluded that these defences (splitting and projection) against the destructive unconscious phantasies had to be dealt with immediately, otherwise there was a threat to the treatment. To simply reassure the child would only reinforce the defences while leaving the unconscious destructive phantasies and fear of Klein undisturbed. Interpretation of the negative transferences (i.e. the hatred of Klein and the anxiety this evoked) became the keystone of the therapeutic work (Klein, 1932). The destructive play of the children followed from their having internalized (introjected) the mother representation (object), who had become "bad" and vicious as a result of projection. In identification with this "bad" object, the children attacked their toys. The play enacted a psychic situation in which the "bad" internal objects destroyed the "good" object. At the same time, however, the most strenuous efforts were made through splitting, to save the "good" object from irreparable injury.

Klein (1932) identified similar unconscious phantasies in adult patients suffering from symptom and character neuroses. Projection and splitting of the object acted as defences, as in the children, to protect the "good" objects. Again as in the case of the disturbed children, the patient tried to preserve the "good" objects from his psychic destructiveness by projecting this onto figures outside the analysis. The analyst was converted into an idealized figure. The essence of Klein's technique was to analyse this defence of idealization brought about by splitting. As the analyst became the object of the patient's projection of his destructive phantasies, his task was to direct the attention of the latter to this defence (projection) and the unrealistic anxiety it caused.

The concept of unconscious phantasy is fundamental to Klein's theory of normal and abnormal mental life (Isaacs, 1952). Unconscious phantasies have their sources in the life and death instincts (Freud, 1920g) and they form the content of unconscious mental processes. Instinctual activity and phantasies proceed concurrently. Unconscious phantasies are sensory, concrete, non-verbal experiences that ultimately become the basis for thinking and the affects. Instinctual as they are, unconscious phantasies are innate and constitutionally determined. They appear at the moment of birth, hence their independence from somatic developmental processes (Freeman & Freeman, 1992). Splitting and projection are unconscious phantasies no less than, for example, the phantasy of scooping out the contents of the mother's breast and body. Splitting, which divides the object into "good" and "bad" objects, is experienced by the infant as a physical cutting of the object into bits. Projection is a physical expulsion of poisonous faeces that otherwise would damage the "good" internal object.

Klein (1932) further postulates that the pathological mental events that she identified in the disturbed children were but an exaggerated version of the mental processes of the healthy infant. According to Klein infantile sadism reaches its maximum intensity during and after weaning (the phase of maximal sadism). This sadism is a threat to the "good" nourishing breast (a part object), which has been incorporated (introjected) on the basis of satisfaction gained from the breast. The sadism is directed to the breast and the penis. As these part objects become endowed, through projection, with anal and acquisitive phantasies, their introjection leads to efforts to expel them as if they were faeces. The aim of the expulsion is to preserve the "good" part object (the breast). This aim is pursued throughout the developmental process. The danger is that once the "bad" objects are expelled, they become the source of dangerous and damaging attacks. Klein likened the nature and intensity of the anxieties of the 3- to 5-month-old infant to those of the adolescent or adult schizophrenic patient. This similarity warranted the description of the healthy infant's anxieties as psychotic or persecutory.

Female and male infants have identical acquisitive and destructive aims, innate or accentuated by real oral frustrations. The sadistic acquisitiveness is transferred, Klein (1932) hypothesizes, from the mother's breast to the father's penis, which is believed to be inside the mother following the parental coitus. The boy, like the girl, initially has a feminine receptive attitude to the father's penis. However, his perception of the penis inside the mother is influenced by the attacks he has directed against the father's penis. The father's penis is, therefore, particularly frightening because of the male infant's wish to have the mother to himself, possess everything that she possesses, and exclude the father (the Oedipus complex). The female infant dreads the mother because of her wish to rob her of the father's penis and of the babies believed to be inside the mother. She envies the mother and her fecundity. The boy also envies the mother because of her ability to have babies and suckle them. This envy of the creativity of women continues throughout life as an unconscious envy of women.

As a consequence of her belief that the anxieties of the infant and those of the adult psychotic patient are virtually identical, Klein (1932, 1935, 1946) has made extensive use of psychiatric nomenclature to describe developmental processes. In her later work, she was influenced by the fact that the ego is split in the schizophrenias. She attributed the persecutory delusions and the passivity experiences (ideas of being con-trolled mentally and physically by a persecutor) to splitting of the ego and to the free use of the unconscious phantasy of projective identification. The content of this destructive phan-tasy consists of the penetration of objects by split-off parts of the ego. However, the objects penetrated by dangerous bits of the ego become a threat to the ego, which is now subject to violent attacks. Passivity experiences result when the ego is itself penetrated by the object containing the split-off parts of the ego. These schizoid mechanisms (splitting and projective identification), as Klein (1946) called them, are elements of the psychic complex (paranoid–schizoid position) constituted by the part objects and the anxieties they generate.

In the case of manic-depressive psychoses, Klein identified the presence of phantasied attacks on the introjected whole "good" object (the mother) in contrast to the attacks on the "good" part objects as in the schizophrenias. The whole object is psychically destroyed by these attacks. Guilt and remorse occur. To relieve these reactions, the object is omnipotently healed and brought to life. At this point the patient's depres-sion turns into a maniacal state. This manic defence—as Klein (1935) calls it—is a complex composed of the denial of psychic reality (i.e. the killing of the "good" object) and omnipotence leading to restoration of the object (reparation).

Again Klein (1935) postulated that the pathological mental events occurring in the schizophrenias and in manic-depressive psychoses are exaggerations of the developmental processes occurring in the healthy infant. In the first three months of life, the infant comes to a psychic state which Klein (1946) called the paranoid–schizoid position because schizoid mechanisms as described above are predominant. Object relations being part object in kind are directed by splitting and projective identification. There is a continuing struggle between attacks on the "good" part objects (breast, penis) and attempts to preserve them. At about the fifth month the infant enters the depressive position where the anxieties are concerned with introjected "good" whole objects rather than the part objects, as in the paranoid–schizoid position. The Oedipus complex arises within the context of the depressive position.

Klein's (1935) preference for the concept of positions rather than developmental stages followed from her theory that the psychic components of those positions—psychotic anxieties, schizoid mechanisms, manic defences—persist throughout life in varying degrees of intensity. Normally the (infantile) psychotic anxieties (persecutory and depressive) gradually attenuate. If for constitutional or environmental reasons they come to predominate, a predisposition is established for the later development of schizophrenic and manic-depressive psychoses.

Klein (1957) attributes the omnipresence of destructive phantasies and the power they exert to the death instinct (Freud, 1920g) deflected from the infantile ego to objects. This externalization of the death instinct saves the rudimentary ego from complete fragmentation. The phantasy in which the ego is split is a defensive manoeuvre to disperse and thus weaken the death instinct as it acts from within. In her last contributions Klein (1957) concluded that envy is the first (externalized) derivative of the death instinct. It is envy that leads to phantasies of sadistically acquiring the contents of the breast and penis. Envy initiates the introjection of the "good" and subsequently "bad" part objects and leads to all the psychic developments that have been described above.

[III]

From the Kleinian standpoint psychotic (infantile) anxieties of varying degrees of intensity are responsible for the different types of mental illness. Persecutory anxiety is at its maximum height in the schizophrenias, but it is also present in the symptom and character neuroses. Depressive anxieties characterize manic-depressive states, as does the manic defence; but they are also active in the neuroses but in a mild form where the psychotic anxieties relate to whole objects rather than to part objects. Where depressive anxieties predominate over persecutory anxieties, the opportunity for the establishment of an analytic process is present. This is in accord with the theory that depressive anxieties make their appearance at a more advanced level of infantile mental development than do persecutory anxieties.

According to Kleinian theory, all relationships with others evoke and provide material for unconscious phantasy. Once the patient has entered into a commitment to undertake treatment, the analyst becomes inextricably involved with his unconscious phantasies (Klein, 1952). These unconscious phantasies will determine the nature and quality of the transference. The hypothesis that the transference arises immediately on the basis of unconscious phantasy is quite different from the concept of transference described by Freud and elaborated later by others (see chapter three). For these psychoanalysts, the real relationship predominates at the beginning of the analysis, and time is required for the full development of the transference neurosis (see chapter three).

Earlier, reference was made to Klein's (1957) theory that patients who participate in psychoanalytic treatment have a need to keep the analyst as a "good" object. This is an onerous and difficult intrapsychic task for the patient because the analyst is already the object of unconscious acquisitive and destructive phantasies. Envy of his possessions, powers, and status are the mainspring of these unconscious phantasies. Schizoid mechanisms (splitting, projective identification) are brought into play to preserve the analyst. Others outside the analysis become the focus of the transference hate, thus turning them into "bad" objects. They are also feared because they have been penetrated by parts of the ego that are destructive in themselves (projective identification). The wish to preserve the analyst as a protective and supportive figure is not successful, because these repudiated destructive parts of the ego are projected into him. He remains an object of fear. Simultaneously, attempts to repair the damage psychically inflicted on the analyst proceed via the manic defence. This reparation goes hand in hand with idealization.

In the Kleinian technique, the analyst must be at pains to avoid those actions and interventions that might reinforce the patient's defences of splitting, projective identification, and omnipotence (manic defence). Reassurance of any kind must be eschewed so that the patient is given every opportunity to become aware of his unconscious transference phantasies of envy, greed, hate, and acquisitiveness. As long as splitting, projective identification, and omnipotence are successful in keeping these unconscious phantasies at bay, they will provide a constant source of resistances to the treatment. Unconscious envy, for example, can lead to a devaluation of the analyst, and to a denigration or failure to understand the content of his interpretations (Klein, 1957).

The analyst's most important interventions are thus those that are concerned with the patient's unconscious transference phantasies and the psychotic anxieties they generate. All the patient's communications have to be drawn into the transference ("here and now" interpretations) because through its analysis therapeutic benefit will accrue. Dreams may be taken as an example. Reisenberg-Malcolm (1981) reports the following dream:

> The patient was in a strange house. She heard a noise and went upstairs. She saw a woman who was looking helplessly at a washing-machine from which water was cascading all over the floor. The seams of the machine had burst.

At this point the patient wakened in fear. Reisenberg-Malcolm (1981) interpreted as follows. Thus far the patient had regarded her as strong and invulnerable, imagining that she was machine-like. As long as she could do this, she had no fear of the damage she had psychically inflicted on her (Reisenberg-

Malcolm). Reisenberg-Malcolm was the washing-machine—the object of the patient's destructiveness. Through interpretations of this kind, the patient becomes aware of how fearful he is of his destructiveness. There is a concomitant lessening of anxiety and a recognition of the unrealistic nature of the transference phantasies. Transference interpretations of this kind help the patient to abandon his need to split his objects into "good" and "bad".

Fairbairn's object-relation theory

[I]

Fairbairn (1940, 1944) has derived the explanatory and developmental concepts that comprise his theory of object relations from patients whose symptomatology and behaviour differed significantly from those suffering from the neuroses (anxiety hysteria, conversion hysteria, obsessional neurosis). The symptoms his patients complained of consisted of a profound sense of inferiority, inability to concentrate, work difficulties, de-realization, depersonalization, compulsive masturbation, psychosocial inhibitions, and impulsive and antisocial behaviour. Fairbairn (1940) discerned that these patients entertained phantasies of omnipotence that were either overt or latent. They isolated themselves from others and were unrealistic in their view of life. A characteristic feature of their mental life was an ability to tolerate contradictory thoughts, intentions, and actions. In Fairbairn's opinion this was the result of splits in the personality structure. The diagnosis of schizoid personality seemed appropriate for these patients.

Fairbairn (1940) noted that his patients were fearful of the demands they made on him. They feared his disapproval and loss of regard for them. They reacted to weekends and other breaks in the analysis with fear and anger. Fairbairn concluded that the patient's relationship with him was principally characterized by wishes for and fear of dependency on one hand, and wishes for and fear of independence on the other. All patients, even those who presented as typical cases of neurosis, were burdened by a sense of inferiority, but they were nevertheless egotistical and grandiose. They over-valued phantasy and intellect at the expense of reality.

Fairbairn (1940) was also impressed by patients' fear that they had exhausted him because they could not be satisfied with his efforts to help them. They felt endangered by their insatiable hunger and potentially destructive greed. Only by isolating themselves from others—and from Fairbairn also—could they ensure the safety of their love objects. This was why they had to turn to phantasy for consolation. This was the basic schizoid position to be found in all patients irrespective of the clinical diagnosis.

The ability to tolerate contradictory attitudes to reality, to the self, and to others and to keep affect apart from thought was, in Fairbairn's opinion, the result of a split in the ego. This splitting (the schizoid position) was least obvious in the symptom neuroses and most apparent in cases of multiple personality, in hysterical amnesic states, and in the schizophrenias. Fairbairn observed that patients' anxieties arose within the context of interpersonal relationships being vividly demonstrated in the analytic situation. This led Fairbairn (1944) to reject Freud's sexual theory of the neuroses. Instead, he proposed that the predisposition and immediate cause of mental disorders were to be found in disturbances affecting (endopsychic) object relations—not from unconscious conflict between unacceptable (childhood) wishes and the remainder of the personality.

In order to describe the endopsychic object relations characteristic of mental illnesses, Fairbairn (1943, 1944) delineated a series of explanatory concepts that can be illustrated by reference to clinical data.

A married female patient in her early 30s was totally dependent on her husband, but this dependency had a controlling, demanding character. She rejected him in different ways, and this led him to doubt himself and his masculinity. During psychoanalytic treatment she produced a plethora of sexual phantasies of a seductive and exhibitionistic nature. She excited the man, frustrated him, and then dismissed him. The content of these phantasies stood in complete contrast to her behaviour in real life, where she was extremely self-conscious, timid, and lacking in self-confidence. Psychic splitting (splitting of the ego) allowed her to deny her sense of inferiority and through phantasy enjoy a sense of superiority.

Dependency initially characterized her attitude to the analyst. She feared being criticized and rejected. When this anxiety passed, her need to control the analyst and punish him for not meeting her demands made its way into her behaviour. This, in turn, was a cause of anxiety. In this case these transference manifestations were a repetition of the patient's relationship with her mother. She was tied to her mother because of over-stimulation (the mother as an exciting and needed object) on the one hand, and by the mother's critical and frustrating behaviour (the mother as a rejecting and frustrating object) on the other. Both were combined in the person of the husband and, subsequently, the analyst. As the analysis proceeded, it became apparent that as well as the patient putting the analyst in place of the mother, she also played the roles of the exciting and frustrating mother in relation to him, as she did with the husband (reverse transference—see chapter three).

On the basis of such clinical observations, Fairbairn (1944) postulated that the exciting and rejecting objects normally appear during the phase of infantile dependence on the mother. The hysterias thus present an exaggerated picture of the process that occurs in the healthy infant. The infant inevitably suffers some degree of frustration during the nursing period. This leads to anger with the mother. To dissipate the anger, which makes the mother "bad", her mental representation is split into a "good" (satisfying) mother and a "bad" (frustrating) mother. The anger is confined to the "bad" mother and so relations can be maintained with the "good" mother. However, this mental manoeuvre does not succeed in reducing the infant's vulnerability. To effect control over the real frustrating situation with the mother, the "bad" mother is internalized. There now exists an intolerable internal (endopsychic) situation characterized by need and frustration. This internal situation is dealt with by splitting the internalized object into an "exciting" and a "rejecting" object.

The patient described above had identified with the "exciting" and "rejecting" internalized mother. Such identifications, according to Fairbairn (1943), occur because all object relationships in childhood are based on identification. When an infant or young child is faced with an overstimulating or frustrating situation, identification takes place with the "bad" object that was the cause of the distress. This identification brings about a repression of the "bad" object and the experiences associated with it (Fairbairn, 1944). Mental illnesses arise when there is a failure to maintain the repression of "bad" objects.

Fairbairn (1940) further cites cases of multiple personality and phenomena observable in the analytic situation to support his theory that the infantile ego is subject to psychic splitting. He conceives the infantile ego as splitting into a central (conscious and preconscious) ego, a libidinal ego (childhood type of ego), and an anti-libidinal ego or internal "saboteur". These ego structures are the source of libidinal and aggressive impulses. They stand in a close relationship to the internal "exciting" object and the internal "rejecting" object. The libidinal ego is paired with the "exciting" object, and the "internal saboteur" with the "rejecting" object. These ego structures and objects are unconscious.

In the case of the female patient described above, her need for attention, her dependency, and her insatiable demands, which characterized her relationship with husband and analyst, were an expression of her unconscious libidinal ego in its interaction with the "exciting" object (husband and analyst). Her central ego was so depleted by splitting that it had insufficient strength to hold off the demands of the libidinal ego. In this case, the "internal saboteur" (the anti-libidinal ego) could be discerned behind the "rejecting" object with which it was closely connected. The patient not only assumed the role of the rejecting object when she frustrated and disappointed the analyst and the husband, but she also demonstrated the power of the "internal saboteur" to subdue both the libidinal ego and the "exciting" objects. The resistances, which met attempts to free her from her attachments to her childhood objects (mother as exciting and rejecting), are explained by Fairbairn (1944) as being due to the strong libidinal ties that join the libidinal ego and the "exciting" object and connect the "internal saboteur" and the "rejecting object.

According to Fairbairn (1944), the content of dreams no less than the symptoms of mental illnesses reveal the relationships that exist between ego structures and internal objects. The figures in dreams give representation on one or more ego structures and internal objects. In addition there is the dreamer as observer (central ego) and the dreamer as observing object. The following dream illustrated Fairbairn's (1944) theory that dreams represent dramatizations of situations existing in psychic reality:

A patient, an unmarried woman of 27, dreamt that *she was being teased by her young brother. He tried to shoot her. She telephoned the police but had to speak in French. She could not get through to the police station. She then saw that she had been wounded in the ankle and was bleeding. Someone—a woman in the background—shot a man she believed to be a forger.*

On the day of the dream she had been teased by a male colleague. She had said that she felt so tired she would like to lie down in the Rest Room. He jokingly responded by saying he would come along, too. She felt uncomfortable because she found him attractive. Before going to sleep, she had been reading a "thriller" set in France. A gang of criminals are involved in forging an artist's pictures. The leader of the gang tries to telephone an accomplice but cannot not get through to him. Later someone shoots the leader. These associations from the day of the dream revealed that the patient was identified with the leader of the gang and that the colleague and her brother were identified with one another.

In the dream, following Fairbairn (1944), the central ego finds expression in the dreamer as observer. Her libidinal ego is represented by the leader of the gang, the forger, who commits a forbidden act.

A memory of sexual games in childhood, subsequently recalled, offered support for the hypothesis that the forger represented her libidinal ego. She recalled playing a doctor game. She was the instigator (the leader) and she painted a friend's vulva with a brush dipped in water. Her "internal saboteur" was represented in the dream by the unknown woman who shoots the forger with whom she is identified. The exciting object is represented by her colleague/brother. The libidinal ego and the exciting object are the foci of attacks by the "internal saboteur" and the "rejecting" object.

Fairbairn (1944) points out that these attacks are without moral significance. They lead to anxiety and not to guilt because the "internal saboteur's" attacks are vindictive and precede in development the superego and moral judgement.

As a "short" (Fairbairn, 1944), this dream dramatizes the patient's intrapsychic relationship with her brother/colleague, who is both the "exciting" and "rejecting" object. Such an interpretation, Fairbairn would suggest, finds support in the fact that she and her brother participated in sexual games, which she initiated. At the same time, he was a source of frustration, as she could not meet his physical demands on her as a playmate. The attack upon the libidinal ego by the "internal saboteur" also represents the mother's attack on the patient because of her seduction of the brother. In Fairbairn's theory these endopsychic object relationships have followed the pattern laid down in the course of the patient's earliest interaction with her mother. The frustrating nature of this relationship accentuated the splitting of the ego and determined the quality of the patient's sexuality. With the brother and later with men in general, sexual relationships were exciting, frustrating, and always tinged with anxiety and aggression—hence her failure to establish a satisfactory heterosexual relationship in adult life.

Fairbairn does not make a distinction, as Freud (1900a) does, between the manifest content of dreams and the latent dream thoughts. Fairbairn (1944) utilizes details of the manifest content to provide material for his interpretations of the endopsychic situation as he perceives it in the individual case. This blurring of the distinction between manifest content and latent dream thoughts follows directly from his theory of mental structures as outlined above.

[II]

Fairbairn's theory of endopsychic object relations inevitably led him to revise psychoanalytic technique radically. His clinical experiences led him to conclude (Fairbairn, 1958) that from a therapeutic point of view interpretation was not, in itself, a sufficient instrument for psychic change. He reasoned that as the patient's difficulties arose from an unsatisfying and disappointing childhood relationship with the mother, heightened in inner (psychic) reality, the relationship with the analyst must assume decisive importance therapeutically. The analyst as a real person is in a position to bring about a beneficial alteration in the patient's endopsychic state. What had been denied to the patient in his early childhood could be rectified in his relationship with the analyst and an opportunity afforded of psychic maturation. If such an aim were to be successfully pursued, then drastic changes had to be made to the psychoanalytic method. Fairbairn (1958) asserted that the method, as practised, contained within it anti-therapeutic elements. The requirement that the patient should assume the recumbent position on the couch and the demand for free associations only encouraged the revival of childhood traumatic events, thus heightening resistances. The "couch technique" was by no means neutral, nor was the analyst himself. The technique might offer security to the analyst, but it aggravated the patient's anxieties.

The primary aim of psychoanalytic technique, in Fairbairn's (1958) opinion, is to bring about a synthesis of the personality by reducing the degree of splitting responsible for the symptomatology. This is a difficult undertaking because of the patient's unconscious resistance against an alteration in the psychic "status quo". There is an unconscious need on the patient's part to retain his aggression in an internalized state, so that the external object is protected. This requires that the early splitting of the internalized object (mother) into a "good" and a "bad" object is maintained. An intrapsychic "closed system" (Fairbairn, 1958) has evolved, which perpetuates the relationship between the various ego attitudes (libidinal ego, central ego, internal saboteur) and their respective internal objects ("exciting" and "rejecting"), as well as between one another. The principal aim of treatment is "to effect breaches of the 'closed system' which constitutes the patient's inner world and thus to make this inner world accessible to the outer reality" (Fairbairn, 1958, p. 380).

Fairbairn (1958) concluded that why the recognition and interpretation of transferences was so often disappointing therapeutically was because the phenomena of the transference (see chapter three) were expressions of the "closed system". For therapeutic change to take place, a relationship between two people (analyst and patient) in the outer world must exist. This will lead to a break in the "closed system" within which the patient's symptoms have evolved and are maintained. The establishment of an open system allows the possibility of a correction of the "abnormal" endopsychic object relations and permits realistic relationships with external objects. It follows from this that the analyst must actively intervene in the analytic situation and abandon the detachment insisted upon by the traditional analytic method. The analyst's interventions must be designed to overcome the patient's (unconscious) efforts to force the analyst into the "closed system", through encouraging transferences. Thus transferences (Fairbairn, 1958) act to oppose the analytic process, unless they are identified for what they are— expressions of the "closed system". By disrupting this "closed system", the analyst can help the patient to accept "the open system of reality" (Fairbairn, 1958). In this way, the patient's infantile dependence can be reduced and the hatred of the libidinal object ameliorated. To facilitate this, Fairbairn advocated that all those requirements that are part of the conventional psychoanalytic method must be modified or abandoned. The analyst is to be seen by the patient as a real person who then acts as a corrective to the unrealistic endopsychic objects. To this end, Fairbairn stopped asking his patients to lie on the couch, nor did he sit behind them. Instead, he had the patient sit up with his chair parallel to his. At all times the analytic method had to conform to the needs of the patient.

Freud, Klein, and Fairbairn

The history of psychoanalytic technique reveals the influence of psychoanalytic theories on the therapeutic method itself. This can be seen in the change from the cathartic or abreactive therapy introduced by Freud (1895d, with Breuer) to what became known as defence or resistance analysis (Fenichel, 1941). The former was based on a theory of psychopathogenesis that postulated that the cause of hysterical symptoms lay in repressed memories of traumatic events. The treatment method (see chapter three) consisted of active attempts to recover these memories and in so doing allow the associated affects to be expressed (catharsis). This traumatic theory of neurosis gave way to the theory that the symptomatology of the neuroses have their source in unconscious conflicts generated by childhood wishes that are unacceptable to the remainder of the personality (Freud, 1916–17). The therapeutic task was, therefore, to bring about the removal of the (unconscious) resistances that opposed awareness of the unacceptable wishes. The techniques of treatment recommended by Klein and Fairbairn have similarly been determined by the theoretical innovations described earlier in this chapter. For those who follow Freud, the transference has a gradual development, but floating transferences (see chapter three) are not neglected. The "once upon a time" (memories of childhood and the psychical reactions to them) is afforded equal importance with transference ("here-and-now") interpretations. For Klein and Fairbairn, interpretation of these "here-and-now" transferences must take precedence, ensuring that the unconscious (transference) hate can find no hiding-place. It is not simply that Klein and Fairbairn advocate techniques that are at variance with those that Freud introduced. In his metapsychological (theoretical) papers Freud (1900a, 1915e, 1917d [1915], 1917e [1915], 1920g) seeks answers to questions that lie outside what is described as clinical theory (Thomä & Kächele, 1987). In these studies, Freud is not concerned with the contents of phantasies, dreams, transferences, and memories. Instead he is preoccupied with the origins, characteristics, and constituents of forms of mental activity—observed and inferred. What is the nature of wishing, of the affects, of repression, of the compulsion to repeat, of the hallucinatory quality of dreams and the manner in which the defence mechanisms come into being? It is not appropriate here to detail the hypotheses proposed by Freud, beyond saying that fundamentally these mental events have their origin in the need to avoid the unpleasure created by bodily needs.

Klein and Fairbairn also address these questions. However, they do so in a manner quite different from Freud. They do not subscribe to his theory that wishes, affects, repression, and other defences are basic, irreducible elements of mental life. They envisage these mental events as having been, in development, preceded and formed by elementary psychic processes—unconscious phantasies, in Klein's case. For Klein, depressive anxieties and the manic defence cause wish phantasies of omnipotence and reparation. Persecutory anxieties and splitting are the precursors of repression. These differences in theoretical perspectives can in part be attributed to the fact that Klein and Fairbairn postulate the presence of a rudimentary mind from the moment of birth in which primitive mental representations exist (unconscious phantasies; ego and object structures). Where Klein and Fairbairn differ is in the relative importance they ascribe to constitutional (hereditary) and acquired influences. The inner world envisaged by Klein is one dominated by derivatives of the death instinct and the measures employed to modify them. For Fairbairn, the nature of the inner world is largely determined by the environmental events impinging on the infant. In Freud's theory the earliest forms of mental life are without content—i.e. without mental representations of self and objects. Such mental processes as occur are governed by the pleasure principle—the need to reduce unpleasure arising from bodily needs or other causes. This theory is in accord with Freud's emphasis on the biological substratum of mental processes (Freud, 1940a [1938]). The extent to which these theories differ can be taken as a measure of the differences between the therapeutic methods of Klein, Fairbairn, and Freud.

CHAPTER THREE

The concept of transference: an introduction to its role in the psychoanalytic process

Ruth Freeman

Introduction

The transference is a fundamental concept of psycho-analytic treatment. When considering the transference from a historical and descriptive viewpoint what must be emphasized is (1) that the concept "of transference is one that has developed (*and is observable in*) the clinical situation of psychoanalytic practice" (Sandler, Holder, & Kawenoka, 1969]; (2) that the transference acts as a searchlight, illuminating the patient's forgotten past, and allows restitution of the continuity between the patient's past and present life; and (3) "Psychoanalytic treatment does not create transferences, it merely brings them to light" (Freud, 1905e [1901]) with "transference aris[ing] spontaneously in all human relationships" (Freud, 1910a [1909]).

These statements are of central importance to the understanding of the concept of transference and its role in psychoanalytic treatment. The fact that the transference is observable during the analytic process allows it to be clinically experienced.

In this chapter, an account is given of the evolution of the concept of the transference from its clinical roots. This is followed by clinical examples that illustrate the role of transferences in psychoanalytic psychotherapy.

Development of the concept of transference

Freud first used the term "transference" in the psychotherapy chapter of the *Studies on Hysteria* (Freud, 1895d, with Breuer). The technique of treatment at this time consisted of actively encouraging patients to recall memories associated with the onset of their illness. Experience suggested that the recovery of these forgotten memories of emotionally traumatic events led to the disappearance of symptoms. Freud found that the task of recall was difficult for patients. Interruptions in the flow of thoughts, apparent irrelevancies, silences, and even active opposition to Freud's efforts were commonplace. Freud described these obstacles to remembering as resistances and recognized that these resistances were mostly outside the patient's conscious control (unconscious resistances). Clearly a resistance occurred where a memory of a past event involving shame or embarrassment was remembered. From his experience with hypnotherapy (Freud, 1891d), Freud appreciated that his presence and behaviour must act decisively on the manner in which the patient reacted to his treatment method. Patients could not avoid having thoughts about him, as they would about anyone else they regularly encountered. The difficulty was, as he discovered, that these thoughts could be alarming, so they remained unspoken, and this acted as an obstruction to the further flow of ideas. He (1895d) further noted that some of these thoughts about himself were identical with memories of individuals emotionally important to the patient. Freud concluded that "the patient is frightened at finding that she is *transferring* onto the figure of the physician the distressing ideas which arise from the content of the analysis. This is frequent and indeed in some analyses a regular occurrence. Transference onto the physician takes place through a false connection" (Freud, 1895d, p. 302).

With the introduction of the method of free association, whereby the patient is asked to follow his thoughts while refraining from making judgements upon them, resistances could be easily identified. In the Dora case Freud asks,

> What are transferences? They are new editions or facsimiles of the impulses and phantasies which are aroused and made conscious during the progress of the analysis; but they have this peculiarity, which is characteristic for their species, that they replace some earlier person by the person of the physician. . . . a whole series of psychological experiences are revived, not belonging to the past, but applying to the person of the physician. [Freud, 1905e (1901), p. 116]

Freud (1905e [1901]) draws attention to the fact that psychoanalysis does not create transferences. They occur in the relationships of everyday life, and their presence may be detected in the inappropriate emotional reactions that often occur in these relationships. Transferences onto the person of the physician are not immediately obvious, and so it is necessary for him to be on the alert for clues to their presence. Dreams are valuable in this respect. When the transference is detected, it becomes an ally of the treatment, as it brings to light an important relationship of the patient's childhood and adolescence.

The Dora case taught Freud (1905e [1901]) that when certain transferences are overlooked, the resistances they create may bring the treatment to an end. Dora broke off treatment with Freud because she transferred onto him vengeful feelings that belonged to an older man whom she loved and admired but who ignored her. She left Freud as her wished-for lover had abandoned her. Dora, instead of remembering, in the course of the analysis, the unhappiness and anger she had experienced on account of this older man, lived out these reactions in relation to Freud. Unconsciously, she had made a "false connection". The task of the psychotherapist is to detect these repetitions and to help the patient to remember these past experiences of emotional or traumatic significance. When memories of this type are repeated in actions outside the analysis, they can be damaging to the patient's best interests. The physician (Freud, 1916–17) "obliges [*the patient*] to transform his repetition into memory". This allowed a reconstruction of the patient's earliest experiences, restoring continuity between the past and the present. Therefore "the greatest threat to the treatment [*the transference*] becomes its best tool, by whose help the most secret compartments of mental life can be opened" (Freud, 1916–17, p. 444).

It is necessary at this point to emphasize, as Freud (1912b) does, that it is impossible to understand the phenomena of transference in its expression of resistance unless a distinction is made between positive and negative transferences. There are transferences of affectionate and loving feelings as well as of hostile ones. Positive transferences may be purely friendly and caring, and these are acceptable to the patient, or they may be of such a nature—as, for example, erotic or dependency feelings—that they result in being inadmissible to the patient's consciousness. It follows that transferences will only act as resistances to the analysis if they are either a negative or a positive transference of a sexual or dependency nature.

In the *Introductory Lectures* of 1916–17, Freud describes the development of the transference during the psychoanalytic treatment of the hysterias and obsessional neuroses. At the beginning of the psychoanalytic process, the analysis is making good progress, since the patient has made an attachment to the physician. The transference is, therefore, the "most powerful motive in its advance" (Freud, 1912b). The patient is experiencing a positive transference to the physician (Freud, 1912b), and this cements the treatment alliance (Greenson, 1967) between patient and physician. This phase of the analysis is referred to as "fine weather" (Freud, 1916–17). However, this does not last. The positive feelings the patient had for the treatment and the physician make way for difficulties. The patient becomes silent, having no more to say. The transference is evolving as the physician becomes of greater importance to the patient, unconsciously representing the parents. The patient becomes sensitive to the words and behaviours of the physician. Alarming and embarrassing thoughts about the physician cannot be mentioned, since they would betray feelings of hostility, ambivalence, dependency, wishes to be loved, and so forth. The patient is now experiencing negative transferences. These can be combined with warm positive feelings, which have also to be defended against. The transference is acting as an obstacle to the progress of the analysis—a resistance. However, as Anna Freud (1936) points out, the transference is being used as a protection against anxieties and painful outcomes of childhood sexual and aggressive phantasies.

Such clinical observations as these suggested to Freud that the psychotherapist and the treatment had become the centre of the patient's neurosis. If the patient were to terminate the therapy, then he would be free of all the difficulties the treatment has provoked. Freud remarked that

> When the transference has arisen to this significance, work upon the patient's memories retreats far into the background. Therefore it is not incorrect to say that we are no longer concerned with the patient's earlier illness but with a newly created and transformed neurosis which has taken the former's place. We have followed this new edition of the old disorder from its start, we have observed its origin and growth, and we are especially well able to find our way about it since, as its object, we are situated right at the centre. All the patient's symptoms have abandoned their original meaning and have taken on a new sense which lies in a relation to the transference; or only such symptoms have persisted as are capable of undergoing such a transformation. But the mastering of this new artificial [transference] neurosis coincides with getting rid of the illness. [Freud, 1916–17, p. 444]

By 1920, Freud had amplified the concept of the transference neurosis. The neurotic patient in psychoanalytic treatment is compelled to repeat past experiences rather than remembering them. This "compulsion to repeat" is the core element of the transference neurosis. The patient can be observed "invariably act[ing] out in the sphere of the transference" (Freud, 1920g). The behaviour of the patient on the couch is another expression of the transference neurosis and the "compulsion to repeat". The patient who finds it impossible to lie on the couch frequently repeats an experience of being assaulted in childhood or adolescence. Her behaviour demonstrates her fears of the psychotherapist and her discomfort arising from the original trauma. Once the memory has been recovered, the patient can lie down without difficulty.

Other patients repeat repressed memories outside the consulting-room (acting out). Patients who are under the influence of the negative transference can act in such a way to be injurious to themselves. The anger may be turned against the self and result in self-destructive acts. Freud (1914g, p. 153) warned that these patients had to be protected from these impulses: ". . . people whom one cannot restrain from plunging into some quite undesirable project during the treatment, and who only afterwards become ready for, and accessible to, analysis". It was these observations of acting out in the transference that caused Freud to obtain a promise from his patients that they would make no major life decisions during treatment (Sandler, Holder, Kawenoka, et al., 1969].

Acting out of the transference, either in or outside the treatment sessions, is an indication that the transference neurosis has established itself. However, as Glover (1955) has described, the transference neurosis does not come in to existence immediately the analysis begins. At this time the patient relates to the psychotherapist as a real person. In fact, throughout the therapy the real relationship exists although it may be influenced and overshadowed by the transference neurosis. In the first few months of the analysis there will be sporadic indications of both positive and negative transferences. Their presence is not obvious, as they usually find conscious expression through allusions to figures in the patient's current life situation. They only require interpretation (brought to the patient's attention) when they are potential sources of resistance. In other words, the patient relates to the psychotherapist in the same way he relates to his wife, friends, employer, and those whose services he requires and pays for. Glover (1955) has called these transferences "floating transferences" and distinguishes them from the transference neurosis. On the basis of life-time experience he states that the transference neurosis does not develop in every case under analysis: "the analytic transference neurosis is seen in characteristic form only in the transference neuroses, the hysterias, conversions and obsessions" (p. 114). It is important to note at this point that not all psychotherapists would agree with Glover's distinction of floating (spontaneous) transferences and the transference neurosis. Indeed, Klein (1952) (see also chapter two) insists that powerful transferences operate from the very beginning of the treatment.

The transference neurosis (Freud, 1916–17; Glover, 1955), which describes the patient's conscious, pre-conscious, and unconscious preoccupation with the psychotherapist, develops quietly and slowly. Its unobtrusiveness may be such as to result in its being overlooked. The transference neurosis does not automatically reveal itself in a manner convincing to the patient. Dreams give expression to the transference neurosis (transference dreams), and they can be used to help the patient to understand, intellectually and emotionally, the nature of his relationship to the psychotherapist and to the emotionally significant figures in the past. The following dream is illustrative of this point.

A woman patient dreamt:

She is standing in a dress-shop with her younger sister, admiring herself in a dress she is trying on. Two female shop attendants are watching her. They are older, and smartly dressed. First they are smiling at her, but then one of the women starts to point, to laugh at her image in the mirror, to humiliate her. She rushes out of the shop.

Asked if the two smartly dressed women reminded her of anything, the patient was able to say that her two older female cousins had visited on the evening of the dream day. One of these cousins is kind and appreciates her difficulties, the other makes smart comments that humiliate her. She rushed upstairs to avoid this woman's comments about her appearance.

The psychotherapist said that the two women in the dream were like the psychotherapist and the dentist she regularly attends. The patient said she feared that both the dentist and the psychotherapist will terminate treatment because they will tire of hearing of her difficulties. She said how her two older sisters had cared for her when she was a child. The psychotherapist reminds her of Jane, her eldest sister.

She was with Jane when she was 4 years old and fell off the swing, breaking her arm. Jane was very upset and had fainted. Jane had not looked after her properly. The psychotherapist said that she feared that she would be humiliated here as in the dream and as by her cousin's smart comments. The psychotherapist, like her sister, would not cope or look after her properly, and she would be sent away to manage on her own. This intervention enabled the patient to tell the psychotherapist that she did not want to worry her and so had found it difficult to speak of things, since she feared she could not cope. This reminded her of her mother, with whom she had pretended everything was all right, since she believed her mother, too, was unable to cope if she knew how scared she had felt during her parents' violent arguments. The interpretation of this transference dream facilitated the further expression of the transference neurosis. The patient recognized her emotional reactions to the psychotherapist—fear and anger—and this enabled her to recall painful memories of her forgotten childhood.

Fenichel (1941) has drawn attention to several misunderstandings about the role of the psychotherapist. He is not simply a mirror onto which the patient "projects" his transferences. Neither is he silent, aloof, and unresponsive. The personality of the psychotherapist inevitably influences the transference. Different psychotherapists react differently, and this influences the patient. The sex of the psychotherapist, for example, is of decisive importance for transference reactions in many patients. With other patients the sex of the psychotherapist is unimportant. They can react with both mother and father transferences to a psychotherapist of the same sex as themselves.

With the introduction of the structural model—id, ego, and superego (Freud, 1923b)—transference manifestations could be ordered in terms of these concepts. Thus there are superego transferences, transferences arising from the ego, and id transferences. Superego (conscious and unconscious) transferences account for much of the resistance in the first few months of an analysis. The patient attributes (externalizes) his own superego values to the psychotherapist and fears his reaction to disclosures that evoke guilt. The patient can equally transfer onto the psychotherapist wishes—id [repressed] impulses—that frighten him and give him a bad conscience. The psychotherapist is now "the devil's advocate". He fears the psychotherapist is encouraging him to think and act in ways he finds unacceptable. Transferences that can be related to the ego have been described as transferences of defence (A. Freud, 1936). The patient uses, in his relationship to the psychotherapist, defence mechanisms that developed in childhood and that have become character traits. Illustrative is the defence described as "the identification with the aggressor" (A. Freud, 1936). When faced with anxiety due to forbidden wishes, these patients characteristically become aggressive. In the analytic situation the patient, in identification with the angry parent, berates the psychotherapist as he was criticized and attacked in his childhood. This is an example of the phenomenon of "reverse transference". The resistances are often difficult to overcome.

The pre-requisite for the analysis of the transference, when it comes to act as a resistance, is the patient's ability to both experience his reactions and also observe them with the aid of the psychotherapist. This is the essence of the treatment alliance. Without a capacity to detach the observing from the experiencing part of the ego, the patient is destined to believe that his emotional reactions to the psychotherapist have only the psychotherapy as their cause. This interferes with the patient's ability to understand that these emotional reactions are repetitions of painful and forgotten memories.

Clinical illustrations

The floating transference

Glover (1955) demonstrated that the transference neurosis evolved slowly, but even in the first few months of the analysis there were indications of both positive and negative transferences (floating transferences).

Such transferences only require interpretation when they become a source of resistance to the therapy. Their presence is not obvious, and they find conscious expression only through allusions to individuals in the patient's current life situation.

The two clinical examples given here are cases in which the floating transference acted as a source of resistance. In the first instance the figure alluded to was a family member, in the second a person whose services were paid for.

EXAMPLE 1
THE FLOATING TRANSFERENCE
WHERE THE PERSON ALLUDED TO IS A FAMILY MEMBER

Christine, a 35-year-old woman, had been married for eight years. She had one small child, Bill, and it was one year after his birth that she started to complain of depressive thoughts and anxiety. Although self-critical, she did not suffer from loss of appetite or sleep disturbance.

During the first few weeks of the treatment, she complained bitterly about her mother-in-law. She was overbearing. She constantly interfered in her life, wanting to know all the goings-on between her husband and herself, but the final straw was telling her what to do and how to behave. Her mother-in-law was curious about how much of her husband's money she was spending, what she was feeding him, whether Bill should be learning the piano, and so forth. She found it difficult not to have an argument with her. The previous week-end things had got out of hand; she had lost her temper with her mother-in-law and had told her to stop interfering. Her mother-in-law had become silent, refusing to speak or to accept her apology.

The psychotherapist recalled that Christine had said that she was concerned about divulging details of her personal life with her husband in the sessions. It felt that she was betraying her husband, but if it was the way to get well, she would try. The psychotherapist pointed out that although she wished to be as helpful as possible, she nevertheless felt that the psychotherapist was curious about her personal business, just like her mother-in-law. When the psychotherapist made any suggestions as to why she had reacted in a particular way to some event, she felt that the psychotherapist was like her mother-in-law, telling her how to act and how to behave. Christine agreed; she had had that thought while coming to the session. She feared losing her temper with the psychotherapist.

EXAMPLE 2
THE FLOATING TRANSFERENCE
WHERE THE PERSON ALLUDED TO IS AN INDIVIDUAL
FROM WHOM A SERVICE WAS REQUIRED AND PAID FOR

The patient, Jim, a married man of 47, had complained of chronic facial pain since a car accident ten years previously. His atypical facial pain, which caused him much anxiety, had been thoroughly investigated, and since no physical cause could be found, he decided to come for psychotherapy. For the first few weeks Jim was taken up with thoughts that his symptoms were physical. He complained about the discomfort in his face and how he felt unable to manage since the pain was unbearable.

Jim had been attending for several months when he told the psychotherapist that he had been out with his wife. They had decided to go to see a faith-healer, for a bit of a lark. He went up and let the faith-healer lay his hands on him. He felt better, he felt it had really done him some good, and he was glad that he had gone. He had to admit that he was very sceptical about going and felt that it was a load of nonsense. It was a waste of his time and money. These faith-healers were charlatans.

The psychotherapist recalled that he had said previously how sceptical he was about coming for treatment, and that it seemed clear that he saw psychotherapy in the same way as he had the faith-healing. Like the faith-healer and faith-healing, he saw psychotherapy as a waste of time and money and the psychotherapist as a charlatan. He had to admit that it was so.

The positive transference as resistance

The first example of a positive transference acting as a resistance resulted from a patient's unconscious homosexual wishes. The second example is from the case of Christine.

EXAMPLE 1
THE POSITIVE TRANSFERENCE:
UNCONSCIOUS HOMOSEXUAL FEELINGS FOR THE PSYCHOTHERAPIST

Paul was a 35-year-old unmarried man. He had had difficulty coming to terms with the break-up of his engagement. This had occurred four years previously, and now that his ex-fiancée had married, he could not get the thought of her being with another man out of his mind. Paul felt that by this time he should be over it and was frightened by the "compulsiveness" of his thoughts.

Paul was the elder son in a family of two boys. He felt that his younger brother, Jim, was more handsome, more talented, and more valued by his parents. It was he who was given gifts, new clothes, and special treats. He scolded himself for talking like a spoilt child. In reality, Paul had been neglected by his parents. Since the birth of his brother (three years his junior), his mother had frequently been ill, with little interest or energy to spend time with her elder son. His father was often away on business, and so the patient saw little of him during his childhood and adolescence. The hostile feelings he had for his brother were combined with a wish to be friends with him. During periods of unhappiness in his childhood Paul turned to his brother for friendship.

After a year of three-times-weekly psychotherapy, with a male therapist, Paul stated that he did not wish to remain in treatment. He still felt unhappy about his failed relationship, and now could not get the idea of his ex-fiancée being married to someone else out of his mind. He could not bear the thought of them together. He realized that this other man stood for his brother. This man was also three years his junior. He complained about his ex-fiancée and why had she left him. He started to have the thought that if he had dressed better, had been more handsome and more talented, then she would have stayed with him. Paul started to comment on how some of the men in the office where he worked dressed very smartly. He reckoned the psychotherapist also dressed well. The psychotherapist would be thinking that he fancied him and be worried that he was a homosexual. Paul felt uncomfortable. He then remembered being lonely as a boy, sitting in a room on his own, reading and playing. He shared a room with his brother, and when he felt scared at night, he would creep into his brother's bed and cuddle him. The warmth from his brother's body reassured him that he was not alone. The psychotherapist said that he feared the wish to re-create this situation with him, and this made him want to terminate treatment. He was now withdrawing from the psychotherapist, as earlier he had withdrawn from his brother.

EXAMPLE 2
THE POSITIVE TRANSFERENCE:
FEELINGS OF DEPENDENCY ON THE PSYCHOTHERAPIST

Christine (see "floating transference", Example 1) was the second-eldest in a family of four siblings. She got on well with her older and younger sisters, but she had always had a difficult relationship with her youngest sibling—a boy. She felt that when he was born, none of the rest of them mattered. Her mother had no time for any of the girls. Even as a small child, she had found women of her mother's age group to befriend. She remembered that before she started school, one of these women would have taken her for ice-cream and away for day-trips to the local town. When she was an adolescent, she remembered another woman whom she had befriended. This woman became her confidante. If she had worries at school or fell out with her girl-friends, then she would tell her rather than her mother.

Prior to a break of a month, she became very low-spirited. She felt that the psychotherapy was doing her no good; she was just as depressed as when she started. It was all right for the psychotherapist, she was going away on holiday, and although she knew if she had any problems she could contact another psychotherapist, she felt loath to do so. She scolded the psychotherapist for leaving her: what good would it do to see a person who did not know her? She wished she was cared for. The psychotherapist said that it was difficult for Christine to admit how much she relied upon her. Christine cried, saying that it was just a job for the psychotherapist, she did not care for her, and now she was saying that she would need to see this other person during the break if there was a problem. This proved that the psychotherapist was indifferent; after all, she was leaving her. She felt that she was being "dumped". Just like her mother, the psychotherapist was abandoning her to someone else—another mother substitute, as in childhood. Christine agreed. She hated saying it, but it was true.

After the break Christine came to the session smiling, but she was unable to say how glad she was to see the psychotherapist. She had asked her older sister about her mother's holidays when they were children. The sister confirmed that when their mother went away, they all stayed at home with their father. Mother only took her brother. She felt that she had been forgotten by her mother.

The negative transference as resistance

Both of the illustrations given in this section are again from the case of Christine. In the first vignette, the negative transference manifests itself during a session; the second gives an example of acting out in the transference.

EXAMPLE 1
THE NEGATIVE TRANSFERENCE:
HOSTILE FEELINGS FOR THE PSYCHOTHERAPIST

Christine arrived ten minutes late to the session and complained that her depressive thoughts were as bad as ever. The treatment was just hopeless—a waste of time. Christine became silent, saying that she had no thoughts and then asked why she was like this, how long would it last, why could she not be given an answer. She started to talk about how bossy her husband was and how she must fall in with what he says. Then her mother came into her mind, standing in front of the range in the kitchen, wearing her apron, and with her arms across her chest, holding a leather strap. She felt frightened.

The psychotherapist pointed out that she wished to get her own back on anyone who had hurt her. Christine saw this as a criticism and was angry. The psychotherapist did not have depressing thoughts. She did not have to cope with them at home on her own, and all she could do was to say how Christine wanted to hurt people who had hurt her. This frightened Christine, and she feared that the psychotherapist would punish her in the way her mother had punished her in the past.

EXAMPLE 2
THE NEGATIVE TRANSFERENCE:
ACTING OUT IN THE TRANSFERENCE

As the treatment continued, Christine's relationship with her mother predominated. Christine felt that her mother never cared for her. It did not matter how many things she did for her, she still was ignored and unloved. These feelings became more apparent as the treatment continued. It was the holiday breaks that Christine found most difficult. Frequent phone calls during these breaks allowed Christine to know she had not been forgotten and that the psychotherapist was still alive.

After a holiday break Christine said that she had been to see her general practitioner. She had begged him to give her anti-depressants. She had taken them for a few days, felt worse, and had stopped them. The psychotherapist said that Christine had found a substitute for her during the break. She felt that the psychotherapist had no time for her; after all, she was away, busy with her own family. Christine's feelings towards the psychotherapist were similar to those towards her mother. Christine had found another doctor—another mother—to take care of her during the break, as she had done as a child, when she looked to women of her mother's age.

Christine recalled that she would sit up and wait for her mother to come in at night because she was frightened that something might happen to her. She remembered standing beside her mother's bed to see that she was still breathing. Christine was fearful that her furious thoughts of wishing her mother dead for rejecting her would actually cause her mother harm. In the same way, she phoned the psychotherapist, to make sure she was still alive and had not succumbed to her angry thoughts (death wishes).

Transferences in terms of psychic structures

Transference manifestations can be classified in terms of superego, id, and ego (Freud, 1923b), as mentioned, previously.

EXAMPLE 1:
A SUPEREGO TRANSFERENCE

Christine found it difficult to disclose details of her sexual life. As demonstrated previously ("floating transferences", Example 1) she felt that the psychotherapist was intruding into her personal affairs. Nevertheless, she was able to disclose that sexual matters had never been discussed in her family home. Her embarrassment and difficulty in talking about such things provided all the ingredients for a resistance, based upon a superego transference, to develop.

She came to one session talking about a radio programme. Adolescents were talking about their sexual experiences. She could not speak; she felt too embarrassed. She feared that the psychotherapist would think she was dirty. She could never remember being told about her periods. She had thought she must have cut herself. She fell silent. The psychotherapist suggested that what was so difficult to say was that she had masturbated as an adolescent. Christine agreed and had feared her mother's response if she were caught. She had the phantasy that God and her dead relatives were looking down from heaven, thinking what a disgusting girl she was. She recalled her mother saying, "stop doing that, it's dirty". Christine feared that the psychotherapist would be as angry and as judgemental as her mother had been if she told her of her masturbation and her phantasies.

EXAMPLE 2
AN ID TRANSFERENCE

Jenny, a 25-year-old unmarried woman, came into psychotherapy as a result of panic attacks she experienced when going out. Outside the house, she experienced feelings of de-realization, and this was accompanied by panic attacks. Her first attack happened when she was kissing her boyfriend on the street corner. She became agoraphobic.

During the course of the psychotherapy the meaning of her symptoms became apparent. When she was out on the street, she was absent psychically. She could satisfy her unconscious wish to be sexually provocative and seductive, but also conform to the demands of her superego by not being there (de-realization). This understanding of the de-realization became apparent as a result of an id transference.

She had been in psychotherapy for two years when the symptoms started to decrease in their severity. She had met a man she found attractive. Her sexual feelings upset and frightened her. She did not know how to deal with them. On the way to an engagement party, she stopped for a drink. A man in the pub was offering women money if they would kiss him. This disgusted her. At the engagement party there was a kiss-o-gram girl. She could never do such a thing. She became silent. She recalled a discussion at work about prostitution. How could these women stand in the street and be provocative and seductive. The psychotherapist said that there had been thoughts about sex and payment in what she had told her. Jenny then revealed that she had had an orgasm with her boyfriend after the party. After this orgasm she felt panicky. She nearly forgot to come to the session.

The psychotherapist reminded her that "to come" is a slang term for an orgasm, and Jenny was frightened that if she became sexually excited and provocative, then she would be like a prostitute. Jenny angrily said that this was dirty talk and that the psychotherapist was putting ideas into her head. She never thought of such things. Jenny wanted to make the psychotherapist responsible for her sexual thoughts: Jenny felt guilty and was frightened by them. She feared being the seducer, soliciting men. It was no surprise that her symptom of de-realization occurred in the street. Unconsciously, she was the provocative, soliciting woman.

Jenny, in this instance, transferred onto the psychotherapist the sexual wishes (id impulses) that frightened her and gave her a bad conscience.

EXAMPLE 3
REVERSE TRANSFERENCE—TRANSFERENCE OF DEFENCE

The patient, Kate, was an attractive, well-dressed married woman of 39. She entered treatment on the suggestion of her general medical practitioner. Kate complained of a burning mouth and burning vulva of 18 months' duration, which she associated with a hysterectomy two years previously. During this time, her sisters and husband had done everything possible to help Kate through her crisis. Although no physical cause could be found for her symptoms, Kate was convinced that her symptoms were physical. The secondary gain from her symptoms, together with her insistence that they were physical, became the major resistances to psychotherapy, which she terminated after the six-week trial period.

During this time, any suggestion that her symptoms were anything other than physical resulted in Kate shouting at the therapist, stating that the therapist was talking rubbish, telling lies, and was accusing her of malingering. This aggressive, verbally abusive behaviour was intermingled with spells of crying. She asked why the therapist did not believe her—she was telling the truth. Any attempt to explain that she treated the therapist as she had been treated by her mother (identification with the aggressor) resulted in further critical attacks from Kate.

She continually told the therapist how much she hated the treatment, and that it was doing her no good. A dream she brought at this time suggested that the psychotherapist was like a cat she could not shake off. She dreamt that *she was sitting in her kitchen. Suddenly her next-door neighbour's cat was on her back, sticking its claws into her; try as she might, she could not shake it off.* On the dream day she had made herself a cup of coffee and was drinking it, looking out of the window. She had seen a cat. Her husband was away on the night of the dream. They had talked about the treatment on the telephone, and her wish to finish after the trial period. Her next-door neighbour was a nice woman, with odd notions. Her cat was always about the place. It was a curious animal. As much as she hated it, she had to admit that there was something nice about it, something reassuring and safe when it sat on her lap. The therapist said that she had the same feelings about the treatment. On the one hand, she hated it like the cat she could not get rid of it; it had its claws in her. On the other hand, she could say what she liked in the sessions and found this reassuring and safe.

The cat in the dream also represented Kate, as well as the psychotherapist. Once Kate got her claws into something, she would not let go. Her insistence that her burning mouth and vulva were physical in their origin, and her clawing attacks, were a rejection of what the therapist said.

In this example of reverse transference, Kate attacked the psychotherapist as she was once attacked. Kate characteristically became aggressive in identification with her angry (cat) mother and berated the psychotherapist as she had been verbally abused and attacked as a child (identification with the aggressor).

CHAPTER FOUR

Countertransference: some clinical aspects

Siobhan O'Connor

In 1910, Freud first wrote of countertransference: an emotional response that arises in the analyst as a result of the patient's influence on his unconscious (Freud, 1910d). He had first seen the transference as a resistance and viewed the countertransference similarly. He noted that the psychoanalyst can go no further than his own complexes and internal resistances permit. Unlike his concept of transference, he did not develop the concept as a therapeutic tool—an idea that was to come much later. The concept has also been much broadened from Freud's original definition. The literature on the subject has led to a much greater understanding of the different emotional reactions occurring in the therapist, but some of it is confusing, particularly for those who have no experience of analysis. I would like to illustrate with clinical examples a link between the emotions of the therapist and their experience with patients. Sometimes this says more about the therapist than the patient, but at times it helps to understand the interaction.

It is relatively easy to understand the idea that the analyst's capacity is limited by his own complexes, but it is not always easy to define in a specific situation whether the limitation is caused by an emotional inhibition or any other factor. For example, in general psychiatry the inexperienced trainee frequently omits to take a psychosexual history, and the excuse given is often that the trainee feared embarrassing the patient. One might quickly interpret a projection of the trainee's embarrassment onto the patient, and this may well be the case. However, there may be other factors. The previous training may be of a rather restricted medical model, and the doctor may be taking a history with a view to ascertaining biological and environmental factors to support a specific psychiatric diagnosis, with only a search for a broad outline of "premorbid personality". Or the trainee may have correctly assessed the inappropriateness of getting such details at that time but may not have the experience to describe this assessment accurately. In the general clinical setting it may be difficult to assess whether there is a specific emotional response influencing the clinician's approach and differentiating that from other issues, such as training.

The psychoanalytical psychotherapist is more alert to possible emotional factors at play in the interchange with the patient. A psychotherapist described how she had been missing rather obvious references to menstruation in her patient's material until she recognized in her training analysis her denial of her own reactions to menstruation. This had led to her neglect of any psychological relevance to the phantasies surrounding such an important biological occurrence. Another psychotherapist described how she had a tendency to attribute her patient's emotional response in therapy to the transference to the mother, often corrected by her patient as more specifically related to her father. In this case the therapist's father had died when she was very young, and she tended to neglect the significance of the father.

The countertransference may be seen as the analyst's transference to the patient, but it includes more. In the example of denial of menstruation, the patient's material was impinging on something that the therapist had not resolved in herself. In the same way another therapist might have difficulty with an angry patient because of a tendency to placate arising out of the therapist's own difficulties with aggression. In the example referring to the father transference, the therapist was identifying with the patient, enacting her own transference in the therapy. In both instances the countertransference has acted as a resistance to understanding the material, and in the second case has actively influenced the response to the patient.

The definition of countertransference became more obscure, as did that of transference, when many used it to describe all aspects of relationships. For some it became a term describing anything which revealed the personality of the analyst (Balint, 1949). A major development in the concept was made when it was seen as a therapeutic tool to be used to further understand the patient's material.

Paula Heimann (1950, 1960) was the first to describe this. She began by regarding countertransference as including all the feelings that the analyst experiences towards his patient. The analyst has to be able to "sustain his feelings as opposed to discharging them like the patient" (1960, p. 10). She had recognized in the trainees she supervised a defensive attitude towards the patients at times—an attempt to retain a "cool detachedness". In exploring the feelings they had experienced but tried to suppress, they were able to discover the aspects of the patients to which they were responding and understand more about the patients' communications. In this supervisory experience the candidates also became aware of their own unresolved problems producing the transference to the patient, and they could take this back to their training analyses. She went on to illustrate the importance of an emotional sensitivity to the patient. "Along with his freely and evenly hovering attention, the analyst needs a freely roused emotional sensitivity." But violent emotions blur the capacity to think clearly, and if the analyst's emotional response is too intense, it will defeat its objective. "He must wait until he understands what is happening."

Kleinian theory on transference places emphasis on the role of projective identification, and later work linked Heimann's views of countertransference as a response to the patient's projective identifications. Bion (1952) described projective identification: "The analyst feels he is being manipulated so as to be playing a part, no matter how difficult to recognize, in somebody else's phantasy" (p. 149). He describes a psychological–interpersonal event in which the patient projects his phantasy onto the analyst and then interacts by exerting pressure so that the analyst experiences himself in congruence with the projected phantasy. Bion goes on to describe the psychological state of the analyst, using the term *reverie*, in which he can serve a "containing function" for the projection of unwanted feelings of the patient. He links this to the way a mother experiences the crying infant's unthinkable thoughts as her own, and she makes herself psychologically available to the infant in her appropriate responses to the infant's needs.

Sandler (1976) writes of "role-responsiveness" as a way of understanding these countertransference reactions, which are more specific to the patient. He describes the interaction between patient and analyst as determined in large part by an "intrapsychic role relationship" that each party tries to impose on the other. The patient's unconscious wishes are expressed intrapsychically in unconscious images or phantasies, in which both self and object in interaction are represented in particular roles. In the transference, the patient attempts to gain gratification of these wishes by trying to impose a role onto the analyst. He does this via rapid unconscious (including nonverbal) signals. Sandler describes a "free-floating responsiveness" in the analyst in which he allows himself to suspend his own self-control to experience the patient emotionally. He allows himself a reflexive acceptance of the role that the patient is forcing on him, and he may at times recognize that his reactions to the patient are out of keeping with his usual tendencies. Sandler emphasizes that he is opposed to the idea that all countertransference responses of the analyst are due to what the patient has imposed upon him.

In a review of the writings on countertransference, Kernberg (1965) pointed out that the broadening of the term to include all emotional responses in the analyst is confusing and causes it to lose specific meaning. In this chapter, I use the concept as a psychological phenomenon that is experienced by the therapist or by anyone who works in a therapeutic setting. It may be recognized particularly when a therapist departs from his or her usual practice or that which is therapeutic. It may be observed in the general clinical setting but more specifically examined in psychoanalytic work.

Countertransference
in the clinical setting

Unresolved complexes in the therapist

In order to demonstrate how an emotional reaction in the professional interferes with good practice, I first give an example from the general psychiatric setting. A further example in psychoanalytic practice then shows more clearly how specific complexes in an individual therapist can give rise to a countertransference response.

GENERAL EXAMPLE

In general psychiatry most trained professionals know to accept the psychic reality of the deluded patient. They learn not to respond with argument or try to reason with their delusions.

A peculiar response was observed in the nurses of a long-stay ward towards an 83-year-old patient who had a relapse of her recurrent depressive illness. The presentation was similar to previous episodes in which she had become withdrawn, refusing food and expressing depressive delusions. These episodes had not responded to ECT, but she had shown gradual improvement over time. The psychiatrist on this occasion decided to let the illness run its course without active intervention. She had become withdrawn and was refusing to eat. She said that the food was rotten, the potatoes were like water, and the meat was like leather. She said that she was being poisoned, and she also refused her medication. At the same time she was neglecting her personal hygiene, complaining that the nurses were injuring her while combing her hair. Finally, she refused to get out of bed. She said life wasn't worth living anyway, and she hated the new ward she was in. The psychiatrist interviewed her as she lay in bed and was surprised at the interruptions of an experienced nurse who had accompanied her. The nurse constantly argued with the patient, pointing out that they had offered her other fresh food, and there was nothing wrong with it.

The psychiatrist then encouraged the nurses, who had been over-vigorous in their cajoling of the patient, to let her withdraw, omit the medication and simply ensure that she had fluids. Within 24 hours the patient had reversed the decline that had set in, and she had started eating small amounts, still complaining that she was being poisoned. The nurses were much relieved, and at this point, for the first time, they told the psychiatrist that, in fact, the potatoes really were like water and the meat like leather. They bemoaned the cut-backs and the poor quality of the food that was served to the patients. Her depressive episode had set in when the patients were moved from an open, comfortable ward to an older, cramped ward, and the nurses were under threat of redundancy.

Here is a rather simple example of how these experienced nurses had been unable to accept the delusions of the patient because they were too close to reality. The nurses' responses, which ran counter to their usual practice, were based on a sense of responsibility and guilt towards the patient. They could not accept the projections of the patient because they fit too closely with their psychic reality. By denying the patient's reality, it is possible that they were forcing her to withdraw further.

The psychiatrist suggested to a senior nurse that they should agree with the patient in the same way that they accepted other delusions and let her complain about the ward and the food while offering it to her. The nurse jokingly replied that there was a danger they would end up with a lot of depressed nurses, thus verbalizing the "countertransference" reaction. But she did see clearly how their own concerns had influenced their approach.

In the same way, in the analytic situation, a patient will project aspects of herself onto her therapist. If it fits with the therapist's inner reality and there is an unresolved conflict, the therapist is liable to experience conflict and have difficulty in containing and reflecting on the projection.

Miss J, a 35-year-old woman with a character neurosis, came into analysis because of difficulties in relationships. She was anxious and timid in the work setting, constantly expecting criticism and avoiding meetings. She was always late in presenting her written work and would try to cover up her inadequacies by skimming over details. In her therapy she was late for every session, apologizing and giving excuses. The therapist had looked at this in terms of resistance, fear of criticism, and avoidance of difficult material. The patient's response was to accuse the therapist of anger. The therapist's supervisor asked her repeatedly whether it was not annoying to have the patient regularly late and cancelling so many sessions. No, replied the therapist, giving her view of the patient as vulnerable and anxious, sympathetic to her difficulties. Her lateness persisted over four months. Eventually the problem came up in the therapist's own analysis, when she was feeling low after a session with the patient. The therapist discovered how much she had been struggling to get the fact of the patient's lateness across to her without her feeling criticized. She could see how frustrated and angry Miss J made people with her behaviour, but she had been turning her own anger back on herself. She had been stopping herself from telling the patient what she needed to know.

The therapist recognized a repetition from her own childhood, in which she was tolerant and passive with an angry sister. Following this, she was able to discuss the patient's avoidance behaviour with her, and although this was initially taken as a criticism, the ensuing work enabled the patient to see how her behaviour influenced others. The therapist had not wanted to "criticize" the patient. Avoidance of the recurring problem had not dealt with the patient's projection of anger in the therapist, but had left the patient more convinced of the therapist's anger. The countertransference may be seen here as an enactment of the therapist's own transference to the patient. It was unconscious in the therapist, and only by becoming conscious of it could the therapist allow herself to act more freely.

Countertransference
as a tool to understanding the patient

The concept of countertransference has been developed with the "widening scope of analysis". Many more disturbed patients are treated in analysis than had previously been considered appropriate. Those patients who are described as coming under the general heading of "borderline personality" have been found to regress more easily in therapy and project very primitive phantasies, making it difficult for the analyst to remain with neutral free-floating attention. The patients actualize their experience, repeating early conflicts within the session, often making demands on the therapist to respond. The verbal material may be hard to follow and at times may appear like disjointed associations. The focus of the therapy is usually on the "here and now", on what is happening in the session, because of the emotional difficulty the patient has in reflecting on her behaviour. It is particularly in the work with these patients that analysts have found the concept of counter-transference a positive therapeutic tool.

Mrs E, a 40-year-old woman who had experienced early sexual abuse, presented her therapist with a vivid account of dreams and observations of people with whom she came in contact. She was very controlling, with a fear of allowing her sexuality to get out of control. She repeatedly acted out demands on the therapist to show affection. She tried to prolong sessions, persistently asked questions, and often left in the middle of a session in a rage, returning to express disappointment that the therapist had not followed her. This acting out was contained and reflected upon, but her demands increased. During a week in the second six months, the therapist had found particular difficulty in following the material. On the Friday session the patient arrived a few minutes early, stating that she was not going to sit in the waiting-room. She sat on the couch, smoking a cigarette. As she looked down on the therapist, Mrs E remarked casually that she would wait the few minutes if the therapist had anything else to do. After five minutes' silence she started to speak. The therapist had difficulty following the associations and decided to reflect instead on the emotions she was experiencing in response. She became aware that it was a feeling of being totally out of control of the session, vulnerable to the patient, with a feeling that she would be abandoned by the patient as of no worth, incapable of helping her.

As she began to see that Mrs E was enacting a powerful role, the verbal associations became comprehensible. Mrs E was demonstrating in her associations that she knew exactly what the problem was, as if she had complete psychological insight into herself and others. Her comments suggested that any intervention by the therapist was an irritant and quite worthless. It became clear that the patient was projecting the vulnerable and humiliated aspects of herself and dramatically behaving in the way that she experienced the therapist. Interpretation of the projected aspects of worthlessness brought acknowledgement by the patient. Mrs E agreed, with relish, that she found the therapist quite worthless and was thinking of finishing therapy. She elaborated on her projection, telling her how anything the therapist said was known to her already, outlining mistakes she felt the therapist had made, and generally describing the whole experience of therapy as useless to her. But then Mrs E had the thought that the therapist might feel worthless because of the way she had been behaving towards her. She went on to describe the same feelings of worthlessness as her own. She described her humiliation and vulnerability to the therapist and her fear that she would be thrown out for her behaviour. The therapist had not demonstrated or spoken of her feelings—the patient presumed that if the therapist were sensitive, she might feel that way. By identifying with the projected phantasy, Mrs E could re-internalize it. In other words, after the therapist had verbalized the meaning of the patient's behaviour, Mrs E could recognize how the therapist might have felt in response and then accepted the feelings as her own.

In the classical view, countertransference is unconscious, and in this case the feelings in the therapist were conscious. It may be seen as "role-responsive" in that the patient enacted the wished-for role of a powerful, independent, and insightful individual who had no need of others and scorned the therapist. This was done verbally and physically, with subtle expressions of disdain. The therapist responded to the role in phantasy. Taking Bion's view of containment, the therapist identified the projected phantasy of a worthless person who was to be discarded, having responded empathically to the interaction. She contained the feelings until she could verbalize them in a way that the patient could understand and accept.

It could be argued that the feelings were initially unconscious and interfering with the therapist's understanding until a self-analysis in the session. But this does not do justice to the experience of dealing with borderline patients. As Kernberg describes,

> when dealing with borderline or severely regressed patients, as contrasted to those presenting symptomatic neuroses and many character disorders, the therapist tends to experience rather sooner in the treatment intensive emotional reactions having more to do with the patient's premature, intense and chaotic transference. [Kernberg, 1975, p. 54]

In current usage, the term "countertransference" is applied to such conscious feelings. This has obscured the definition, like so many in the analytic literature, but it has come with an increased awareness of the relationship between patient and therapist, with less emphasis on the idea of "resistance". Reich (1951, 1960) separates "permanent countertransference" reactions from "acute countertransference" reactions, referring to the former as being due to character disorder of the analyst, and the latter as being determined by the different transference manifestations of the patient. In the above case, the patient's behaviour frequently fluctuated according to different projections. She would behave as if the therapist was sadistic one day, a potential sexual abuser another, and so on. The experience of the therapist described above was recognized by her as unusual and relevant to the experience of the moment. Paula Heimann writes:

> The moment occurs when [the analyst] understands what is happening. The moment he understands his patient, he can understand his own feelings, the emotional disturbance disappears and he can verbalize the patient's crucial process meaningfully for the patient. [Heimann, 1960, p. 10]

Often the ability to contain such feelings depends on the experience and the psychological integration of the therapist. The capacity to reflect when "under attack" may depend on a general experience of difficult patients. The significance of countertransference may be misunderstood in difficult cases when the therapist becomes fearful with such patients. An inexperienced therapist who feels out of control may, for example, fear an actual physical attack by a patient and have difficulty differentiating between a truly risky situation and one in which their own projected phantasies obscure the picture. In the above example, the therapist waited until the feelings she was experiencing could be linked to the patient's associations and behaviour. They were not too disturbing or intense. Undoubtedly the therapist's feelings arose from her own experience, but it is recognized that in dealing with these patients the reactions in the therapists have more to do with ability to withstand psychological stress and anxiety than with any particular, specific problem from the therapist's past. In other words, any therapist dealing with such patients is likely to experience similar reactions.

Applications in the general psychiatric ward

The traditional psychiatric approach has concentrated on phenomena observed in the patient. The training in psychiatry has improved from seeing the psychiatric interview as a scientific examination to an increased awareness of the importance of the attitude of the interviewer. "Interview-skills" training attempts to reflect on the trainee's approach, but the analytically informed psychiatrist becomes much more aware of the possible complexes that may inhibit him. Emotional defences interfere with good practice from the initial interview on, and throughout treatment. A professional may have difficulty in speaking of particular topics, inhibiting the patient in the process, and later problems may occur because of emotional reactions experienced towards particular patients over time. The practice of concentrating the enquiry on the patient often obscures the therapeutic possibilities that arise when the emotional reactions of the professionals are reflected upon.

The management of "difficult patients" is one that taxes many, and increasingly they are referred to the psychotherapist. Often it is found that formal psychotherapy is not appropriate, but a dynamic approach informs the psychiatrist. Main (1957) has described a group of patients who evoke a particular type of response in the medical and nursing staff of a psychiatric hospital. In the following example, the reactions of the staff were not unusual but may illustrate a common response in which emotions evoked can lead to increased frustration with a severely dependent patient.

> Mrs M had been an inpatient on frequent occasions, with a history of benzodiazepine abuse and parasuicidal attempts, including overdoses, self-cutting, and tying a cord around her neck, enacted on the ward as well as at home. On one occasion, when walking with a nurse, she threw herself in front of a car—taking care to choose one that was distant enough and going reasonably slowly. On the ward she would regress and complain frequently of various somatic complaints and pseudo-hallucinations, with attention-seeking behaviour. She identified with symptoms and behaviour she had observed

in other patients, re-enacting them. Her demands for attention increased particularly when the nurses were busy with other patients.

The nurses' responses varied from concern for her in which they responded to her demands to confrontations in which they chided her for her behaviour. They felt compelled to call the doctor frequently for symptoms that they doubted were of significance, but they feared missing something important. The patient was generally well liked, despite her behaviour. The nurses spent a lot of time with her, listening to her concerns and trying to encourage her in more appropriate behaviour. In individual interviews she would regress, becoming preoccupied with her childhood, in which she had experienced severe deprivation. In group situations and generally on the ward her behaviour then became so disruptive that there was discussion about sending her to a locked ward. The nurses were reluctant to ask for this. They feared that the patient would see it as a punishment, although they found it increasingly difficult to manage her in the admission ward.

At this stage a new approach was introduced by a consultant psychiatrist who had just taken up post. She undertook responsibility and outlined to the nurses a structured plan. The underlying approach was to give the patient responsibility for her behaviour. The issue of a transfer to the locked ward was described as an alternative that the patient would be offered if she did not control her behaviour, with the message that it was only necessary for the sake of other patients on the ward and not for her benefit or punishment. A timetable of various therapies was set up, with skills training in cooking and budgeting, recreational activities such as the weekly ward outing to the swimming pool, and specific times to go home and visit her family. She was given very structured tasks and was not included in relaxation or discussion groups. The nurses were asked to give only specific sessions of time, reviewing her progress with her and discussing in particular how she coped at home. Outside of that, they were to respond with the minimum of intervention. They were not to call the doctor for her symptoms unless they were particularly concerned. If she did not partake in the activities, she was not to be given any special time with nurses or doctors. The consultant agreed to take responsibility for any medical problems that might arise and made it clear that she intended to continue responsibility for her care long after she had shown improvement. Regular marital sessions were arranged to concentrate on current problems.

Immediately the nurses felt relieved of the guilt that they would have felt if the patient had received the "punishment" of transfer. The situation never arose, as they were able to become firmer in their attitude, impressing responsibility on Mrs M with no sense of guilt. Mrs M responded by more direct angry comments, which had previously been enacted in attention-seeking behaviour. On one occasion, when the nurses refused to call the doctor, she threatened to get herself admitted to another hospital with an overdose and in doing so make sure she got a different psychiatrist. The nurses correctly assessed her attitude as an angry outburst without true suicidal intent. (She went home and made the tea and came back at the correct time, very pleased that she had overcome a hurdle and not carried out her threat.) She progressed from making threats she did not carry out to co-operating and starting to deal with her difficulties.

On reviewing the change in the nurses—they had previously been responding to Mrs M's enactment of the needy child projecting hostility and neglect onto them. They responded to her childlike behaviour as if they were caring parents. They had given her time and empathized, but when the demands were too great, they had scolded. They had fully recognized that the patient could control her behaviour, but they had been reacting to projections. It could be seen as "role-responsive" in which they responded to the projected representation of the moment. If they were particularly busy and could not react, they could occasionally get her to behave by a quick comment of "I haven't time for that now". One nurse described having done this while Mrs M was having a pseudo-seizure on the floor with good response, but noted that she didn't like doing it and didn't think Mrs M would respond if it were done too often.

I have chosen this case because I would like to illustrate the dangers of a "little knowledge". In this case, although one could argue that the responses were based on Mrs M's behaviour, the true "countertransference" lay elsewhere. The relatively simple intervention of the consultant allowed the nurses to do exactly what they thought was good practice. They had no difficulty with the treatment plan, even to the point of being able to let her walk out of the ward with threats of suicide, because they knew it was appropriate to let her go.

In this case the apparent "countertransference" was actually more to do with professional responsibility than any manipulation by the patient. The staff could assess very accurately the suicidal risk and the significance of physical symptoms, but they had been inhibited by the problem of ultimate responsibility. The fears were of the legal implications if they did not respond to symptoms or threatening behaviour, and the ever-present possibility of a mistake. When given the security of the consultant's support, they had no difficulty in managing the patient. The consultant had to face the risk inherent in any patient who shows parasuicidal behaviour, but assessed the risk to be small if the patient was given the assurance of long-term interest. After discharge the patient had one brief re-admission at the time when a social worker left, but there was no further suicidal or attention-seeking behaviour. At the time of writing two years later, she still attends with her husband for an hour's session, now once every three weeks, and she has been working in a part-time job. For the first year the consultant had to withstand various attempts to get extra sessions including very alarming symptoms. But it was felt that the most important aspect of therapy was to provide a model for her to identify with, and to give her the security of long-term interest, without giving in to her demands. The focus had been on practical difficulties, including management of the children, and is now mainly on the marital relationship; she no longer presents "symptoms".

The countertransferences arising from feelings of responsibility and the associated fears are seldom seriously considered as a major obstacle to good therapy. They are often thought to be reasonable responses and not questioned. The response to suicidal risk is naturally given priority, but there are times when it is at the expense of good treatment. In some cases it is quite clearly out of proportion to the actual risk and quite irrational if one considers the risks that doctors will accept on behalf of patients when putting them on drugs that may have serious and potentially fatal side-effects. Similarly, known hypochondriacs are regularly subjected to excessive investigations that in time may produce their own iatrogenic effects, the doctor ever-fearful of "missing something" and inhibited from following an appropriate psychological approach. (In the above case of Mrs M, every investigation for physical symptoms had merely increased her anxiety.)

The case was chosen to demonstrate a very common "countertransference" reaction, which shows itself in muted form in other cases. A similar response occurs in inexperienced therapists when dealing with a difficult case. Often they respond to the patient's projections, not because the projections are so powerful, but because the therapist is fearful of upsetting the patient or of losing them through their own mistakes. And this may help to demonstrate another learning point in this case. There is a danger that with a little knowledge of "countertransference" the inexperienced may attribute their feelings to the patient without considering a more powerful unconscious motivation in themselves. The analytic method is a very strict discipline, and although a "countertransference" response may be observed and reflected upon, it can always only be another tool to understanding.

How to manage the countertransference

A persistent theme in the psychoanalytic literature is that countertransference phenomena are essential concomitants of psychoanalytic treatment. A. Reich (1951) pointed out that without countertransference, the necessary talent and interest in the analyst is lacking. Spitz (1956) and Little (1960) described countertransference as essential where there is empathy. Similarly, in the general psychiatric setting concern for the patient is essential in the "caring" professions, and an emotional response may help or hinder treatment.

For the psychoanalyst, Freud initially recommended self-analysis, but he soon took the view that this was difficult because of the analyst's own resistances to self-understanding. He recommended that the analyst undertake an analysis by another—a "training analysis". Later, believing even this to be inadequate, he suggested re-analysis every five years.

In practice, all analysts undergo a training analysis, and this is concurrent with their training cases. In this way, the analyst may come to recognize his own "blind spots", as well as being presented with the opportunity to have an analysis of his own reactions to his patients. Many analysts do undergo a second analysis, but most training analyses today are much longer and consequently more thorough than when Freud's recommendation was originally made.

However, it is well recognized that there can only be a "good-enough" analysis (to borrow a term), and there is no such thing as a completely analysed individual. In practice, therefore, analysts are recommended to continue a self-analysis, and there is a general acceptance that peer supervision is essential in order to recognize countertransference difficulties when they arise.

This leads to the alternatives when a training analysis is not available or practical for the psychologically minded clinician. Some undertake an experience of psychotherapy in which they learn to recognize "blind spots" that they may not have resolved but may consciously stay alert to. In such cases supervision may help to recognize when such responses have interfered with therapy.

An example was of a counsellor who had undertaken personal therapy and had told his supervisor of his difficulty in any situation where there was abuse of children. One of his patients subsequently confessed during a session that he had hit his daughter on a day when he was feeling particularly tense and his daughter misbehaving. The counsellor had responded by outlining to the patient how harmful it is to abuse children. He was met with an angry response at the end of the session. Despite the counsellor's previous awareness, to the extent of having told his supervisor, he had reacted in the countertransference. The patient did not need to be told he was guilty, and he reacted with understandable anger. The exchange can be seen to be irrational in that the counsellor allowed no opportunity to explore the behaviour, even to the extent of not having discovered whether the problem was persistent. But supervision helps to stay alert to such reactions.

The multi-disciplinary team in the general psychiatric setting allows different perspectives on the patient's problems. For those who are willing to see another's point of view, it may counteract a tendency to identify too readily with one aspect of the patient. Supervision of cases may help in that the supervisor can aid reflection on the trainee's responses to the patient. This may be done in an individual or group setting, either in direct supervision or experiential groups.

PART TWO

PERIPHERIES
OF PSYCHOANALYSIS

Psychoanalysis
and
psychoanalytic psychotherapy

A psychoanalytic approach to the treatment of the schizophrenias in hospital practice

Thomas Freeman

P sychoanalytic concepts, both descriptive and explanatory, can materially contribute to the understanding, management, and treatment of the schizophrenias. It is true that chemotherapeutic agents can beneficially influence some of the most disturbing manifestations of schizophrenic psychosis at the onset of the illness and in chronicity. Prior to the introduction of chemotherapy, remissions occurred, but where the illness was of long duration, patients were fearful and disturbed in their behaviour. The management of these abnormal mental states taxed the resources of the hospital staff.

Chemotherapeutic agents have their disadvantages and limitations. They tend to obscure the clinical phenomena and interfere with the natural course of the illness, and therefore it is less easy to decide whether or not the disappearance of a delusion or a catatonic sign is, in fact, indicative of a remission of the illness. Equally, it is difficult in long-standing cases to determine whether the potential for further improvement is being hampered or assisted by the drug treatment. Of greater importance is the fact that chemotherapy does not alter the

115

prognosis in the long term. It has become apparent that while chemotherapy can dispel those manifestations that are thrown up by the pathological process—i.e. the hallucinations, delusions, and catatonic signs—it is incapable of influencing the morbid process itself—hence the failure to bring about the recovery of patients whose illness had entered a chronic stage. It is important not to confuse an aetiologically based form of treatment with a symptomatic measure. That is what chemotherapy is, no more and no less. Effective in remitting cases, they give the impression of cure.

The clinical phenomena provide the basis for an understanding of mental events that imitate the morbid process and how the morbid process has affected the patient's mental life. It is through this interest in what has happened to the individual patient as a person that the psychoanalytic approach transcends the organic view of the schizophrenias and contributes to management and treatment. The symptomatology at the onset gives little indication as to the course the illness will follow. Because of this, there has been much controversy amongst psychiatrists about what constitutes a schizophrenic psychosis. For the present purposes it is best to adopt the classification of remitting and non-remitting cases because at the onset, usually occurring between the ages of 13 and 25, all patients present signs, sometimes ephemeral, of that systematic splitting that led Bleuler (1911) to describe these psychoses as the schizophrenias.

For Bleuler (1911), systematic splitting is a descriptive concept, and it should not be confused with the splitting that is hypothesized as playing a major role in the object relations theories of Fairbairn and Melanie Klein (see chapter two). Systematic splitting describes the fact that the patient no longer values reality. His judgement is no longer influenced by it. He is now taken up with another reality—a psychic reality. In this autistic state, the self is split, in that aspects of the mental and physical self are transposed onto others (transitivism), and the physical and mental aspects of others are located in the self (appersonation). The sign (the verbal idea) is split away from the signified (the object), and affect is split off from thought. It is in the established case that this splitting is to be most easily observed.

It is important to note that the delusional content that occurs at the onset of non-remitting cases disappears as the illness continues. In contrast, the delusional ideas that then appear tend to remain unchanged over many years. This stability of content is a feature of what Manfred Bleuler (1978) describes as "end states". This term does not mean that the process of illness has come to an end, is incapable of further developments for good or ill, or that further changes may not occur. Only when an illness had continued in this relatively unchanging condition for five years can it be designated an "end state". Bleuler (1978) distinguishes three types of "end state": severe, moderately severe, and mild. In recent years there has been a shift from severe to mild and moderately severe end states, and this may be due to the effects of chemotherapy. Periodically the quiescent state is disturbed by acute attacks characterized by hallucinations and delusions with a persecutory content. They are usually transient and, while in progress, are not necessarily contained by anti-psychotic medications.

Disinterest and inattention characterize patients whose illnesses terminate in severe or moderately severe "end states". They are often silent, and answers to questions are either irrelevant or incomprehensible. The immediate environment is confused with the past, and misidentifications are common. It was these manifestations that led Freud (1911c [1910]) to say that transferences did not occur in the schizophrenias. This is not to say that these patients do not make attachments, because they often do to nurses whom they have known for a long time and to doctors also. This was more common in the days when nurses remained on the same wards for long periods and doctors lived within the hospital grounds. However, experience has shown that these ties are so tenuous that they cannot support a psychotherapy that exposes the patient to painful memories and to affects that occur as a reaction to frustrations and disappointments.

An example is that of a divorced woman of 40, who had been in hospital for more than ten years. Her illness began after her husband left her for another woman. She was usually withdrawn, inattentive, and neglectful of herself.

Her speech was often illogical, and neologisms were frequent. She was responsive to a particular nurse and would sometimes try to please her by improving her hygiene and going to occupational therapy. From time to time acute attacks occurred, when she was restless and impulsive and hallucinated. During one of these acute attacks a nurse began to see the patient daily for a fixed period of time in the hope that this contact might bring the attack to an end and that something might be learnt about the cause. She did, in fact, become quieter, and her speech became more normal. She expressed her resentment about being kept in hospital. She told the nurse about her husband's infidelity. She put great emphasis on the fact that the other woman was more intelligent and better educated than she was. Her husband's family had not approved of her, because she was of a "lower class". She frequently interjected, "I wish I had been educated to be a nurse or something". Another remark was, "I'm reading so that I can be educated like a nurse. You see, I'm not educated in skin and hair and things like that."

After about two months during which she showed a greater interest in her surroundings, she became low-spirited. She sat with her eyes closed. When asked why she did this, she replied, "There's nothing for me to see, there's nothing for me". Gradually a hostile tone appeared in her voice. She was no longer friendly. One day she shouted at the nurse, "You can't make me a nurse, it's a dirty profession. You are my slave, I'm a princess don't forget that . . . you can't make me a nurse." Her speech began to deteriorate, and she became negativistic. She would not speak to the nurse any more.

The nurse's interest and attention promoted what remained of the patient's healthy mental life. However, this brought her face to face with a disagreeable reality. If she had been intelligent and educated, she would have had a husband and a profession like the nurse. Was the relapse provoked by envy and hatred displaced from the woman who stole her husband to the nurse? Had a transference been created, the intensity of which led to a falsification of reality? The nurse was now perceived as an enemy and hateful. It is not uncommon in the psychoanalytic treatment of character neuroses to find patients who have the greatest difficulty in perceiving the analyst as he really is, rather than as a figure of the past who was frightening and hated. Here the intensity of feeling does not destroy the therapeutic alliance, but it provides a powerful resistance against progress. In long-standing cases of schizophrenia such an alliance is precluded by the patient's autism. This clinical example illustrates that transferences do occur in the schizophrenias, but they are not "working transferences".

The woman patient's denial of her helplessness to alter a painful reality by reversing the nature of her relationship with the nurse—"You are my slave, I'm a princess"—is typical of patients whose illness has reached a moderately severe or severe "end state". In quiescent periods the content of delusions consists of wishes fulfilled. They are usually phantasies characteristic of later childhood and adolescence. A male patient believes he is a great inventor but a malevolent persecutor has had him incarcerated in hospital. A female patient believes she is married but enemies prevent her and her husband coming together. This protective or defensive use of wish delusions is similar to the way in which young children deny reality by making use of wish phantasies in which they assume—directly or through imagined figures or animals—the power and strength of the parent who is both loved and feared. The control over the parent, which the child gains through wish phantasies, is no different in nature from the omnipotence and omniscience that are at the core of the wishful delusions of patients in "end states" (Freeman, 1988a).

The similarity that exists between the mental life of healthy young children and that of schizophrenic patients demonstrates the principle that nothing new is created by the morbid process. At first sight the opposite seems to be the case, because the way in which schizophrenic patients think, feel, and perceive is completely unlike that of the mentally healthy. The disruption in the continuity and quality of the patient's mental life can be regarded as the result of a far-reaching psychic dissolution. The most recently acquired achievements in mental development—self-awareness, the capacity to reflect, abstract thinking, and selective attention—are lost. The psychic dissolution leads to the exposure of elementary forms of mental activity. Adult cognitive functions fall under influences of the same kind that affect the thinking, remembering, and perceiving of the mentally healthy while they dream [Freud's (1900a) primary process].

This is important because it is necessary to know what mental events initiated the psychotic attack. Once in possession of this knowledge, ideas about management and treatment can be formulated. In the case of symptom and character neuroses, it is always possible to get an idea of the psychic dangers and the subsequent inner conflict that led to the onset of the symptoms from dreams, memories, phantasies, and transference reactions. Schizophrenic patients at the onset of the illness are not so obliging. They do not volunteer recollections of the period prior to the beginning of the psychosis. It is as if they are no longer important. There is usually a repetition of delusional and/or hallucinatory experiences. Even questioning fails to evoke memories of the recent past. Katan (1975) has revived the idea, originally proposed by Minkowski (1927), that it is possible to reconstruct the phantasies, conflicts, and danger situations that occupy the patient's mind immediately prior to the break with reality, i.e. in the pre-psychotic phase. This is achieved by treating the content of the delusions and the hallucinations in the same manner as the manifest content of a dream.

The following examples are illustrative. In the first case the delusional ideas and the misperceptions of reality arose from an identification that had taken the place of a real object relationship.

The patient was a young woman, a nurse by profession. She fell ill suddenly. She was restless and anxious. She claimed that colleagues were calling her a prostitute. When admitted to hospital, she expressed doubts about her sexual identity—"Am I a woman?" she asked. She thought the women patients were men dressed as women. She complained of dimness of vision and of having a squint. She believed that she was being hypnotized and made to feel sexual excitement. She accused a doctor of making her act the part of a prostitute; she behaved in a seductive and erotic manner in the presence of men.

According to the patient's mother, she had been in low spirits for about two months. She had been keeping company with a young man for over a year, and he had broken off the relationship. She had met him when he was a patient in the ophthalmic ward where she was a nurse. He had been admitted for the correction of a squint. Later she revealed that she had regular coitus with him. He had promised to marry her. Her belief that she had a squint and her doubt about her sexual identity demonstrated her identification with her former lover. Through the psychotic reality she fulfilled her wish for the past to become the present; for a return to the first meetings with him. This psychotic identification suggests that the pre-psychotic phase began when the loss of the beloved was compensated for by an identification with him. In the delusional content displacement led to an unknown persecutor (the hypnotist) taking the place of the lover. She blamed the persecutor for the sexual arousal. It may be fairly claimed that in the pre-psychotic phase she felt herself threatened by her sexual wishes and feared giving way to masturbation. Her sexual need had become acute owing to the lack of the satisfaction to which she had become accustomed with her lover. In the psychotic attack her erotic behaviour showed that through the identification with her lover she had become a seducer (a prostitute).

In the second case the reconstruction of the pre-psychotic phase pointed to unconscious homosexual wishes as the danger that provoked the psychic dissolution.

This was the case of a 20-year-old unmarried woman. The psychotic attack began with erotomania. She believed that her college lecturer was in love with her. After a little while she began to feel that she was being watched and followed and that her conversations were being recorded. She had noticed that the lecturer was taking an interest in her flatmate, with whom she had a close relationship. One day she came to the conclusion that the college lecturer had turned against her and was behind the unpleasant attentions she was having to experience. She attributed the change in his attitude to her—from love to hate—to his wish to begin a relationship with her friend. He wanted to get rid of her before she warned her friend of his lecherous and deceitful intentions.

Her fear of the lecturer became so intense that she left college and went to stay with relations. When she arrived at her aunt's house, she felt herself possessed by a "wonderful spirit". Society was going to change for the better. Christ was about to return, and she would be one of his followers. During the night in her aunt's house she began to think about Adam and Eve—was she Adam or Eve? Was she the snake who enticed Eve to persuade Adam to eat the forbidden fruit? Next morning she looked at herself in the mirror. Her face was black. She felt afraid—was she the devil? Suddenly she thought she must be Cain. She had murdered Abel. Later, when she saw her uncle take a bread-knife out of the drawer, she was certain he was Abel, come to life to murder her.

This patient was an only child who had lived much of her life with her mother and grandparents. Her parents had separated when she was an infant. She was devoted to her mother, but there had been many separations. The mother had had several bouts of psychotic illness. She committed suicide when the patient was 11 years old. The patient accused her father of causing her mother's death. She resented men. They only made use of women. An uncle had tried to seduce her when she was about 14 years old. Men had a more interesting life. As a child, she had envied boys and their freedom, and she enjoyed those times when she was with them, because she could do as she liked.

At the onset of the acute attack, she believed the lecturer loved her (erotomania) and then she feared that he hated her and wanted her out of the way. At the height of the attack, she feared retaliation for a murder, which she had committed in the role of a man. In the pre-psychotic period she feared that the lecturer was coming between her and her girl-friend. This made the lecturer a rival, and she hated him. She wanted to get rid of him and have the girl-friend for herself. To resolve her problem, she wished to separate him from her girl-friend by getting him to love her.

This wish became a reality with the onset of the psychotic attack—he now loved her. By making the man the object of her sexual wishes, she could maintain the repression of her homosexual attraction to the girl-friend. As the attack proceeded, the death wishes were projected first onto the lecturer and then displaced onto the uncle. Now she feared being murdered as a punishment for her death wishes. Support for this reconstruction comes from recognition of the fact that she always feared separation from the homosexual love object (the mother). This was repeated with her girl-friend, whom she loved as she had her mother.

The effect of anti-psychotic medications, in modest doses, was to remove her persecutory fears. In daily meetings these women were able to speak about their unusual experiences. As the anxiety subsides, there is an opportunity to get a glimpse of the more intimate aspects of the patient's life. However, as is so commonly the case, the disappearance of the delusional ideas is accompanied by a resistance against further disclosures. There is an urgent wish to leave hospital and return to normal life.

There are psychoanalysts who regard this resistance as no different from that encountered in neurotic patients and that it should be treated as such by means of interpretation. There may be another reason for this powerful resistance against further disclosures. It may be that it springs from the fear of re-experiencing the acute psychotic attack. A psychotic patient's ability to persevere with a therapeutic relationship depends on the weakening of the memories of these attacks. The anxiety may be enhanced by the very means by which it is hoped to cure the illness. The analytic method encourages psychic regression. In non-psychotic patients this regression allows the repetition of anxieties in the transference, whereas in the schizophrenias regression accentuates the destabilization of psychic structure. As the patient emerges from the acute attack, there is a constant dread of a return to that mental state where there is confusion between phantasy and reality, and between self and object representations.

Over 80 years ago Bleuler (1911) drew attention to the frequency with which sexual phantasies comprise the content of delusions at the onset of the schizophrenias. More particularly, he pointed out that the sexual element manifests itself in unpleasant forms, as in the second case described above. Sexual intercourse is represented by murder, as in the case of a patient who, while shouting, "I am being murdered", passionately kissed her hands and made unmistakable sexual gestures. There is much support for the theory that the content of persecutory delusions gives expression to masturbatory phantasies, but the sexual excitement is replaced by anxiety (Freeman, 1989).

This theory is based on the masturbatory phantasies reported by neurotic patients during psychoanalytic treatment. The content of a commonly encountered delusion consists of the complaint of being photographed in a compromising position by a persecutor for the purposes of blackmail.

> This delusion was present in an unmarried man who believed that a female colleague was in love with him. He was convinced that he had been photographed with his imagined lover, who, he believed, had been in bed with him. The husband had arranged this because he was jealous and wanted to ruin him.

> After much resistance, a male neurotic patient in psychoanalytic treatment described the following masturbatory phantasy: He is watching two women undress. He gets into bed with one and tells the other to photograph them while they have coitus.

During the psychoanalytic treatment of the neuroses, the patient tolerates his resistances, and, with the help of the analyst's interpretations, the unacceptable wish phantasies that provoked the symptoms come to consciousness with beneficial effects. It is often possible then to discover the childhood psychic events that provided the material for these phantasies. Such a sequence does not happen in the schizophrenias. This is largely due to the way in which the patient perceives and experiences the psychiatrist and himself. The patient may believe that the psychiatrist is also affected by the persecutor(s); there may be other transitivistic manifestations. Mis-identifications are common, and there is an emotional egocentrism analogous to that of the young child. This causes the patient to blame the psychiatrist for disappointments and frustrations. The patient often comes to view the psychiatrist as an agent of the persecutors.

There are psychoanalysts who regard these manifestations as expressions of a transference psychosis—comparable to the transference neurosis (see chapter three). It is more believable that these psychotic phenomena are simply the result of the psychic dissolution that has taken place. This makes it impossible for the patient to re-translate the content of the persecutory delusions back into the language of the pre-psychotic phantasies. The delusions, therefore, continue to exert their influence over the patient's emotions and behaviour.

There is a small number of patients with whom it is possible to establish a working therapeutic relationship, once the acute attack has subsided. A gradual strengthening of the healthy aspects of the patients' personality takes place. Within the shelter of the therapeutic relationship, the patient can gain insight into his anomalous reactions and can come to recognize his vulnerability to losses and disappointments and why he fell ill.

A psychological understanding of schizophrenic psychoses leads to better treatment and to a better outcome in the long term (Jackson & Cawley, 1992). To achieve this end, we must know as much as possible about the symptoms, the behaviour, the patient's life experiences, and the psychic reactions that they engendered. When a patient is admitted to hospital, there is always the likelihood that there will be someone to whom he will become attached. It may be a nurse, an occupational therapist, a social worker, or a ward maid, rather than a psychiatrist. Where such a relationship springs up, it can be the source of much information. This means that all staff members concerned must be involved. In this way it is possible to reconstruct the mental events of the pre-psychotic period. The reliability of these reconstructions is often enhanced by what is learned from relatives and friends as well as from the prodromal symptoms. Conflicts due to ambivalence in relation to siblings, incestuous wishes, object loss, acquisitiveness, and death wishes are some of the immediate causes of the break with reality.

In the vast majority of cases a remission follows the first attack, and today this is speeded up by chemotherapy. The difficulty is that the chemotherapy only acts on what is brought forward by the pathological process and not on the pathological process itself. This is the reason why the incidence of re-admissions has risen so steeply since the introduction of drug treatment. There is also the current emphasis on early discharge from hospital. Treatment then consists solely of regular injections of long-acting medications. In the instance of the long-standing cases these drugs, while removing the more disturbing manifestations of the disease, only enhance the volitional defect that is a prominent feature of chronicity. In these "end states" a psychotherapeutic approach can act against further psychic disintegration by encouraging the development of what remains of healthy mental life, without disturbing the wishful delusional reality that compensates for an unsatisfying and frightening external reality.

Experience suggests that where a serious attempt is made to identify the psychic dangers specific to the individual patient, within the context of a relationship with doctor, nurse, or social worker, and where the relationship is continued after discharge from hospital, the risk of relapse and readmission to hospital is greatly reduced. The need for large amounts of medication is no longer necessary. Such an approach ought to be easier since the introduction of community psychiatric nurses and community care. When patients relapse after hospital treatment, this is not simply due to a lack of sympathetic interest on the part of the family. In many instances the return home intensifies psychic dangers. They are the very same dangers that had initiated the psychotic attack. Where this hazard is identified during the period of hospitalization, the patient should be encouraged, in co-operation with his relatives, to find accommodation outside the family home. This is not always easy to arrange because of the limitations of the community psychiatric services.

Everyone who works psychotherapeutically with schizophrenic patients is conscious of their lack of rapport and of interest. The absence of emotional involvement on the patient's part and the paucity of productive responses to interventions is disappointing and discouraging. These difficulties are frequently compounded by the fact that the home background of these patients is often replete with mental pathology and behavioural disorders. The hospital psychiatrist cannot select the patient he is expected to treat. There is sometimes a sense of irritation and anger with the patients' unwillingness or inability to join in the therapeutic venture. These reactions of the psychiatrist may be even more pronounced with cases of the non-remitting type. Some psychoanalysts believe that these reactions on the psychiatrist's part are unconsciously induced (projective identification) by the patients and represent an important element of their psychopathology. They believe that these reactions provide material for important interpretation. This an attractive hypothesis, and it may be of value in dissipating the sense of helplessness and frustration so often experienced by those trying to treat these patients.

Morale is the indispensable element in the psychotherapeutic treatment of the schizophrenias. In the psychoanalytically sophisticated hospitals in the United States and Switzerland, morale was maintained by psychiatrists supervising one another's patients. In this country it can be fostered by the team approach referred to earlier. Such an approach permitted work with long-standing cases of schizophrenia in the days immediately prior to the introduction of chemotherapy (Freeman, Cameron, & McGhie, 1958).

Comprehensive psychoanalytic profiles of individual patients (Freeman, 1988b) can be drawn as clinical material becomes available. While these profiles may not give an accurate description of the psychic terrain, they do give direction and interest to those working with the patient. This work encourages the growth of what remains of the patients' healthy mental life and the development of an affective tie between patient and doctor or patient and nurse. At the end of the day, therapeutic success or failure depends on how far it is possible to revive these ties with reality.

CHAPTER SIX

A psychotherapeutic approach to the understanding and treatment of a psychosomatic disorder: the case of burning mouth syndrome

Ruth Freeman

Introduction

Burning Mouth Syndrome (BMS) is described as a burning sensation of the oral mucosa, tongue, palate, lips, and pharynx. The aetiology of BMS was first suggested to be multifactorial in the 1930s (Fox, 1935; Schroff, 1935) being due primarily to physical factors (deficiency states, disturbances in salivary and gastric secretions, and local causes including trauma) and secondarily to psychogenic factors.

In the terminology of today, Schroff (1935) and Fox (1935) are, in essence, proposing a psychogenic–physical aetiological continuum for BMS. However, the role of psychogenic causation versus physical causation remains an area of contention for BMS.

Since the prevalence of BMS varies with age (Basker, Strudee, & Davenport, 1978; Hugoson & Thorstensson, 1990) and is five times more common in post-menopausal women (Grushka, 1987), it was proposed that BMS was due to deficiencies in hormones and vitamins. Research has demonstrated that deficiencies due to hormones (oestrogen/progesterone) and vitamins (especially the Vitamin B12 complex) are of subclinical proportions, and replacement therapy may be little more than a placebo effect (Grushka, 1983).

Some patients with BMS do experience problems with disturbances in gastric secretion (Lamey & Lamb, 1988); however, the majority complain of dry mouths. Hugoson (1986) has suggested that this is secondary to anxiety states and/or the use of psychotrophic drugs such as protheiden. He stated that the dry mouth was, therefore, secondary and not a primary cause of BMS.

Local causes include tongue thrusting and teeth-clenching. These can be alleviated with hypnotherapy (Lamey & Lamb, 1988), again suggesting a psychogenic dimension to the disorder.

The psychogenic element in the aetiology is further supported by the work of Hammaren and Hugoson (1989). They have related major life events as important predictors of the onset of this condition, while previous studies (Schoenberg, 1967; Schoenberg, Carr, Kutscher, & Zegarelli, 1971; Ziskin & Moulton, 1946) had suggested that BMS was associated with the loss of a loved one as well as repressed aggressive wishes and sexual phantasies.

Therefore, while the physical causative factors initially appeared to be primary in the aetiology of BMS, more recent research has pointed to an increased importance for a psychogenic dimension.

However, what relevance can the consideration of dental conditions, such as BMS, have for psychotherapists? The importance of discussing such conditions as BMS is that it allows a reappraisal of the value of using psychoanalytic constructs as a means of understanding the mental representation, symbolization, and psychopathology of conditions of a psychogenic nature. Conditions such as BMS can, therefore, be illustrative of the psychoanalytic theories used to explain the origins of psychosomatic disorders.

For some time there has been a debate about the place of psychogenic factors in the aetiology of psychosomatic conditions. Various psychoanalytic theories have been proposed to explain them. There are those who postulate that the functional changes in a bodily organ (organ neurosis: Fenichel, 1946; psychosomatic disorders: Glover, 1949) result from a "damming-up" of affects that are denied conscious expression and find an outlet through a process of somatization (affect equivalents). Others (Alexander, 1950; Dunbar, 1943; Engel & Schmale, 1967) propose that psychosomatic disturbances are physiological processes that have acquired mental representation through a process of symbolization, as a result of repressed wishes and unresolved conflicts, whereas Gaddini (1982, 1987) suggests that what remains fundamental for psychosomatic disorders is the fact that a "mind–body continuum" exists. This is a closed system in which the mind is located throughout the body and not restricted to the brain (Gaddini, 1987). Therefore, according to Gaddini (1982), phantasies and wishes in illnesses of a psychogenic nature can be expressed through the body (phantasies of the body) enclosed within this "body–mind–body circuit". Gaddini (1982) further suggests that this is a more primitive form of functioning, and the role of psychotherapy for such conditions is to allow the "fantasies of the body" to gain psychic imagery, as found, for example, in dreams.

Can these psychoanalytic constructs explain the observable and clinical manifestations of BMS? If BMS has a psychosomatic dimension to its aetiology, the mental representation and symbolization of the burning and site "chosen" needs to be examined in order to provide a psychopathology of such conditions. The clinical material presented here with one patient illustrates a psychogenic element in the aetiology of BMS. Conclusions are constructed on the basis that the patient's material suggested that the recovery of memories played a part in the resolution of her symptoms. The emergence of dreams and phantasies towards the latter part of the first year of treatment further suggested that a psychic shift had taken place from body to mind, in the mind–body continuum, thus providing a psychic hypothesis for the remission of the burning tongue.

The psychotherapeutic experience

Psychotherapeutic experience with patients suffering from BMS is difficult because of their reluctance to recognize that psychological influences may have been instrumental in creating the symptomatology. Occasionally, however, a patient is encountered where it is possible to initiate and sustain a psychotherapeutic relationship with beneficial results. This was the case with Betty, a 45-year-old married woman.

The preliminary interview

The patient was a pleasant, intelligent woman who talked freely and without difficulty. She was low-spirited on account of her symptom but not anxious or clinically depressed. She reported that her tongue had been burning for four years. She associated the burning with having toothache in a lower left molar. This started on a Saturday when her husband, Peter, was out. He had refused to take her with him or to tell her where he was going. When he eventually returned, they went to an emergency clinic, where the filling was removed and the tooth was dressed. She stated that the dentist told her that the tooth was healthy and that the filling should be replaced. But the pain became worse, and she persuaded her own dentist to take the tooth out. A few days after the extraction, the burning started in her tongue. She and Peter were not getting on at this time. He would be out of the house all the time. She suspected and feared that he was having an affair with a woman with whom he worked. She feared that he would leave her. He would keep her short of money and refuse to pay bills. She was now working as a nurse in a local hospital. She paid the mortgage and other household bills. She told the therapist that they rarely, if ever, had intercourse. He was violent towards her, and she was able to associate her facial pain with the many times he had hit her. She stated that she wished that "Someone would send Peter to Kuwait [the war] and that he would never come back".

Personal History

Betty was the youngest of three children. Her sister was ten years her senior and her brother five years older. Her father was dead but her mother was alive. She described her childhood as being uneventful and recognized that she was her parents' favourite. During her childhood she had lived in an isolated house in the country. She went to the local primary school, which she enjoyed, although she was frightened of a female teacher. She went to secondary school, which she also found frightening. She was teased about her appearance. She had her upper incisors extracted when she was 14 years old, because of their prominence. She described this experience as a traumatic event and recalled coming home on the bus with her mother afterwards.

Her husband had lived in the next house along. She had known him all her life and started going about with him when she was 15 years old. She left school, trained to be a nurse, and was married when she was 20 years old. They lived a few miles from her parents, and when several years later they decided to move to a local small town, she was fearful.

Her husband is five years older than Betty. He is moody and, as mentioned above, can be violent. He wishes to sell their house and build a house in the grounds of an isolated farm that he owns. This was and remains an area of conflict between them. Her first child, a son, was hydrocephalic and was still-born. She has two living daughters. The eldest is 22 years old and is recently married. Her younger daughter is aged 20, a student, and she is to be married in the near future.

The sessions

The psychotherapeutic sessions took place weekly and have continued over a period of three years. The sessions can be divided into four phases. During the first phase, which lasted for 12 months, the content of the sessions was mainly taken up with enabling Betty to express her disappointments, frustrations, and lack of satisfaction in her marital relationship. She was able to say how Peter embarrassed her and how he abused her physically when he was angry. It emerged that she had filed for a personal protection order prior to divorce proceedings but could not go through with it. She had believed her husband when he said he would change. She felt guilty, as if she had committed a crime. The way she described her physical reactions to the distressing events with Peter made it possible to say to her that, under the circumstances she "burnt" with embarrassment, "burnt" with fury, and "smouldered" with unresolved passion. She readily accepted the idea that her sense of guilt was caused by the wish that her husband would die. It was at the end of this first phase that Betty remembered her dreams and brought them to the sessions. The dreams, at this time, illustrated her sexual frustration and aggressive feelings for Peter.

The first dream was of *a woman washing an old man. She looks on. In the dream she is aware of her distaste for this old pathetic man.* Her associations revealed that at work, on the dream day, she had been bathing an old man in the hospital. She thought how these old men never have erections, even when they are being bathed. She assumed they were just not up to it. Betty stated that she then thought about Peter and when they were in bed together. He was like the old men, incapable of having an erection. In fact, when she was in bed beside him, she was aware of having the same feeling of distaste for him as she had experienced in the dream. It occurred to her that Peter was just a useless, hopeless old man.

The second dream revealed her wish to have a virile young man who could satisfy her sexually. She dreamt of *going to see the dentist. On the way down the stairs she is hosed down by two boys; she is soaked through.* Betty recalled that the day before (the dream day) she had thought that she needed to have a dental check-up. She had also seen the little boys next-door playing with their father's hose, soaking each other. She had been at a meeting at work about sexual problems—premature ejaculation. She had thought of Peter—was this his problem? Her daughters would soon both be married, and their husbands seemed so young, just like boys. It was possible to link the imagery in the dream—to be hosed down by the "boys"—to her wish to have a young, virile husband, like the husbands of her daughters and like the dentist who cared for her needs. These young men would not suffer from premature ejaculation but be able to maintain their erections, "hose her down", and satisfy her sexual needs.

The second phase, which lasted for six months, was characterized by a pronounced symptomatic improvement. Her relationship with Peter was better. He promised to be more understanding. They spent more evenings together and went out for meals. They had happy 25th wedding anniversary. A dream reported at this time reflected her happier frame of mind. In the dream *she is with her father in a field and crossing a stile. She runs on in front of her father to a house. It is a cottage; it is lovely, it is a place where she feels happy.* She could not think where this cottage was or what it reminded her of. At the next session she told me that her sister had been in and had been talking about their grandmother's cottage. It dawned on her that it was the cottage in the dream. With this came many memories of visiting her grandmother and a maiden aunt, who would spoil her, and of happy times spent there. It was during this phase that many of the details discussed in the personal history came to light.

The third phase was initiated with the return of the symptom. The analysis of two dreams led to an understanding of the cause of the relapse and to thoughts, feelings, and memories that had not yet been disclosed. In the first dream *she is walking in a town, wearing her gold chain; a dark man (a Spaniard) snatches it from her neck, and she begs him to give it back. When he does, she realizes its just lead.* Her associations to the dream were that, as with Peter, all that glitters is not gold. Peter did not want her sexually, and she did not want him.

In the second dream *someone—a man—is trying to get at her through a window. The window is smashed; she is frightened and wakens.* On the day of the dream Peter had been arguing with their daughter. She was frightened by this and feared he would turn on her. The previous evening (the dream night) he had wanted to have intercourse with her. She rejected him angrily because she was menstruating. She had a heavy loss and a discharge. She then went on to say that she had bled freely and extensively during the birth of her last child. Subsequently she had a uterine prolapse. She had tried to use a coil for contraception, but it was painful and she bled. She had a need for coitus, but she was fearful when Peter approached her and terrified when he got angry. Her dream gave representation to the way in which she perceived coitus as damaging and destructive. She could see, with little help, that she feared that Peter would damage her internally through coitus and childbirth. She hated him for it. She recovered a memory of her first pregnancy. She remembered that she had thought that Peter was the cause of the deformed baby. It was his sperm that was defective, and it had damaged her and had caused the baby to be malformed. She could now understand that her relapse was related to these fears and the threat of coitus.

Following these disclosures, the tongue-burning disappeared. During this time she recovered many childhood memories, one of which concerned her mother's frugal nature. As a small child she had yearned for a pair of red shoes, which her mother thought a waste of money. She remembered throwing a tantrum and being chastised for doing so. As an adolescent, she wished for a television set, and she would hope that it would have arrived in the house as if by magic. She also wished that her parents were young. She rarely if ever asked anything from or of her mother, since she hated being disappointed. She complained of Peter's meanness and how she would not ask him for anything, be it money, a lift to the shops, or coitus. She feared being disappointed by him. It became possible to link her inability to ask Peter for things with her childhood experiences. Her feelings of disappointment and the subsequent rage she felt for Peter had its origin in her childhood relationship with her mother.

She was able to recall how when she first went about with Peter that she had been told that he was having coitus with an older girl who lived near her in Ballycorr. The woman she feared that he had been having an affair with lived in Carncorr. It became possible to identify why the burning had started when it did, since fears of her husband's affair rekindled old memories of previous infidelities. It also became apparent that Peter was a transference object for her mother, who, she felt, was unfaithful to her, since she took her sister's part in her violent rages against the patient.

Furthermore, she recalled that as a small child she had wished for her older brother to take her with him when he went out. He would refuse to do so. She would try to think of ways of getting her own back on him. This always back-fired. It was possible to connect Betty's attempts at being cool and off-hand with Peter with her wishes for revenge on Jim. Furthermore, her fury of being left behind by Peter had its origin in her childhood—disappointment and rage with her brother Jim. She recalled how alike Jim and Peter were in their personality and looks and the fact that they were both five years her senior.

As a result of this psychotherapeutic work, she became more confident and more forceful in her dealings with Peter. She became less frightened of him and refused to tolerate his aggressive behaviour. He appeared to acknowledge that she also had her needs and anxieties, which he must try to understand, particularly with regard to her sexual life.

A fourth phase to the treatment started prior to a summer break. Betty was able to tell the therapist of how jealous she felt when her husband looked at other women. She felt bitterly ashamed. After the summer the burning in her tongue reappeared. This time the burning only occurred on the way to sessions or during the sessions themselves.

She slowly admitted how furious she was with the
therapist for bringing up the question of her jealousy. She
was fearful of her anger. In childhood her older sister's
rages had left her frightened and helpless. Now she was
fearful of the therapist's retaliation. The therapist was an
unknown quantity. She might explode with anger if she
knew of the extent of Betty's fury against her. In the
transference the therapist became the raging older
sister.

The analysis of this transference resistance allowed her to
connect her fear of her husband's explosive rages with
those of her sister. She was also able see that her fears
and dislikes of her line manager were related to the fears
she had of her female primary-school teacher, who had
also raged at her. Furthermore the therapist reminded her
of a friend—a school-teacher who had little time for her
own children. She would shout at them and make them
cry over the smallest unimportant incident. It was now
clear that from the beginning of the psychotherapy
progress had been impeded by these resistances due to
the transference.

Why was this patient, in contrast to others with BMS, able
to cooperate and benefit from the therapy? A working
alliance developed despite of her anxieties. She began to
identify with the therapist and adopted an analytic
attitude to her symptom. Thus she came to appreciate the
connection between the appearance of the symptom and
its immediate cause. This development may have been
based on the special position she occupied in her family.
She was the youngest sibling by five years and considered
by all to be her mother's favourite. She would be taken for
special outings by her parents.

Was the symptomatic benefit the outcome of an
idealization of the therapist or a catharsis of disagreeable
memories, some of which were expressed via the
transference? After the sudden death in a car accident of a
favourite nephew, she noted that her tongue began to
burn. She related the immediate cause to her husband's
old car breaking down on the way back from the funeral.

She became aware of the thought that she wished it had been Peter who had been killed in the car accident and not her nephew. She was also able to link the old broken-down car to her husband's premature ejaculation and her young nephew's fast car to the perceived dangers in coitus. Improvement followed the retrieval of this death wish.

The nature of BMS

Can any conclusions be drawn from this case about the nature of BMS? The data that appeared in the course of the psychotherapy demonstrated that psychic factors played a major role in the symptom formation. The relief that occurred was the result of the reduction of the anxiety and guilt that had interfered with the free expression of aggressive and sexual affects. It was thus reasonable to hypothesize that until this occurred these affects were represented by the burning sensation in the tongue. Rather than experiencing rage or sexual excitement Betty suffered with a burning tongue as her phantasies and wishes were expressed through her body (Gaddini, 1982, 1987). Consequently, Betty was unaware of the depth and quality of her emotions—as, for example, the death wishes towards her husband. She was, to quote Betty, the "type of person who just does not argue or feel angry about things". Only later was Betty able to appreciate her feelings of rage. She stated that her "tongue was like a barometer—the angrier [she] felt, the hotter it got".

The psychotherapeutic experience also revealed a further series of data that must be taken into account with regard to the nature of the symptoms. Preconsciously or unconsciously, she had entertained the phantasy that her internal genitalia had been damaged by coitus and childbirth, perhaps by masturbation, but this was not gone into. This frightening phantasy was activated when Peter approached her for coitus. This resulted in her rejection of him and led to subsequent violent rows. When alone, she was safe and could experience a sexual excitement that, unsatisfied, contributed to the burning tongue.

A case can be made for the hypothesis that the burning tongue was the result of displacement of phantasies and affects from below upwards—from the genitals to the tongue—after the fashion of a hysterical conversion symptom. By thinking in this way, some progress may be made towards answering the question of the choice of symptom. Did the tongue come to represent the active aspects of her sexuality (phallic sexuality) on the one hand, and the phantasied danger to the genitalia on the other hand? Can the burning tongue come to represent (Engel & Schmale, 1967) symbolically feelings of anger and sexual excitement?

While controversy remains as to the role of symbolization and representation in psychosomatic disorders (Taylor, 1989), the clinical data support the view that Betty's repressed aggressive and sexual wishes were expressed as affect equivalents (Fenichel, 1946; Glover, 1949) through the burning of her tongue. The clinical material also supports Gaddini's (1982) hypothesis that psychosomatic disorders are phantasies and wishes expressed as bodily symptoms—"fantasies of the body"—rather than as psychic images. Therefore with increased awareness of the antecedents of the symptoms, the psychic shift that occurs relocates phantasies and wishes from existing within the symptomatology (the burning tongue) to the affects.

However, in a sense it is immaterial whether or not such a case is to be categorized as psychosomatic in Fenichel and Glover's sense or as one of conversion hysteria, where psychic contents (wishes, phantasies, etc.) can be identified as existing between the affects and the symptomatology. The question is whether or not psychological factors are operative and decisive in all cases of BMS. It is no accident that BMS is designated a syndrome. This concept allows accommodation of a number of different causative factors with a psychogenic–physical continuum being proposed for the aetiology of BMS. In some cases of BMS, psychological factors predominate, as in the case presented here; in others, physical elements; while in still others there is a mixture of psychic and physical causes. The question remains, nevertheless: is there one cause or a spectrum of them? Only further psychotherapeutic research will answer this question.

Psychoanalysis
and
the study of culture and society

Freud, religion, and the Oedipus complex: some reflections on the infantile origins of religious experience

Peter Torney

Since the time of Freud, the religious landscape of late-twentieth-century advanced industrial society has changed considerably. The years following the Second World War have seen the emergence of a plethora of new religious movements and cults, many of Eastern origin (Beckford, 1985, 1986; Wallis, 1984), and the fragmentation of the major Christian denominations into a multitude of sects of various kinds, emphasizing now this and now that element of their traditional religious past (Wilson, 1976). While the main Christian denominations remain on the surface organizationally intact within this burgeoning field of new salvational paths, they appear riven within by conflict as they attempt to adapt their traditional views to the ever-changing demands of modern culture.

In addition, the post-war years have seen the emergence of many new psychotherapies, all purporting to offer their adherents some form of self-transformation. Unlike religion, these latest secular revelations offer a form of "psycho-salvation" (Wallis, 1979) as a solution to the problems of modern living. These new "technologies of the self" for "governing" the modern soul (Rose, 1990) have entered perhaps unwittingly into competition with traditional religion. They, too, line the shelves of the new "religious" supermarket from which individuals can select the appropriate salvational package with which to construct some sense of meaning and purpose in what is fast becoming for some commentators a fragmented "post-modern" world (Frosh, 1991; Lasch, 1991; Sennett, 1977).

That psychoanalysis has become implicated in this, at least in the popular imagination (Persaud, 1993), should give serious cause for concern to those working within the field of psychoanalytic practice and research. It is true that many of these new therapies emerged as a reaction to or divergence from psychoanalytic orthodoxy and can be subsumed under the title the "human potential movement" (Brown & Pedder, 1979, pp. 166–179; Wallis, 1985). But like their religious counterparts and unlike psychoanalysis, they are imbued with a certain utopianism and therapeutic optimism that goes beyond the boundaries of individual neurotic misery to posit implicitly or explicitly some solution also to the social problems of everyday unhappiness.

The point is made well by Richards (1989) when he compares this humanistic psychological optimism with the essentially tragic vision of Freud. A similar critical juxtaposition, though in different terms, is evident in the work of Chasseguet-Smirgel and Grunberger (1986) and Rieff (1966).

It is clear that Freud saw psychoanalysis as no *Weltanschauung* (1933a, pp. 158ff). He was loath also to rise up as a prophet:

> I have not the courage to rise up before my fellow-men as a prophet, and I bow to their reproach that I can offer them no consolation: for at bottom that is what they are all demanding—the wildest revolutionaries no less passionately than the most virtuous believers. [Freud, 1930a, p. 145]

This search for consolation is the common denominator that links both the search for psycho-salvation and its more traditional religious counterpart. At heart it is a search for meaning, for certainty, for security in a modern world that has become increasingly complex and bureaucratized, and where traditional certainties and values seem to have withered.

Regardless of how the malaise is defined, the fact is that individuals in modern industrial society have a far wider range of potential ideational and material products with which to pursue some form of consolation and happiness than has hitherto been the case. Of course access to these cultural artifacts is differentially distributed across economic classes and this will determine for many the measure and type of consolation pursued. Whether they find it or not may have more to do with politics than with psychology or religion.

This said, however, the problem remains as to what purchase can be exerted by psychoanalysis on the phenomenon of contemporary religion as broadly defined. To be sure, Freud wrote much on the topics of culture in general, and religion in particular (1907b, 1912–13, 1921c, 1927c, 1930a, 1939a). While he may have been loath to act the prophet (1930a, p. 145), he was certainly not inhibited in offering diagnoses of the "disease". For Freud psychoanalysis was a critical tool that could be applied to a range of cultural phenomena without at the same time offering a solution, or some form of *ersatz* consolation. In the end pathological social structures can only be changed politically. If psychoanalysis has any contribution to make, it can only be from the clinical domain where those people who seek relief from their neurotic misery can hopefully be strengthened so as to transform tormented passive endurance into a creatively active participation in the political theatre of their everyday lives. But from this clinical domain there spring also those concepts that facilitate both a critique of, and commentary on, wider cultural processes.

As mentioned above, a common denominator of the various salvational paths available today is the search for consolation. The consolation may take many forms, but it is nonetheless consolation. The remainder of this chapter looks for clues as to why this should be so by focusing principally on the psychoanalytic ideas of Freud. The argument eschews a focus on Freud's main papers on religion, except for passing reference, and concentrates instead on looking for interesting ideas in other parts of his work not normally highlighted in this regard.

A central theme in the writings of Freud on religion is the key role of early childhood experience. At times this thread is implicit, at other times it is explicit. In a number of places in his writings Freud states his view that a person's image of God is motivated by early childhood attachments that form the prototype.

> It has its infantile prototype, of which, in fact, it is only a continuation. For once before one has found oneself in a similar state of helplessness: as a small child in relation to one's parents. One had reason to fear them, and especially one's father; and yet one was sure of his protection against the dangers one knew. [Freud, 1927c, p. 17]

One of his earliest and best known, and indeed hotly disputed papers on religion was *Totem and Taboo*. Here we find expressed forcibly the same theme:

> The psychoanalysis of individual human beings, however, teaches us with quite special insistence that the god of each of them is formed in the likeness of his father, that his personal relation to god depends on his relation to his father in the flesh and oscillates and changes along with that relation, and that at bottom god is nothing other than an exalted father. . . . If psycho-analysis deserves any attention, then . . . the paternal element in that concept must be the most important one. [1912–13, p. 147]

Later in the same text he pins his colours to the mast and states:

> . . . the beginnings of religion, morals, society and art converge in the Oedipus complex. [1912–13, p. 156]

It is therefore necessary to unpack clearly what is meant by the Oedipus complex. Such is no easy task, and in what follows I am trying only to sketch briefly a broad model of early development that leaves much unsaid and many by-ways unexplored.

In order to enter into the world of the child, a good starting-point is to imagine oneself as an infant and attempt to grasp the primitive character of its thoughts, desires, and feelings. It demands of us that we bracket the fluid capacities of our adult minds; the capacity to think of a future or to contemplate a past; the capacity to use language and imagery to conjure a picture of our experience, etc. Such are not available to the infant. In this life-world there is no word for hunger or thirst, no word for pleasure or pain, no capacity to articulate thwarted wishes or fulfilled desires, no words for love or hate, just naked experience. Gradually the infant begins to build a primitive picture of its experience, and these images become attached to what must be deeply felt bodily states and desires, which we, with our adult language, can describe as pleasurable or painful, happy or sad, intolerable or overwhelming, frustrating or satisfying. But the infant has no such linguistic capacity to map out its experience, just an ever-increasing range of images conveyed through the senses that become attached to its bodily feelings states.

In addition, those parts of the body and bodily functions such as ingesting food and urinating/defecating become woven into this primitive symbolic world of the infant and are usually described and discussed in the literature under such headings as orality, anality, and pre-Oedipal attachments. The physical experience of incorporating food, retaining or excreting waste, of close physical contact with a primary carer or its absence, have an intensity that can only be guessed at from our adult point of view. How the infant manages to deal with these intense states will have a lasting effect on the personality. For these states are not just passively experienced. On the contrary, they are built up into an internal representational world that is as intense as it is chaotic, involving an attempted synthesis of extreme physical states with crude imagery. It is a form of primitive symbolism, where the desire to preserve and retain pleasurable imagery has its bodily prototype in oral incorporation, and the desire to escape from or to expel unpleasurable imagery has its bodily prototype in anal expulsion.

Indeed, some psychoanalysts would argue that these primitive bodily-based prototypes are the foundation of our human capacity to think and to symbolize. Developmental failure at this pre-Oedipal stage can have catastrophic consequences for later development, inflicting sometimes irreparable damage on the persons capacity to symbolize meaningfully. Whether it be described as a failure to negotiate the move from the paranoid-schizoid position to the depressive position described by the Kleinian school or the pre-Oedipal distortion in character/personality formation described by the contemporary Freudians will be no doubt a matter of continuing and fruitful debate. The fundamental point is, however, not to lose touch with, and empathy for, the profound human experience that lies behind such descriptive and explanatory categories.

The genesis of the child's internal reality continues through this world of primitive pre-verbal imagery. But all the time it is in a dialectical relationship with the outer world of social reality, which, in turn, domesticates this experience progressively into the categories of a socially accepted cultural world. A world of language, of real objects, real values, real moral codes is gradually overlaid upon and woven into this primitive object world. It is at this time that we can see the beginnings of a moral sense being laid down in the child's mind, and it is these momentous happenings that are of signal importance.

At this stage the child has achieved some degree of object constancy. The parents are seen as real and separate objects, a developmental achievement that is as momentous as it is precarious. Indeed, it could be said that this capacity is always under threat; for not a few it collapses in later life, and the primitive, now unconscious, symbolism of the early period manifests itself in the hallucinations and delusions of psychotic states.

But for the sake of our discussion let us assume that the capacity for real object relations has been sufficiently developed. The child's desires and wishes continue to be directed towards its parents in both an active and a passive manner. Passively the child longs for the attention and ministrations of mother and father, for example, and actively pursues strategies to achieve this result.

But what is of cardinal importance from the psychoanalytic point of view, is not so much the observable behaviour, but the internal intensity of the child's desires, and its attempts to manage this potentially chaotic internal world by means of synthesis and defence.

For the purposes of this chapter I focus on the vicissitudes of the male child and leave the discussion of female development to another time. The male child's desires seem to become progressively focused on the mother or other primary female carer. The desire for close physical touch, for union, for the pleasure attached to such experiences—all are vitally alive in the child in an intense manner. These libidinal cathexes are directed primarily at the mother, and the child tends to identify with the father by wanting to be like him. But the father is now being perceived as a competitor and an intruder—as, indeed, are other children in the family.

Father is now someone with whom the child would like to dispense—someone to be got rid of, someone indeed to be annihilated. The conflict between a primitive longing love for the father and an equally primitive murderous hate of him is now in place. Perhaps this is symbolically represented in the mind of the child in terms of a wish to expel and destroy thoughts of the father (oral/anal expulsion) and to retain and preserve thoughts of the mother (oral/anal retention). If he actively pursues his desires for his mother, then he risks the imagined wrath of his father and his own possible destruction.

How does the child resolve this conflict? The boy's narcissistic self-interest triumphs, and the erotic cathexes of his mother are renounced. Faced with a loss of such tragic proportions, the child deals with the crisis through the mechanism of identification, introjecting both parents into his ego.

It is important to note that these identifications are with both parents, and this is such a momentous happening in the mind of a young child that it is worth dwelling on at some length. Although the identifications are with both parents, it is necessary to differentiate between them. The child's identification with mother is motivated by fear of his father; and it must surely be coloured by the profound loss entailed in having to renounce an external attachment to his mother that is as dear as it is intense—it is the prototype that textures the quality of all future libidinal disappointments. All losses such as this seem to involve a defensive manoeuvre of this type, where the lost object is introjected as a means of defending against the psychic pain involved. The mother, therefore, becomes more deeply embedded in the unconscious psychic structure of the child. The intense libidinal desires are renounced, to be replaced with a conscious aim-inhibited affectional bond.

Fear also is the motivating force for identification with father; a defence against fear of him becomes transformed into a desire to become like him and imitate him. But he may imitate him in all things should he wish, save one—the free exercise of his intense sexual desires for his mother. To pursue that strategy raises many fears in the mind of the child, not least of which is the terror of castration, if not annihilation. As a consequence, the boy's attitude to his father is also accompanied by a certain defiance and hate—usually muted, if not completely crushed and driven underground by terror.

Although these two identifications can be separated in this way for the sake of discussion, they are intimately related. The fundamental question is which identification will predominate—that with the mother, or that with the father. This is not an idle speculation, for the child not only fears and hates his father, he also loves and longs for him in a manner not dissimilar to the manner in which he desires his mother. This particular phenomenon gives rise to the view that the Oedipus complex has both a negative and a positive component. The positive aspect of the complex relates to the libidinal desire for mother (later renounced) and an imitative identification with the father. However, the reverse is also possible; the child may take his father as a love object and identify with his mother by wishing to be like her. This is the negative aspect of the Oedipus complex.

In essence, it is a series of object relationships that are internalized, coloured by intense desires and highly ambivalent feelings of love and hate. Within the drama of this internalized representational world the child's ego can cast itself in many roles. At one time the little boy can cast himself in the homosexual role and take his father as a love object and identify with mother; at another, he can switch to the heterosexual role and take mother as his love object and identify with father. That this latter is the final outcome of this internal drama should not blind us to the fact that the former drama is also laid down in the unconscious, albeit in a much muted form. If I may continue the dramatic metaphor: it is a stage upon which many potential catastrophes are permanently waiting to happen—and, indeed, do happen for not a few in later life.

These are momentous happenings indeed in the internal world of a young child. Freud describes the general outcome of the process in the following way:

> The broad general outcome of the sexual phase dominated by the Oedipus complex may, therefore, be taken to be the forming of a precipitate in the ego, consisting of these two identifications, in some way united with each other. This modification of the ego retains its special position; it confronts the contents of the ego as an ego ideal or super-ego. [1923b, p. 34]

With the emergence of the superego, a key feature of the child's experience has moved from the outside to the inside, so to speak. That is, the power, strength, authority, severity of the parents are now set up in the internal world of the child, and for the first time perhaps it begins to experience a sense of guilt as a discrepancy emerges between this ego-ideal and the actual performance of the ego. It is the beginning of conscience—a critical agency which, like the tortoise its shell, the child and later the adult can never escape.

Indeed, it is clear that the foundations of morality have been firmly if primitively laid down at this stage, involving crude experiences of conscience, guilt, and punishment. The intensity of this guilt, however, can seem out of proportion to the nature of the child's peccadilloes, and this needs to be accounted for. The clue to answering this puzzle lies in the nature of the child's wishes towards its parents that now lie buried alive, so to speak, though in an unconscious state: to wit, incestuous desire and murderous hate. Given that children of this age rarely distinguish between a wish and its realization, a mechanism referred to as "omnipotence of thoughts", the conditions are created in the mind of the child that in his unconscious he actually believes himself guilty of some dreadful deed.

Further to this, however, we must account also for the severity of the superego, which seems out of proportion to what would usually be internalized at the resolution to the Oedipus complex. To explain this, we must turn to the notion of fusion/defusion of instincts. When Freud was writing at this time, he was thinking in terms of the life and death drives. In normal development the two drives are fused together, with the destructive drive being bound and contained by libidinal forces. But he argued that a transformation occurs during the process of identification that unbinds the destructive instinct from the control of Eros. This aggressiveness, if not expressed outwardly—and there is a strong cultural prohibition against this—is taken up by the superego, making it more cruel and severe towards the ego. As Freud notes:

> The more a man controls his aggressiveness, the more intense becomes his ego-ideal's inclination to aggressiveness towards his ego. [1923b, p. 54]

It is clear that the character of the child's personality has undergone a significant transformation during these years of development. If there has been an unsatisfactory resolution to the many conflicts with which the child has had to deal, then they will return in various guises in later life.

The vicissitudes of each individual's developmental biography are in a sense unique to them and involve many factors. It is not just the internal world of the child that is important, but also the significant others in his early life; whether the parents were kind or cruel; whether they related well or badly to each other and to the child; the degree of actual loss in terms of bereavement; all these and other factors will have a significant role to play. For the inner world of the child is in constant dialectical relationship with the outer environment, and it is the resolution of the internal and external trauma arising from this series of relations that will set the agenda for character formation and leave a legacy in the adult unconscious. Cultural institutions can provide the stage where the individual defensively re-enacts unresolved conflicts of love and hate or finds in them consolation for his losses.

From the perspective of adult life, such early childhood experience presents itself as hazy and opaque, hidden behind the shadow of amnesia. Because of this, it is difficult for many to accept that it plays any significant role in our conscious adult lives and in our common patterns of thinking, feeling, and acting. From the point of view of psychoanalysis, this is because this experience is now consigned to the state of being unconscious.

The reality of unconscious mental processes is a fundamental proposition of psychoanalysis. The idea that we are not masters or mistresses of our own psychological house is a deep wound to our narcissism, and it is not surprising that many reject the notion. That such mental processes are unconscious means that they are invisible, and the critical capacity of persons of common sense leads them to doubt their existence.

But from a psychoanalytic point of view the starting point is, and surely must be, this fundamental proposition. An important point to emphasize at this stage is the problem of referring to the unconscious as if it were some sort of entity in its own right, like a *thing* existing in the mind, for example. Indeed, so common is this perception that it is not surprising people are sceptical as to its reality. They have every right to be! The fact is that although this meaning predominates in the popular imagination, the unconscious is not a separate element as such, but a quality attributed to mental processes and contents that are not immediately available to consciousness, but which have an effect on our thoughts and actions. In this sense, therefore, it is the *unconscious character* of our *biographical* experience that is central.

That this unconscious biographical experience is relevant when it comes to exploring people's religious beliefs and attitudes seems to me to be beyond question. It is at this point that the contribution of psychoanalysis comes to the fore.

From this point of view, unconscious biographical experience becomes deeply and unwittingly woven into many individuals images of God, the Devil, or even fate or destiny. The internalized parental imagos of early childhood become transferred onto these external deities or forces, and it is these that hold clues not so much to their external referents, but to the internal world of the individual and the vicissitudes of his or her previous relationship with their parents.

It is clear that, whatever else Freud said about religion—and he said much—a key theme was his view that the image of God, the Devil, fate, providence, destiny were in essence projections of unconscious images of the father (Freud, 1974, pp. 283–284). These religious images are rooted primarily in the Oedipus complex, both in its positive and in its negative forms. In his paper on Leonardo Da Vinci, Freud states quite clearly his view on the relationship between the father-complex and belief in God, and it is worth quoting in full:

> Psycho-analysis has made us familiar with the intimate connection between the father-complex and belief in God; it has shown us that a personal God is, psychologically, nothing other than an exalted father, and it brings us evidence every day of how young people lose their religious beliefs as soon as their father's authority breaks down. Thus we recognize that the roots of the need for religion are in the parental complex; the almighty and just God, and kindly Nature, appear to us as grand sublimations of father and mother, or rather as revivals and restorations of the young child's ideas of them. Biologically speaking, religiousness is to be traced to the small human child's long-drawn-out helplessness and need of help; and when at a later date he perceives how truly forlorn and weak he is when confronted with the great forces of life, he feels his conditions as he did in childhood, and attempts to deny his despondency by a regressive revival of the forces which protected his infancy. [Freud, 1910c, p. 123]

Perhaps a good way to grasp the meaning of what Freud is saying here is to focus on an extreme example, which can throw into sharp relief many of the elements involved. A striking example of the childhood origins of religious delusions is evident in the case of Daniel Paul Schreber. This case is one that has received close scrutiny over the years by numerous psychoanalytic authors starting with Freud (1911c [1910]). This present discussion of Schreber is based on his memoirs of his nervous illness, which he published in 1903 (Schreber, 1988). This text is a most vivid account of psychotic experience and contains a complete account of Schreber's delusional system.

While Freud and his colleagues were primarily interested in the case from the point of view of understanding the mechanism of paranoia, the highly religious nature of the content of the memoirs provides a fine illustration of Schreber's conception of, and relation to, God.

From his own reading of the original text, Freud identifies four features that are important about the character traits of Schreber's God and of his relationship to him: the fact that God does not understand living men (Schreber, 1988, p. 75); the resulting persecution of Schreber because of this misunderstanding (p. 198); God's incapability of learning anything (p. 154); and the attempts by Schreber to find a justification for God's behaviour (Freud, 1911c [1910], pp. 25–28).

Freud argues that in the whole of Schreber's book there runs the constant and "bitter complaint that God, being only accustomed to communication with the dead, does not understand living men" (1911c [1910], p. 25). Here is Schreber's own comment:

> A fundamental misunderstanding obtained however, which has since run like a thread through my entire life. It is based upon the fact that, within the Order of the world, God did not really understand the living human being and had no need to understand him, because, according to the Order of the World he dealt only with corpses. [Schreber, 1988, p. 75]

Later in the memoirs Schreber again makes the same complaint. This time, however, it is after having had "the most wonderful impressions" (p. 124) over several days and nights. During one of these visions he saw "God's complete omnipotence in its complete purity" and simultaneously heard a "mighty bass" voice saying, among other things, "wretch" (p. 124). What is important in the memoirs at this point is that Schreber had to hold himself in a state of complete immobility. He did this when he was in the garden of the Sonnenstein Sanatorium and despite the attendants' remonstrations to walk about, and also when he was alone in his room.

> That rays could ever expect me to remain totally immobile ["not the slightest movement" was an often-repeated slogan], must again be connected I am convinced, with God not knowing how to treat a living human being, as He was accustomed to dealing only with corpses or at best human beings lying asleep (dreaming). There arose the almost monstrous demand that I should behave continually as if I myself were a corpse, as also a number of other more or less absurd ideas, which were all contrary to human nature. [Schreber, 1988, p. 127]

The same reproach against God is stated in chapter 18 (p. 188), and this idea of God led Schreber to the view that this misunderstanding of men was behind God's persecution of him.

Schreber describes these plots against him as threefold: God was trying to "unman him" and turn him into a woman; God was killing him; and God was attempting to destroy his reason. "Always the main idea behind them was to "forsake" me, that is to say abandon me" (p. 99). The mechanism by which these effects were to be achieved by God was through "miracles" and the "uninterrupted influx of God's nerves into my body", which lasted over a period of six years (p. 60).

These miracles were many and various and are described in detail throughout the book. Such things as miracled mechanical fastenings, whereby his own nerves were stretched across the planetary system by means of rays, are referred to in his text as "tying-to-rays" or "tying to celestial bodies" (p. 118). These miracles were allied to others that made him experience intense states of heat or cold, regardless of whether he was in the garden or in his room (p. 145). In addition, all that he had ever said, thought, or done was recorded through the miracle of the "writing-down-system" (p. 119).

In chapter 11 of his text, Schreber describes in detail the "miracles" perpetrated on his body, and which caused him intense pain. These include his graphic descriptions of the process of unmanning him, together with miracles enacted against his internal organs, especially his heart, lungs, stomach, gullet, and intestines. In addition, Schreber describes the "compression-on-the-chest" miracle; the devastation to his head by the "flight-rays", which made him feel as if his head were sawn asunder; the attacks on his eyes; and the coccyx miracle, which made sitting or lying down impossible.

What emerges from this book is an image of a person tormented by auditory and visual hallucinations of the most appalling kind, and it would be all too easy to dismiss them as just the ravings of a chronically disturbed man and of having little or no meaning. However, the pioneering work of William Niederland (1980, 1984) has enabled a very strong connection to be forged between Schreber's early childhood experiences and both his persecutory delusions and his image of God.

Niederland takes as his starting point the biography of Schreber's father. Schreber senior was a social, educational, and medical reformer, who authored numerous books and lectured widely. He was specifically interested in child-rearing practices, and Niederland focuses especially on one of his works, entitled *Kallipäde oder Erziehung zur Schönheit* [Callipedics or Education for Beauty] (Schreber, 1858), later reprinted and renamed *The Book of Education of Body and Mind*. Niederland observes:

> I have chosen this volume for particular consideration because it is almost exclusively about the upbringing of children from infancy to adolescence. It also contains passages which indicate that the methods and rules laid down by Dr Schreber were not merely theoretical principles offered in book form for the public, but they were also regularly, actively, and personally applied by him in rearing his own children—with telling effect, as he reports with paternal pride. [Niederland, 1980, pp. 253–254]

Niederland warms to his task, gradually piecing together all the various elements from this and other sources, that appear to make sense of the inchoate welter of Daniel Paul's delusions. Space does not permit an extensive account, but the following may serve as examples.

Schreber talks about the miracles associated with heat and cold in his "miracled-up" world (Schreber, 1988, p. 145). He also observes at this point: "From youth accustomed to enduring both heat and cold, these miracles troubled me little . . ." (1988, p. 146). In Schreber senior's book, Niederland discovers the advice to use only cold water in the ablutions of infants of three months of age; cold baths from aged five were to be the rule.

However, it is in the "compression-of-the-chest" and "coccyx" miracles and the "immobility" problem that we see the sinister influence of Schreber's father. He had manufactured and used a range of metal orthopaedic apparatuses the design of which was to instil correct posture into the user. Niederland gives a series of diagrams of these sinister apparatuses in his presentation and shows that these were used regularly on the Schreber children. For example, one device demonstrates how children are to be strapped onto a bed in such a manner as to keep them supine and immobile (Schreber's "immobility" problem).

With regard to the "writing-down miracle", we learn from Niederland that the father encouraged the keeping of a blackboard upon which were to be tabulated all the child's peccadilloes and departures from discipline. This was hung on the child's bedroom wall, and the issues were dealt with forcefully on a monthly basis (Niederland, 1980, p. 258).

Niederland argues convincingly on the basis of the evidence that many of Daniel Paul Schreber's delusions can be clearly explained through such reconstructions. His father's sadism seemed thinly disguised under the veneer of a child educator and social reformer, although, it must be said, his ideas were hailed at the time as innovative.

On the basis of Niederland's evidence it is clear that the God of Schreber is but a projection of his internalized sadistic father, and the persecutory miracles but archaic memories from his childhood, woven into his delusional system. This was a projection outwards of an internal representational world that was as intolerable as it was overwhelming, consisting of painful physical experiences attached to an internalized image of an overbearing and sadistic father, towards whom he could only adopt a passive, masochistic attitude. His delusional system represents a valiant attempt to defend himself from what must have been from an early age fragmenting and annihilating experiences.

At this point an objection may be raised that the God of Schreber bears no resemblance to the Deities of the world religions and can be dismissed, therefore, as just the ravings of a psychotic. But that is not the point at issue. What is clear is that this man's religious delusions have an infantile and childhood origin; they are woven out of real historical experience. In the extreme form of human experience that was his psychosis, his past returned from repression in this florid form.

It is the historian Roy Porter (1989) who has argued that Schreber's religious system also reflects many of the concerns of late-nineteenth-century culture. On closer examination, the memoirs appear not to be as bizarre as would first be thought on a casual reading. For example, with regard to Schreber's end-of-the-world delusion (1988, p. 85). Porter argues that the science of the day was predicting a heat death of the universe, and this formed one of the deepest anxieties of this period:

> The death of the sun and the end of time formed one of the gravest anxieties of the contemporary sciences of cosmology, astronomy, geology and so forth. [Porter, 1989, p. 157]

Porter advances similar arguments regarding Schreber's worries of moral decline—another late-nineteenth-century pre-occupation, as was the burgeoning discussion of comparative religion and evolution (1989, p. 157), about which Schreber demonstrated a considerable knowledge. Against this background, Schreber's system seems to be an amalgam of early childhood experience and contemporary intellectual debate. His misfortune was that he was consigned both to an asylum, and to the psychiatric gaze of the day, which had the effect of amplifying the lunatic elements of his discourse at the expense of the sane.

In our day, there are numerous cult cosmologies of a strange and bizarre nature, from "flat earthers" to flying-saucer cults, from elderly gentlefolk with sandwich boards proclaiming the end of the world to large organizations that peddle some form of unifying cosmic consciousness. The content may be different to that of Schreber, but the underlying unconscious dynamics are perhaps the same. These cults, however, are in the public domain. Schreber's religion was, of necessity, a private one, constructed as a defence against intolerable wishes and experiences. He had no disciples to proselytize, given his incarceration in the asylum. Nevertheless, one element cannot be neglected in looking at paranoid versions of religion, and that is the grandiose features embedded in the system. Implicitly or explicitly, delusions of grandeur seem to parallel the feelings of persecution. For example, Schreber comments:

> . . . he who has entered into a special relationship to divine rays as I have is to a certain extent entitled to shit on all the world. [Schreber, 1988, p. 177]

This notion of "specialness" is not uncommon in religious thinking, as are accompanying feelings of omnipotence, sometimes articulated in terms of having a special power or a direct line to cosmic influence. Perhaps a content analysis of various religious and pseudo-religious ideologies would enable a clear dividing line to be established between those forms of belief that, in their ritual aspect, have an uncanny parallel with obsessional neurosis (Freud, 1907b), and those that tap into latent paranoid structures in the personality related to persecution and/or grandiosity.

One feature of many religious cosmologies, and one that I have left until now to discuss, is the division of the supernatural into two opposing forces, usually in terms of good and evil or, more traditionally in Christian terms, God and the Devil. Some clues can be gleaned in this regard from a paper published by Freud on "A Seventeenth-Century Demonological Neurosis" (1923d [1922]). His interest in such themes as witchcraft and possession, can be traced back to his period of study under Charcot. Freud's interest in the case of Christoph Haitzmann, with which this paper deals, was stimulated by Dr Payer-Thurn, who had sent him a copy of a seventeenth-century manuscript that he had discovered in the monastery of Mariazell, some 80 miles south-west of Vienna. The text consisted of copies of the paintings by Haitzmann of his visions of the Devil, together with a fragment from his diary, and a report written by a monastic scribe.

What is relevant in terms of the argument in this chapter is Freud's discussion of the Devil as a father-substitute. Indeed he devotes a whole section to this issue (1923d [1922], pp. 83–92). The essence of his argument is familiar. The child has two sets of impulses directed towards his father—those of an affectionate and submissive nature, and those that are both hostile and defiant. In terms of the former, these tend to be projected outwards in later life and become attached to the benevolent and righteous God. The hostile attitude to the father, coloured as it is by hate and fear, becomes transposed onto representations of evil, which in the Christian tradition usually means the Devil or Satan. In other words, a unified parental imago, laid down in the unconscious biography of the individual and associated with intense feelings of love and hate becomes resurrected, split, and projected outwards to become these two opposing images of good and evil.

This phenomenon of ambivalence is extremely well illustrated in both the first and second paintings by Haitzmann of his visions of the Devil (see illustrations in *Standard Edition, Vol. 19*—frontispiece and facing page 69). In the first painting, the Devil is represented as an elderly man, dressed in the attire of the day and leaning slightly on a walking-stick. The only sinister aspect seems to be a black dog on the left of the picture as we look at it; the dog, in fact, has a strange face—more that of a bird of prey, like an eagle or a vulture.

In the second painting, however, the elderly man has been transformed into the Devil. The walking-stick is the only significant element that remains. Instead of a hand on top of the walking-stick, we now see what looks more like a claw; and the legs of the figure are now not human legs, but those of a bird of prey with large talons. The figure's head, with glaring eyes, is topped with horns.

It is not unreasonable to see both pictures as representing the two sides of Haitzmann's internalized image of his father, projected outwards and amplified by his own feelings of love and hate. However, there is one other striking feature in the second painting. The Devil is endowed with a pair of female breasts. Freud makes the point that this, too, is a projection onto this satanic view of the father (1923d [1922], p. 90). Not only does Haitzmann project his own hate and destructiveness onto this figure, but he also repudiates his own feminine attitude towards his father by projecting these symbols of femininity onto this figure as well. In this sense it is a repudiation of what most males perceive unconsciously to be the consequence of a passive loving relationship with their father—the threat of being turned into a woman, and the consequent male phantasy of castration. The illustration from Schreber above exhibits a similar conflict in more florid terms.

For Haitzmann, the hallucinations that the pictures represent must have been frightening in the extreme, and it is clear that he was a very disturbed man, to whom the label "demonological neurosis" seems hardly to do justice. Nevertheless, Freud expounds clearly the view that these hallucinations have infantile origins.

To be sure, in our day images of the Devil appear conspicuous by their absence in the popular imagination. Freud appears aware of this but suggests that:

When a boy draws grotesque faces and caricatures, we may no doubt be able to show that he is jeering at his father in them; and when a person of either sex is afraid of robbers and burglars at night, it is not hard to recognize these as split-off portions of the father. The animals, too, which appear in children's animal phobias are most often father-substitutes, as were the totem animals of primaeval times. [Freud, 1923d (1922), pp. 86–87]

While Christoph Haitzmann was living in a social context where demonology was a dominant cosmological motif, we are living in an age where belief in the Devil seems consigned to a marginal position. Perhaps it is the case that we are looking in the wrong places for such symbolic representations. A casual browse through the shelves of one's local video store would leave one in little doubt that this symbolic imagery is anything but defunct. On the shelves devoted to the horror-film genre one can find the most exotic phantasmagoria on offer, from gremlins to ghouls, from exorcists to poltergeists, all seeming to capture the imagination of not an insignificant number of the viewing public. Steven Spielberg's movies such as *Jaws* and *Jurassic Park* perhaps owe their popularity to the symbolic meaning of the content, the former dealing with a marauding monster from the deep in the form of the voracious shark, the latter with ferocious monsters from the distant past in the form of dinosaurs. The symbolic significance in terms of the argument above is as plain as a pike-staff!

In order to understand the unconscious processes involved in the representations of evil, whether externalized and personified in grotesque form or in impersonal forces, it is necessary to return briefly to some points raised earlier in the discussion of childhood development. Allusion was made there to the process of the defusion of the instincts that occurs during the process of identification. According to Freud, all such identifications seem to release destructive energies that tend to be taken up by the superego making it more cruel towards the ego. The alternative is for this destructiveness to be split off and projected outwards rather than for it to be contained in the internal dynamics of the personality.

But it seems that this destructive potential is always waiting to find an outer object with which it can resonate. This is clearly achieved in the cathartic experience of watching a film, regardless of whether the imagery is relatively crude or finely textured and woven into a plot about good and evil, domination and powerlessness, heroes and villains. It is another matter, however, when the scenario moves from the phantasy world of the cinema and begins to involve real human beings.

The history of religion is littered with examples of these projective mechanisms in terms of real—as opposed to imagined—social relations. The sixteenth-century witch trials, the Spanish Inquisition and its use of juridical torture, the religious genocide evident in our own day, all betray, amongst other things, the projection onto others of a hate and destructiveness that has its origins more in the heart of the perpetrators than in their victims. Onto such are projected all the unconscious detritus of the in-group that must be warded off and fought against. The victims are no longer perceived as human beings, but as instances of a discreditable category, to be shunned or destroyed. They have become the new folk devils, the construction of which profoundly implicates deep unconscious fears from the past and against which moral outrage must be marshalled. In some of its various institutional forms, religion can sometimes betray such a tapestry of malice, hidden neatly behind a screen of dogmatic self-righteousness. As Freud seems to be suggesting, just as man appears to make God in his own image, so, too, does he seem to make the Devil (in whatever guise), and in both images he can catch a reflection of his own personal past.

How often it is, though, that we hear tales of individuals who have led either violent or debauched lives, who have engaged in numerous horrendous activities, suddenly turning to religion with a massive conversion experience. A Christian prototype was the dramatic conversion experience of St Paul on the road to Damascus, and the history of religion is full of many other such instances of a no less dramatic nature.

A clue to a possible answer to this phenomenon is provided by Freud in a short paper written in the latter part of 1928, with the title, "A Religious Experience" (Freud, 1928a). In this text, Freud discusses a letter he had received from an American physician, who had read an account of an interview with him by the journalist G. S. Viereck, in which his lack of religious faith and his indifference to survival after death had been mentioned. The physician in question had written to Freud describing his own Christian conversion and expressed the hope that God would reveal the truth to Freud if he approached the problem with an open mind (1928a, p. 170). A short correspondence between the two followed, but Freud had been intrigued by the letter, and it provided him with "food for thought" and seemed to demand "some attempt at interpretation" (ibid.).

Briefly told, the physician's story is as follows. One day when in the dissecting-room of his university, his attention was attracted by a "sweet-faced dear old lady who was being carried to the dissecting table". The thought came to him that there is no God, for how could He allow such a thing. After this time, he ceased going to church, but he continued to wrestle with his doubts about the doctrines of Christianity. However, while meditating on the topic, he heard an inner voice urging him to consider the step he was taking, and over the next few days, and after meditation on the Bible, he became convinced that Jesus Christ was his personal Saviour, and Jesus was man's only hope.

In seeking an explanation of this experience, Freud looks to the Oedipus complex. This physician would have seen many dissections in the course of his work; why was it that this particular "dear old lady" should have moved him so? Freud argues that this experience resurrected in him Oedipal feelings from the past in relation to his own mother, together with feelings of hostility towards his father. These became transferred onto the present situation, with the old lady standing for his mother, and his reproach of God echoing his hostility for his father. Just as in the past the outcome of the Oedipus conflict was submission to the father and identification with him, so, too, in the religious sphere the same outcome is evident in this man's experience: "complete submission to the will of God the Father" (1928a, p. 171).

Freud is careful to point out, however, that not all conversion experiences may have the same genesis.

> The point which our present observation throws into relief is the manner in which the conversion was attached to a particular determining event, which caused the subjects scepticism to flare up for a last time before being finally extinguished. [1928a, p. 172]

Religious conversion is sometimes perceived as an either/or event, so to speak: either one is converted and becomes a believer, or one remains a non-believer. In the contemporary climate of advanced industrial society, this does not hold sway. Sociologists talk more in terms of "conversion careers" when looking at this phenomenon in modern society, particularly in relation to the new religious movements (Richardson, 1978). If I may return to the "religious supermarket" metaphor employed at the beginning of this chapter, it is the case that regardless of the provenance of a particular religious product, individuals can return to the shelves and try another if the first choice has proved unsatisfactory to their needs.

A key characteristic of many of these new brands of self-realization is the emphasis of not a few on meditative techniques, from transcendental meditation to yoga, and from Buddhism (Zen or otherwise) to Christian mysticism. One may well ask how such a trend as this can be fitted to the parental complex, as so far discussed relative to the work of Freud. In fact, Freud does not attempt to explain such phenomena by any such strategy. Instead, he takes us on another tack altogether.

After writing his essay *The Future of an Illusion* (1927c), Freud sent a copy to his friend, the novelist Romain Rolland. Rolland replied that he was entirely in agreement with Freud concerning his views on religion, but he argued that the true source of religious sentiments was to be found in what he described as a sensation of "eternity":

> a feeling as of something limitless, unbounded—as it were, "oceanic". . . . This feeling, he adds, is a purely subjective fact, not an article of faith. . . . One may, he thinks, rightly call oneself religious on the ground of this oceanic feeling alone, even if one rejects every belief and every illusion. [Freud, 1930a, p. 65]

Rolland's argument led Freud to ask related questions about this phenomenon (1930a, p. 72): (1) What were its origins? (2) Could it be regarded as the origin of the whole need for religion?

In answering the first question, Freud again looks to the past biography of the individual. But on this occasion he does not appeal to the Oedipus complex. On the contrary, his argument focuses specifically on that early twilight period of infancy where the ego is as yet not differentiated from the external world. In this sense boundaries between self and other, or self and external world, are non-existent; the ego has not as yet disengaged itself from the general mass of sensations. This only sets in under the somewhat harsh tutorship of the reality principle, whereby the infant begins to distinguish between an "outside" reality and its "internal" world.

Freud's argument in this instance is not the first time that he had addressed these issues. Indeed, echoes of these ideas are evident in the "Project" (1950 [1895]); in the important chapter seven of *The Interpretation of Dreams* (1900a); in his papers, "Instincts and their Vicissitudes" (1915c) and "Negation" (1925h). It is from these thoughts that Freud seeks to explain the genesis of the oceanic feeling. He comments:

> Our present ego-feeling is, therefore, only a shrunken residue of a much more inclusive—indeed, an all-embracing—feeling which corresponded to a more intimate bond between the ego and the world about it. If we may assume that there are many people in whose mental life this primary ego-feeling has persisted to a greater or less degree, it would exist in them side by side with the narrow and more sharply demarcated ego-feeling of maturity, like a kind of counterpart to it. In that case, the ideational contents appropriate to it would be precisely those of limitlessness and of a bond with the universe—the same ideas with which my friend elucidated the "oceanic" feeling. [Freud, 1930a, p. 68]

Freud cites another colleague who was engaged in research on Yoga. The meditative practices, the methods of breathing, and the fixing of attention on bodily functions evoke new sensations, which are "regressions to primordial states of mind which have long ago been overlaid" (1930a, p. 72). Here we have, according to Freud's colleague, a physiological basis of "much of the wisdom of mysticism" (p. 72).

From the issue of mysticism it is clear that many of the new and not so new meditative techniques are, if we follow Freud, attempts to regain a lost unity. Both in the techniques employed and in the manifest symbolic representations of their content there is an attempt to achieve the lost innocence of primary narcissism. Freud was well aware of the primary identifications that were operative in infancy in relation to the breast, for example. His posthumously published "Findings, Ideas, Problems" has a striking entry for July 12:

> "Having" and "being" in children. Children like expressing an object relation by an identification: "I am the object." "Having" is the later of the two; after loss of the object it relapses into "being". Example: the breast. "The breast is a part of me, I am the breast." Only later: "I have it"—that is, "I am not it". . . . [Freud, 1941f (1938), p. 299]

This distinction between "having" and "being" perhaps characterizes well the whole nature of the life problem to which religion in all its various forms offers some solution. At heart it is a solution to problems and traumas of loss, both internal and external, and the accompanying destructiveness that such loss releases. Here we are at the centre of the tragic vision that Freud would have us accept about ourselves, and against which we will twist and turn, in fact do anything, rather than face. It is this vision that separates psychoanalysis from its optimistic humanistic counterparts in the therapeutic marketplace, and a perspective that gives psychoanalysis its critical distance from its subject matter, preventing it becoming a symptom of the "disease" it has to diagnose.

Those of a religious turn of mind may be of the view that the pursuit of such a strategy as this in the analysis of religion constitutes an attack. It is perceived as an attempt to debunk, pathologize, and disenchant the beliefs of many people. Freud has been accused frequently of this (Wallace, 1983).

Personally, I am not persuaded that it is any such thing. The primary aim of psychoanalysis is understanding, and as such it attempts to peer beneath surface appearances to discover unconscious motivations that influence daily life and our common patterns of thinking, feeling, and acting. The philosopher Paul Ricoeur (1970) has observed that along with Marx and Nietzsche, Freud can be classed as a master of suspicion. All three thinkers in their own way attempted to penetrate beneath the surface manifestations of life, stripping away the humbug and self-deception with which we sometimes clothe our lives.

It is not so much the beliefs that are being criticized, however, as the manner in which they are held and the consequences that ensue for many as a result. Religious symbol systems are essentially attempts to find sources of meaning and consolation, and as such act as homes for our deepest wishes. But such symbolizations of our predicament (Brittan, 1973) can act as carriers of obsessional and paranoid tendencies; indeed, they can become pathological. Rather than articulating all that is good and creating communities that foster true emancipatory communication (Habermas, 1970), they can breed destructiveness and the worst forms of illusion. Perhaps the time has come in psychoanalysis to take up Freud's challenge and "embark upon a pathology of cultural communities" (1930a, p. 144), highlighting from content analysis those elements of an ideological frame that are neurotic or psychotic, in the same manner that is applied to individuals. But that is an agenda for another paper.

In my view, the psychoanalytic exploration of the infantile origins of religion, far from disenchanting religion, issues a challenge also to theologians to be more adventurous in their thinking. Far better to talk of a God shorn of our infantile projections than to worship some composite figure that owes more to our unconscious motivations than to revelation. Maybe we should all bear in mind the quotation from the philosopher George Santayana:

> Those who cannot remember the past are condemned to fulfil it. [1905]

CHAPTER EIGHT

Psychoanalysis and literature: a psychoanalytic reading of *The Turn of the Screw*

Ronnie Bailie

I t is not for nothing that *The Turn of the Screw* has attracted more psychoanalytic attention (inter alia, Brooke-Rose, 1981; Katan, 1962, 1966; Wilson, 1952) than anything else that Henry James wrote. Even without the benefit of a psychoanalytic training, the average reader is likely to have a powerful intuition of extraordinary and murky psychological depths in the piece. No need here to get *behind* the veneer of polite drawing-rooms and elaborate cerebration to the unconscious core, for *The Turn of the Screw* reads like the relatively undistorted unconscious communication that it actually is. By this I mean that its manifest topics and persons have proceeded no great distance from their latent or instinctual sources. It is a question of congruence: the story fits its unconscious determinants like a glove.

This means that what often opposes the successful or convincing psychoanalysis of art is not encountered here. For sometimes the original instinctual and infantile sources are so heavily disguised and their force so successfully attenuated that only an act of intellectual violence—involving flagrant reductionism or leaden implausibilities—can re-establish the appropriate lost links. It is indeed with the critic and his reader as it is with the analyst and his patient: the patient's conscious and reasonable ego cannot accept unconscious contents reached by a brutal frontal assault; these can only be arrived at and accepted when the defensive processes of the ego are analysed and ready to receive them. By analogy, the reader of psychoanalytic criticism cannot see violence done to the ego-like outer rind of the work of art—its surface images and situations—without rebelling in some measure against the blind instrument conducting the investigation. But this important issue of tact and plausibility is perhaps more easily handled with James's famous "supernatural" text. For if displacements, condensations, and over-determinations abound in *The Turn of the Screw*, they are already clearly visible in the surface elements of the story and are not limited to the secret interplay of these elements with their hidden unconscious antecedents. The key ideas and feelings have not (that is) been banished to the periphery of the story, whose centre is thereby robbed of its instinctual charge and left blank and inscrutable to interpretation. In *The Turn of the Screw* James's unconscious speaks directly and in the most distinct tones imaginable.

[I]

The limit of this evil time had arrived only when, on the dawn of a winter's morning, Peter Quint was found, by a labourer going to early work, stone dead on the road from the village: a catastrophe explained—superficially at least—by a visible wound to his head; such a wound as might have been produced (and as, on the final evidence, *had* been) by a fatal slip, in the dark and after leaving the public-house, on the steepish icy slope, a wrong path altogether, at the bottom of which he lay. The icy slope, the turn mistaken at night and in liquor, accounted for much—practically, in the end and after the inquest and boundless chatter, for everything; but there had been matters in his life, strange passages and perils, secret disorders, vices more than suspected, that would have accounted for a good deal more. [*Henry James: The Turn of the Screw* (Kimbrough, 1966, p. 28)*]

This is the most visible corpse, the most clearly advertised and examinable dead body in James's work. It is appropriate that we should find it in *The Turn of the Screw* (1898), for it is here, in his first dictated story, that James's lifelong unconscious concern with the body becomes finally irrepressible. Here his unconscious is clamorous for representation, and finds it in images more troubled and fantastic than any we can meet elsewhere in his fiction. As we shall see, there are good reasons for concluding that the spectacle of Quint's dead body is the heart of the tale, and not simply as that body lies here in all evidence, but as it offers itself to view at other special moments. (And let us not forget that a lifeless male form—Miles, dead in the arms of his governess—is also the last image of the story.) Quint's body holds the key to this fictional labyrinth, and that is why we should come to *The Turn of the Screw* as to an autopsy—to consider the body and establish the cause of death of Peter Quint—an enterprise into which the quoted passage teasingly draws us. There is no deeper "well of unconscious cerebration" (Blackmur, 1934, p. 23) than that out of which rises this ghostman—in life "not quite in health" (*The Turn of the Screw*, p. 27), in death not quite extinct. In the figure of Peter Quint lie locked the closest secrets of James's imagination.

In all of his (most spectral) embodiments we will find complications and oddities. The passage that tells us of Quint's death is as slippery as his path home. "A clear unextraordinary case", says one voice; "More to this death than meets the eye", says another. Considering the scene of his death, it is hard not to recall that, to the "haunted" governess, in his first appearance, the apparitional Quint—strutting and fretting on the

---

*All quotations from *The Turn of the Screw* presented in this chapter are taken from the 1966 edition edited by R. Kimbrough.

crenellated tower—resembled nothing so much as an "*actor*" (p. 24); and that, to her also, autumnal Bly,

> with its grey sky and withered garlands, its bared spaces and scattered dead leaves, was like a theatre after the performance—all strewn with crumpled playbills. [p. 52]

Accordingly, we can almost smell the spirit of the theatre in Quint's cheap catastrophe—that is what is wrong with the perfidious net of words that covers his corpse. There is an all-too-evident attempt to present his body and the story of what has become of it with irreproachable clarity. It is as if bold forensic chalk-marks have already mapped the site and point to the head-wound that is to explain all things. But nothing is clear here—except the attempt at clarity. The words do not *tell* so much as they serve to draw us into a maze—offering, now a certainty quickly punctured, now a doubt hastily suppressed. Certainty about what happened to Quint is at one moment lavishly offered, at the next shabbily withdrawn. And the extraordinary passage ends with an additional convolution: not only may the facts not explain the body, but the body may be more in need of explaining than appears. What perversity of explanation is this, making us doubt an assurance that there is no doubt? What game, to present facts, call them conclusive, yet refuse to conclude? Assuredly the death of Peter Quint is no simple affair.

But whatever mysteries, whatever anatomical puzzles may be enclosed there, it is noteworthy that the body of Peter Quint is not the first to claim our attention in *The Turn of the Screw*. That distinction belongs to his "victim", to the newly arrived young governess, whose first act in her room at Bly is to consider

> the long glasses in which, for the first time, I could see myself from head to foot. [p. 7]

This moment—that of the governess's brief hesitation before the mirror—is not least remarkable for coming and going without insistence. For, properly understood, the business transacted in it is truly momentous. But a perverse rhetoric—a rhetoric that underlines what may be discounted and passes in an instant what is crammed with rich seeds—a *displacing* rhetoric is one of the most persistent characteristics of *The Turn of the Screw*. If the laws of the piece were not thus dictated by the evasions and obfuscations of the unconscious, if the author had here possessed his art rather than been possessed by it, if *The Turn of the Screw* had belonged, for example, to the artificial but daylight world of opera, this moment would doubtless have swollen to an aria before the mirror. For it is both a beginning and an end. The beginning is clear, if surprising: a young girl sees the full extent of her body in a mirror, for the first time in her life. (As if to reiterate the anatomical point, she notes, too, the "figured full draperies" of her room.) Given her love-interest in the Master, her employer, here is a moment of imaginary initiation, a moment announcing womanhood and physical maturation, a moment of delight. Artistically, too, it is a beginning, for a motif enters the story here: the image of the *complete* body.

But this beginning is also an end. What she sees, no one will see again. The complete body, thus ritually presented, now leaves the stage, never to reappear. If, in retrospect, we can call this moment the announcing of a motif, it is one destined to be commemorated by its own absence. For if the banished phrase does not return whole, it insinuates itself in quiet fragments that secretly harp on its dismemberment. This amounts to saying that, in the matter of imagery, *The Turn of the Screw* is a haunted story—over and above its status as the story of a haunting. Artistically and psychically, it is haunted by the image of an incomplete (or damaged) human body—that is to say, by the body of Peter Quint. In common with the governess, we already suspect that Quint is an actor; already we guess at his role: to "fill a vacancy" indeed—to fake anatomical completeness.

But here we presume, or at best anticipate, for our dead man lying by the roadside seemed complete enough. It is not empty clothing that is found in the cold dawn but the body of a man. And is it not the case, moreover, that the dead Quint appears to the governess—stands before her—on more than one occasion? It is true that (as Mrs Grose tells us) his haunting outfit is not his own (p. 24); but have we any warrant for assuming that it drapes a mere fragment of a man? Let us consider Peter Quint's second appearance:

The person looking straight in was the person who had already appeared to me. He appeared thus again with I won't say greater distinctness for that was impossible, but with a nearness that represented a forward stride in our intercourse and made me, as I met him, catch my breath and turn cold. He was the same—he was the same, and seen, this time, as he had been seen before, from the waist up, the window, though the dining-room was on the ground floor, not going down to the terrace on which he stood. [p. 20]

There are variations of place and circumstance in the ghostly appearances of Peter Quint, but they have all in common the remarkable and consistent fact that Quint displays himself only from the waist upwards. His full physical extent is never seen: he appears incomplete(ly). This remains true even in circumstances that present greater representational difficulties than this appearance on the tower or outside the dining-room window. For example, it is the same anatomical story when the governess encounters Quint on the stairs of the sleeping house. Above looking down, she notes that Quint reaches only "half-way up", finding himself "stopped short". In the circumstances, the physical (and representational) difficulties of the intruder's retreat ("cut off" not merely in metaphor) are covered decorously enough by a syntax of cunning ambiguity, as the "figure" goes

with my eyes on the villainous back that no hunch could more disfigure, straight down the staircase and into *the darkness in which the next bend was lost.* [p. 41; emphasis added]

Two things are clear, therefore: first, that Quint is presented as a consistent anatomical image, and, second, that, conformably with the perverse rhetoric we have already identified, the character of that image is essentially secret. For Quint's deficiency is there to be inferred, but it is by no means insisted on. And it was precisely this insight that the stagey spectacle of the ex-valet's corpse with its florid display of a head-wound attempted to obstruct. There is a good deal to put us off our guard. For is it not suggested, after all, that Peter Quint was, while he lived, an incorrigible womanizer, sharing this characteristic with his Harley Street Master, who has "charming ways with women" and whose study is littered with sundry "trophies of the chase" (p. 4)? Peter Quint, we are assured, sinned not by abstinence or incapacity but by *excess*. How may we square our ghostly pseudo-amorous remnant with such a man? Or how, in the face of such a man, can we maintain our conception of Quint's anatomical deficiency? We appear to have worked ourselves into an intellectual impasse.

Happily, this difficulty is more apparent than real, and a solution requires merely that we give due weight to the unconscious determinants of the story. Chief among these is the clearly inferable fact that the body of Peter Quint rose out of a special place in the unconscious phantasy, the unconscious image-making faculty of his creator. It is this that the secret consistency of his anatomy proclaims. And it is this which dictates the teasing reversals of the whole performance. For there is a kind of fiction that is content to flirt with its unconscious determinants, content to rise into the daylight of representation and play there unburdened by the dark energy that lends it grace and power. More plainly said, fiction *can* sublimate its unconscious sources into a lucid and untroubled art: as Freud remarked, "Real art begins with the veiling of the unconscious" (Nunberg & Federn, 1962–75, II, p. 373). But that is emphatically not James's fate in *The Turn of the Screw*. Here his imagination is ridden by the ghosts of his unconscious life, hounded and harried and pursued by them along the passages of the house of fiction. Here they brook no refusal; if he wants their power then they must be on stage with the people of daylight. It is out of this spectral company that Peter Quint emerges as the quintessential expression of James's imagination. But having made no truce with the powers of daylight, and "knowing" that his creator has here, in this ghostly tale, abandoned the fiction of social reality, Quint obeys, in this new place, the laws of the subliminal place he never ceases to inhabit. The unconscious world crosses over into the waking world of mankind in curious disguises. So Quint does not parade his ghostly lack but masquerades as a sexual adventurer: he represents himself as his opposite. To this unconscious witticism he adds a death fit for the theatre of melodrama. He lets it be known that he has died from a fall and a head-wound. As if he were not in any case—in his "extraordinary case" (Aziz, 1973, pp. 227–261)—already essentially dead; as if *that* were the wound.

[II]

It is well known that, in the spring of 1861, at the outbreak of the American Civil War, in which he took no active part, Henry James suffered an injury that—in the most famous phrase of his autobiography—he called an "obscure hurt" (Dupee, 1956, p. 415). It is also well known that, whatever the objective nature and severity of the (sacroiliac?) injury, it became the focus of a great deal of morbid psychological energy in the sufferer. But, above all, the incident appears to have set its seal upon what we may call James's personal mythology, and to have done so by employing a mechanism that Sigmund Freud has characterized as follows:

> It not at all infrequently happens in the case of a person who is disposed to a neurosis . . . that a pathological somatic change (through inflammation or injury perhaps) sets the activity of symptom-formation going; so that this activity hastily turns the symptom which has been presented to it by reality into the representative of all the unconscious phantasies which have been lying in wait to seize hold of some means of expression. [Freud, 1916–17, p. 391]

There is, as we are in the process of discovering, much evidence to suggest that, in his unconscious phantasy, Henry James had long thought of himself as one grievously injured, a man good as dead of an "obscure" wound, over which the spring of 1861 had drawn a too-careless finger. One of the things that we have in the portrait of Peter Quint is a powerful imaginative representation of this important early phantasy of annulment and vanquished power that the incident in young adulthood found itself drawn into. It is the singular destiny of this ghostman, riddled with "secret disorders", to represent his creator with the most appalling intimacy. That is why the body of Quint is anatomized with such meticulous unconscious care and why we cannot consider it too curiously.

It was mostly suspicion that we brought away from our first consideration of the dead body of Peter Quint. The spectacle made us uneasy, it taxed our credulity. On the other hand, there was some foolishness in expecting that the tale of a man "obscurely hurt" should be clear and unequivocal. Better to expect darkness or a specious clarity. And what but a misleading, perfidious clarity stares back at us from Quint's "visible wound to the head"? For here, as everywhere in *The Turn of the Screw*, the mechanisms of representation are those of the unconscious. Things change their names, change places, hide in their opposites. So the vagueness of a "hurt" takes refuge in the graphic determinateness of a "wound"; if the "hurt" was "obscure", the "wound" is not merely *there* but (oddly) 'visible'. But these displacements and inversions subserve another anatomical displacement that is the work's central strategy. We are asked to believe (and it is true) that Quint's "visible" wound is "to the head": but in conformity with a mechanism of (hysterical) symptom-formation, a disturbance of function that is lower (genital)—is subjected to a disguising and "legitimizing" displacement into other—in this case upper—bodily zones. Just as the governess sees Quint from the waist up, so *our* attention is directed upwards, and we are asked to believe that his "deadness" is a matter of damage to the higher faculties only.

But if the governess does not *see* him from the waist down, she by no means ceases to meditate on the nature of his insufficiency—though, here again, the unremitting mechanism of displacement draws a plausible veil over her obsession. When she refers to Quint, her remarks insist on the *lowness* of his social rank. So he is a "base menial"; on another occasion a "low wretch" provided (in a socio-moral pun) with a "villainous back" (*The Turn of the Screw*, pp. 36, 41). These exceedingly vigorous remarks fall a little curiously from the mouth of "the youngest of several daughters of a poor country parson" (p. 4) and seem to uncover an extraordinary social presumption. But it is interesting to notice that all her terms of derision are ambiguous, and ambiguous in the same way—by consistently admitting of a *spatial* meaning. The governess's obsessed emphasis is nothing other than a (convenient) displacement into the socio-moral of a preoccupation that is essentially anatomical. Thus her disapproval may both secretly and openly direct itself at the lower half of Quint's body.

Up to this point I have dwelt so exclusively on the *deficiencies* of Peter Quint, that anyone assembling an account of *The Turn of the Screw* from my words only could be forgiven for making him out a quaking and pusillanimous ghost, remnant of the fraction of a man. And what I have said so far suggests (for the governess) mostly a tale of frustration and lovelessness. In this I have failed to convey the dominant feeling-tone of *The Turn of the Screw* and have neither addressed nor explained the pronounced elements of menace that give the story its considerable power. The Quint who haunts the corridors of Bly may be no sexual predator, but he is a fearful presence and a far-from-extinguished spirit. He is still a predator—after his fashion. We have seen that Peter Quint is apparently condemned to live only as a higher man, anatomically speaking. One way of formulating his menace is to observe that the "higher man" is not without compensating faculties, products, we might say, of a kind of demonic conversion. For the ghostly Quint has retained his predatory instincts, albeit that they have been displaced upwards. To what end does he come, but to look, to fix, to stare? In the ample gardens of Bly the governess acutely figures the "fellow" who was a "hound" now "prowling for a sight"—his new vice (pp. 33, 44).

[III]

It is, of course, difficult to make out an image of unequivocal potency in the stare of a Quint who "hungrily" hovers (p. 46). And if the erstwhile adventurer now preys with his eyes, his essential muteness seems but additional testimony to a predatory faculty that is severely curtailed. This wordless ghost is indeed a most paradoxical offspring of one who gave up his life to the curious and lonely rituals of verbal manufacture that hide behind the bland word "novelist". It is as if Quint's eyes have in some fashion usurped the office of his mouth, as if he suffers some inhibition of speech. How may we connect this characteristic with those of his voluble creator?

One of the things that *The Turn of the Screw*—uniquely—enables us to do is to reconstruct phrases of instinctual conflict in the early development of Henry James. I believe that it is possible to locate such a focus of neurotic development at the time when he was engaged on the acquisition of speech. We know a good deal about his *adult* speech: that it was slow, that it was elaborate, that it was full of pauses—to such phenomena numerous contemporary witnesses testify. That these things were actually the persisting stigmata of infantile conditions seems to me abundantly clear. To prop up this assertion, we can adduce the testimony of Edith Wharton, whose great closeness to James in the last years of his life gives her words special authority. According to her, Henry's

> slow way of speech . . . was really the partial victory over a stammer which in his boyhood had been thought incurable. [Wharton, 1934, pp. 177–178]

This is a rare piece of evidence, but it is not impossible to find half-conscious reminiscences of the same state of affairs elsewhere—in William James's letters, for example. This is from a letter of 1907:

> You know how opposed your whole "third manner" of execution is to the literary ideals which animate my crude and Orson-like breast, mine being to say a thing in one sentence as straight and explicit as it can be made, and then to drop it forever; *yours being to avoid naming it straight, but by dint of breathing and sighing all round and round it*, to arouse in the reader who may have had a similar perception already (Heaven help him if he hasn't!) the illusion of a solid object, made (like the "ghost" at the Polytechnic) wholly out of impalpable materials, air, and the prismatic inferences of light, ingeniously focussed by mirrors upon empty space. . . . [emphasis added]
>
> But it's the rummest method for one to employ systematically as you do nowadays; and you employ it at your peril. In this crowded and hurried reading age, pages that require such close attention remain unread and neglected. You can't skip a word if you are to get the effect, and 19 out

of 20 worthy readers grow intolerant. The method seems perverse: "Say it *out*, for God's sake," they cry, "and have done with it". [H. James, 1920, II, pp. 277–278]

William was, of course, 15 months older than Henry, and it is well known that the younger brother had a perfectly conscious life-long feeling that he would never be able to catch up:

At Cambridge of course, when I got there, I was further to find my brother on the scene and already at a stage of possession of its contents that I was resigned in advance never to reach; so thoroughly I seemed to feel a sort of quickening savoury meal in any cold scrap of his own experience that he might pass on to my palate. [Dupee, 1956, pp. 417–418]

Even without Henry's own statement that he was a "timorous" child, in adolescence "anxiously mute" (Dupee, p. 317), it is not difficult to extrapolate from the observed adult personalities of the brothers—William "is simpler and full of enthusiasms and freshness, whereas Henry is jaded and reticent" (Montgomery Hyde, 1969, p. 128)—and to see with what scorn and impatience an energetic and voluble William must have superintended the halting early articulations of his younger companion. (Edward Emerson, the family friend, gives the interesting impression that Henry's characteristic family pose was silence.) Now I am not implying that Henry suffered early traumatization by William's easier accomplishments: only that William witnessed Henry's early difficulties and on some level remembered them. It remains for us to reach some understanding of why Henry developed and preserved an inability to "say out" his thoughts and feelings. The importance of *The Turn of the Screw* is precisely that it enables us to make this reconstruction.

The last chapter of the story traces the steps that lead to the death of little Miles. It is, in my view, important to see two things: first, that these steps are distinct and definite; and second, that the story stops *abruptly* with the child's death. The question *why* Miles dies is, of course, a *cause célèbre* in the criticism: the exorcism of Quint has left him bereft of the will to live; the governess has frightened (or perhaps squeezed) him to death; or what you will. The fact remains, however, that, if we read literally, Miles dies as a result of speaking certain words that have remained unsaid up to that point. And when he has said them, everything stops dead. This is what I meant when I alluded to the distinct and definite steps that led to his death. These are none other than the steps that the governess takes to make him "say out" the words around which he has "sighed and breathed" for some time. The steps are those in the governess's interrogation of the child.

Let us not forget that, even setting aside the extravagantly tortuous—reluctant—dialogue of the piece, the theme of forbidden words has permeated the story from the beginning. The governess is forbidden to contact her employer ("Not a word. I'm off!"); a letter reporting Miles's offence at school lies for a time unopened; opened, that letter merely alludes to "something" and is promptly locked away; the child, finally questioned, discloses it was a question of "things [he] said", "only to those [he] liked" (*The Turn of the Screw*, p. 87). And it is finally the governess's question, the first direct exigent question of the story, that brings down the house. It needs no Freud to conclude that an anxiety focused on the power of the effect of speech is deeply rooted in James's story.

It is necessary to be quite clear about the exact timing of Quint's appearances in the closing sequence. He appears precisely at the moments when the governess broaches the murky issue of the child's offence *and is requiring the child to speak*. Note the perfect impasse: she requires him to report the forbidden words (from school) but provokes "instead" a speaking of them as Miles is coerced to the naming aloud of Quint. It is at this point that the child dies, destroyed—it seems—by the words that he knew not to say and by the governess's sadistic insistence on speech.

What are we to make of this fatal misalliance? What is the buried wisdom of Miles's refusal to speak, of the anxious muteness he shares with his younger creator? As we have noted, throughout the story, Peter Quint has nothing to say. More precisely, a strict silence is the very medium in which he appears—with this crucial addition: that Quint's presence is actually productive of an awful hush—sound dies before him:

> It was as if, while I took in, what I did take in, all the rest of
> the scene had been stricken with death. I can hear again,

as I write, the intense hush in which the sounds of evening dropped. The rooks stopped cawing in the golden sky and the friendly hour lost for the unspeakable minute all its voice. But there was no other change in nature, unless indeed it were a change that I saw with a stranger sharpness. [p. 16]

It seems to me that Quint's presence is to be understood as an exhortation to silence: he has the force of this specific interdiction. And here we arrive at the heart of the early "speech neurosis" of Henry James. James's early (and persisting) inhibition of speech—his stammer, his hesitations, his silence—marks a disturbance in the verbal sphere caused by a feeling of imminent danger—a danger that threatened if, for example, forbidden words were said out. That his father was the original embodiment of this danger we can infer from the child's evident assumption of the defence of identification, for Henry Senior had a stammer. But it is above all the pressure of oral sadistic phantasies contaminating the verbal sphere that invests spoken words with such destructive power. It is not without significance that, as I noted in opening, *The Turn of the Screw* was the first *dictated* story and that James tried to frighten his (male) amanuensis as he composed aloud (Kimbrough, 1966, p. 178). Nor can it reasonably be considered coincidence that James's dictation era was also the era of his guilty and troubled "Fletcherism", a chewing madness that dogged him for many years (Montgomery Hyde, 1969, p. 138). Conversely, if oral expression meant danger, silence meant the avoidance of destruction, perpetrated or suffered; and it is just such destruction that *ends The Turn of the Screw*.

And here we have the infantile prototype of the extraordinary verbal style of James's maturity—the style that, significantly, only became itself when James created by dictation, by saying. What must he do in dictation but—in the unconditional space of imagination—"say out" whatever comes into his head. *He cannot do it*: he has no facility. The baffling labyrinth of the mature style is a compromise-formation: it represents the fusion of a ferocious oral drive with an immense inhibition on saying out. And the style's fusion of a great expressive urge with an ineradicable habit of lexical and syntactical evasiveness is not merely a *derivative* of instinctual conflict: as a construct of words, it remains embedded in the primitive material of that conflict. "Kind and elaborate as ever" a visitor of 1911 says of the ageing novelist (Montgomery Hyde, 1969, p. 128). The whole issue lies also in this often-noted "elaborate" ceremonial of kindness and courtesy that James used with his guests. Elaborateness mediates his approach to his objects, his hesitations shield them. By 1911 it is an old story.

If Quint's appearance is a kind of paternal exhortation to silent obedience, it is also—as the quotation above clearly illustrates—the determinant of a change in the modality of experience from hearing/speaking to vision. What you cannot say, you may "look". Quint both silently "fixes" his objects and elicits acts of looking. We can say, therefore, that the drive energy that is checked in the oral-verbal sphere is deflected into the visual sphere. And here we rejoin by another route our earlier view of Quint as one who hunts with his eyes.

[IV]

"When I go to Europe again it will be, I think, from inanition of the eyes", announces the young Henry James to a correspondent in 1870 (Edel, 1977, I, p. 286). This image falls gracefully from the pen of one whose verbal invention is so free and copious that it is easy to admire the youthful *jeu d'esprit* and proceed without further thought. But James's cleverness here sports with an image that is tellingly characteristic, for his prose is littered with phrases that associate food and sight. Such images are worth investigating, partly because they will help us further to anatomize Peter Quint and partly because (which is the same thing) they cover and mark the site of a Jamesian *idée fixe*. It is not difficult to turn up examples. In the Hawthorne book of 1879, James can lament "the lightness of diet to which (Hawthorne's) observation was condemned", despite his "appetite for detail". Elsewhere, Hawthorne is "hungry for the picturesque", of which there is, however, no "copious provision" (Tanner, 1967, pp. 54, 73). A letter of 1873 finds James anxious to share his feast of Roman memories with his brother, since otherwise he may "swallow [his] impressions like a greedy feeder" (Edel, 1974–84, I, p. 321). Four years earlier, a letter to his sister Alice represents him as spending his mornings in the Vatican and his afternoons strolling

> at hazard, seeking what I might devour and devouring . . . whatever I have found. [Edel, 1974–84, I, p. 163]

A letter of 1870 finds a repatriated James expressing his enthusiasm for

> a number of Siennese photos, which I have literally devoured. My brother says that to him, for several days, they have been as meat and drink. [Edel, 1974–84, I, p. 243]

In general, repatriation breeds "hungry Eastward thoughts" of the Europe to which he will return for sustenance, for in Cambridge "his sense aches at times for richer fare" (Edel, 1977, I, p. 286).

Now while it is undeniably true that the spirit of most of these remarks is self-consciously sportive, their humour by no means disqualifies them from psychic significance. It is difficult to avoid the suspicion that, in this playful fusion of visual and oral imagery, we have an important adult derivative of the early internal history that we have been attempting to reconstruct. If, at the time of the acquisition of speech, Henry James indeed suffered a deflection of drive energy into the visual sphere, the evidence of this food-sight imagery once again suggests that a predominance of oral sadism primarily determined that deflection and its character. On the secondary level, there is good reason to suppose that the agency of sight was chosen both on account of Henry's visual acuity and the weakness of father's sight, and William's. There is no doubt whatsoever that, not merely in *The Turn of the Screw*, but in Henry's fiction generally, the ego function of looking inherits a sadistic colouring and is frequently represented in oral terms; neither can it be doubted that the associated instinctual pressure was such that James suffered an extraordinary hypertrophy of the scoptophilic instinct. All of this finds powerful representation in the fiction. In *The Sacred Fount*, for example, the cannibalistic curiosity of the narrator leads him to this culpable feast of scrutiny:

My question had not been in the least intended for pressure, but it made her turn and look at me, and this, I quickly recognised, was all the answer the most pitiless curiosity could have desired. . . . Beautiful, abysmal, involuntary, her exquisite weakness simply opened up the depths it would have closed. It said everything, and by the end of a minute my chatter . . . was hushed to positive awe by what it had conveyed. I saw as I have never seen before what consuming passion can make of the marked mortal on who, with fixed beak and claws, it has settled as on a prey. . . . Voided and scraped of everything, her shell was merely crushable. [H. James, 1901, pp. 135–136]

This means that when James creates a Quint who (permitted his creator's preferred term) "fixes" his objects in a deathly gaze after "prowling for [that] sight", the imagery employed is far from casual. It is dictated by internal processes of infantile origin. Extrapolating to later (Oedipal) development, we might say that, after the defeat of his phallic aspirations (the "wound"), Quint has (regressive) recourse to a kind of substitute virility of sight. The "awful bloody beak" of "vindictive intention" that—allied, inevitably, to the issue of "looking"—finds its way, 18 years later, into the deranged deathbed dictations of Quint's creator, serves only as an additional last confirmation of the powerful oral-sadistic character of the drive energy with which the act of looking became invested in the course of James's development (Edel, 1974–84, IV, p. 810).

[V]

If we have now constructed a more satisfactory account of Peter Quint, one that, acknowledging his weakness, can nevertheless attempt to explain his powerful presence, we have still not arrived at a balanced reading of the story. For the governess of this account has up to now figured as the more-or-less passive victim of the ghostman, condemned to frustrations of which he is the author. Certainly, there is much in her portrait—and much in the tradition of governesses out of which she rises—to sustain such a view: she is young, she is poor, she is "untried"

(*The Turn of the Screw*, p. 6). But in the struggle between herself and Peter Quint, it is far from accurate to propose her as a dramatically less vigorous combatant. It turns out, indeed, that the very question that has occupied us to this point—that of what we may call Quint's potency—is not unrelated to the nature of his adversary. The nameless heroine has her own formidable intensity, and an understanding of the place of that quality in the scheme of the story will provide a crucial last turn to the screw of our investigation.

We must return to the appearances of Peter Quint, no longer now to demonstrate their iterative and unchanging characteristics but, on the contrary, precisely to see what changes in them. For they *do* change, though not in essence because Quint does, but rather because the governess presses herself in a particular direction, struggles to assume a particular position, and this is duly reflected in her remorselessly developing relation to the dead valet. That Quint does *not* change, that he, from first to last—for all the intensity of his stare—seems trapped and immobile in his silent and essentially excluded part, this circumstance seems in the end but an additional commentary on the governess's development and, indeed, a strict complement to that development.

She sees him first—her adversary—on the crenellated tower as she walks beneath in the gardens of her new home. Like her Harley Street employer, the elevated stranger "rises" before her, marking a distance that seems like an interdiction (p. 4). We need not return to the fear conjured up in her. What our second scrutiny of the scene selects instead is a thought that flits through her mind: that the figure her imagination (she admits) half expected seems not most "in place" at "such an elevation" (p. 16). Accordingly, Quint is, indeed, never again encountered in a setting that flatters and aggrandizes as this first does. When she next meets him, he has descended to the ground level where she herself stands. (He will never rise again.) He is, we recall, outside the dining-room window, looking in as the governess looks out. Her (reiterated) insistence that he is "the same" does not prevent a crucial modulation: no longer fixed to the spot, she fairly "bounds" out of the house:

> It was confusedly present to me that I ought to place my-
> self where he had stood. I did so; I applied my face to the

pane and looked, as he had looked, into the room. As if, at this moment, to show me exactly what his range had been, Mrs Grose, as I had done for himself just before, came in from the hall. With this I had the full image of a repetition of what had already occurred. She saw me as I had seen my own visitant; she pulled up short as I had done; I gave her something of the shock that I had received. She turned white, and this made me ask myself if I had blanched as much. [p. 21]

Psychically speaking, we are standing here on what must have been familiar terrain to Henry James, the terrain, *mutatis mutandis*, of his well-known dream of the Louvre. As in the dream, an assailant, a "visitant", pressing inward, is himself put to flight by his would-be victim (Dupee, 1956, pp. 196–197). And there could be no clearer indication of the mechanism of defensive identification involved in that rout. The governess's fear is mastered by a literal assumption of Quint's place and his attendant fearsomeness. And that this—impressively active—reversal yields fruit not merely delusive, becomes perfectly clear when one considers the governess's next encounter with Peter Quint.

Since this happens inside the sleeping house, it is again, in appearance, a question of a "forward stride in our intercourse" (*The Turn of the Screw*, p. 20). But this is a phrase that, to attuned ears, is redolent of the simple irony that Quint, while persevering, is now essentially in retreat, and is perhaps, indeed, never other than at bay, like some "baffled beast" (p. 85). We recall that this (first and last) indoors confrontation is on a darkened stairwell on which, as the governess stands *above*, Quint stealthily ascends. She has had, she informs us, some seconds to "stiffen" herself before the predator sees her, and is able to reflect that

. . . dread had unmistakably quitted me and . . . there was nothing in me unable to meet and measure him. [p. 41]

Seeing her, Quint is "stopped short", and they face each other in a "common intensity". In this mutual stare, her stillness perfectly matches that of the ghostman, and her identificatory intentness reaches even to matching him in his deadness, as she wonders whether "*I* were in life". Outfaced, Quint turns and descends. That he had at no point been other than *below* the governess makes this outcome a foregone conclusion. She has usurped the position that was his only at the outset (on the tower), and their subsequent meetings symbolically enact a progressive exchange of power. Readily allied to this are some reflections that, days later, she has on looking down the same stairway, to see the ghostly Miss Jessel seated in a "half-bowed" and defeated posture below:

> . . . I wondered whether, if instead of being above I had been below, I should have had the same nerve for going up that I had lately shown Quint. [p. 43]

This imaginative revisiting of a feminine position makes perfectly clear the extent to which she has now repudiated that position. It also puts us in the position to offer a hypothesis as to the most primitive psychic core of the Louvre dream and this fictional recasting of it. In as much as the dream turns on the night terror of a man threatened by the approach of an assailant as he sleeps, it seems reasonable to view the "admirable nightmare" (Dupee, 1956, p. 196) in broadly Oedipal terms, and to find in it a clear expression of a castration anxiety. But the genetic precursors of the phallic and castrated opposition of the Oedipal level of conflict are the masculine/feminine and active/passive oppositions of earlier development. From this perspective, the dream appears to turn on a masculine repudiation of an imminent intrusion that threatens to produce feelings of intolerable (feminine) passivity. The repudiation is affected primarily by the defence of identification. In essence, what happens in *The Turn of the Screw* is that, in the (profoundly appropriate) imaginative vessel of the "untried" governess, these primitive "feminine" terrors of her creator are summoned up, and the history of an attempt to master them is unfolded. Within the tale, this ancient conflict is charted as the governess's struggle with a questionable man, the "actor" Peter Quint, who dresses in the borrowed robes of his Master. In the surreal mobility of the tale's clothing it is not hard to make out a deep suggestiveness. For the essence of the thing is *her* progressive assumption, *her* putting on of this masculinity, and it is towards this end that the whole ferocious endeavour of the tale is directed.

It is, indeed, only when looked at in this way, looked at from the direction of the psychic history of its creator, that the extraordinary ending of *The Turn of the Screw* can be credited with a meaning that surpasses the intellectual or imaginative whims of the individual reader. What can we say of that ending, first of all, that is more suggestive than the fact that the other women (Flora, Mrs Grose) have been driven out of Bly in preparation for the governess's supreme performance? For that performance is intent on nothing other than the expulsion of the feminine from her own nature, and the driving out of the others, old woman and child, is a bold preliminary sketch, an already extravagant earnest of what is to come. Alone with Miles—"the little gentleman" who shares his uncle's tailor—she waits for Quint, who does not fail to put in one last appearance. The resultant final contest attains an awesome intensity; but, to our heightened understanding, Quint is not merely present as the desperate face at the window. The governess has never seemed more ferocious in the rage of her own intentions, never more "blind with victory" (*The Turn of the Screw*, p. 87) than now, as she tries to press the young man to her body and possess his secrets. Out of this frenzied drama of possession looms a sentence that tells us we are close to the end: she "reddens to the roots of [her] hair" (p. 86). Her hair now the colour of Quint's, there can be little surprise in the last sentence that the "little gentleman" has breath to utter:

"Peter Quint—you devil!" [p. 88]

This is the text's most famous ambiguity, the question of whom these words are hurled at—the governess or the visitant outside the window. But Miles has not merely *uttered* these words: he has made a "supreme surrender of the name", and his dead heart is shortly to be pronounced "dispossessed" (p. 88). Quint also has vanished. It is evidently to the governess that the name has been surrendered, in her favour that the men have been dispossessed. Psychically speaking, there is no ambiguity in Miles's final tribute to his governess. With these four words her awesome assumption of an imaginary masculinity is complete.

But this is not to say that the climax of her history—the ending of her tale—is unequivocally positive for the governess.

For all its savage triumphalism, the closing sequence is shot through with pity and fear. Moreover, from the outset, the story has been offered as that of a woman who is already dead, already entered into the sphere of her strange quarry. This need not surprise us, given her persistent preoccupation with his place. More important, however, is the related recognition that the first (or Quint-centred) sequence of my argument is not unseated by the second, centred on the governess. For her progressive, self-preservative identification with Quint is nevertheless with what we have seen as a damaged object—not a "gentleman" (p. 22)—rather than with some fuller, more complete embodiment of the active and masculine. In other words, her story ends with a *flawed* solution, and a solution that doubtless opens into the reality of her creator and his earliest identifications.

[VI]

Having suffered the amputation of one leg above the knee when he was 17, Henry James Senior was, after all, a man physically incomplete. He had been broken, too, in the first years of his marriage, by the unexpected after-dinner appearance to him of an apparition that was destined to be the prototype of all Jamesian hauntings:

> To all appearance it was a perfectly insane and abject terror, without ostensible cause, and only to be accounted for, to my perplexed imagination, by some damned shape squatting invisible to me within the precincts of the room, and raying out from his fetid personality influences fatal to life. The thing had not lasted ten seconds before I felt myself a wreck; that is, reduced from a state of firm, vigorous, joyful manhood to one of almost helpless infancy. The only self-control I felt capable of exerting was to keep my seat. I felt the greatest desire to run incontinently to the foot of the stairs and shout for help to my wife. . . . [H. James, 1879, pp. 43–44]

We have no account of Mary James's view of this or of the two years that her husband needed for the regaining of his mental and emotional equilibrium. But his use of the word "incontinently" in this (1879) account is striking, as is the imaginary image of the unmanned young husband hobbling to the foot of the stairs to seek help from his young wife above. There is no doubt at all that Mrs James was a person of considerable self-possession and one whose efficiency in all the offices of external management inclined her to be relatively unsympathetic—if not indeed a little obtuse—to the world of feelings. The habit of self-sacrifice and selflessness—creating an accumulating (and undischargeable) indebtedness in others—made her view the vivid expression of ("selfish") feeling as weakness. There can be no clearer indication of this than her recorded attitudes to the bowel movements of children. When her first grandchild displayed a tendency to constipation, she could find no cause for anxiety. It was the malady of *strong* infants: only "the less fine specimens" were likely to be

> troubled the other way [by diarrhoea]—so this is not a weak, but a strong point in the little man—Everything evinces his superiority. [Strouse, 1980, p. 24]

There is little reason for surprise, therefore, that when, for example, in 1874 the *materfamilias* writes to her (frequently constipated) son Henry about his brother William's persistently morbid state of mind, she locates the seat of his trouble in the fact that he "*must express* every fluctuation of feeling" (Strouse, 1980, p. 24). Not for nothing will the reticent mature novelist, wary of first-person narration, speak of "the terrible *fluidity* of self-revelation" (Blackmur, 1934, p. 321). All of which provides the all-too-evident context within which the father "incontinently" asks to be read. It formulates Mary's likely view of the extravagance of his after dinner visitation and of his reaction to it: so he must contain himself and display the placid control to which his wife's whole demeanour was an implicit tribute. We will find no incongruence between this state of affairs and certain of the elder Henry's social ideas. Notably, he held that the nature of social and domestic authority was changing in his time from the old paternal and tyrannical style to a style more maternal. This new masculine authority was to be character-ized by "the utmost relaxation, indulgence, and even servility" (W. James, 1884, pp. 169–170). There can be little doubt that the mother provided a quietly formidable centre in a household riddled with the father-derived cancer of masculine indecision. True control in the James household resided in the "little buffalo" to whom weak backs, weak eyes, weak nerves, uncertain careers, and strong imaginings were unknown (Strouse, 1980, p. 25).

It seems to me to be a short step from these matters back to *The Turn of the Screw*, where the bewildered protagonist attempts, for the mastering of her fears, to "take on" one Peter Quint, who represents a deeply questionable ideal of manhood. It is my conviction that Henry James Senior stands (or falls!) behind Peter Quint, primarily as a damaged, overmastered man. But, as if for corroboration of this hypothesis, many other details of the history of Henry James's father are condensed into the portrait of Quint: his early addiction to alcohol, his irregular dissolute life of that same era, his premature return home from "school"—this all ending when his "fall" deprived him of part of his lower body. And, coming at the thing from the other side, it is significantly (as so often in James) in the imaginative vessel of a *female* protagonist—vulnerable to visitants—that the enterprise of mastery is undertaken. All of which tends to the conclusion that it is in the labyrinth of early (and unsatisfactory) identifications that the innermost meaning of *The Turn of the Screw* is to be sought. But as in analytical treatment, so, too, in a psychoanalytically oriented criticism, this is a meaning we must patiently uncover, not invent.

CHAPTER NINE

Psychoanalysis, cinema, and the role of film in the psychoanalytic process

Richard Ekins

Introduction

This chapter is situated within two sets of related issues: that of the interrelations between so-called pure psychoanalysis and applied psychoanalysis (Chasseguet-Smirgel, 1992; Gehrie, 1992; Schwartz, 1992; Wallerstein, 1992), and that of the interrelations between psychoanalysis in the training institutes and in the universities (Freud, 1919j [1918]; THERIP, 1993).

I introduce what I have in mind with reference to certain remarks of Freud, Anna Freud, and Ella Freeman Sharpe. I then look at my chosen topic—psychoanalysis and cinema—from the vantage-point introduced. This entails a brief review of the literature, which is followed by the presentation of case material in which one particular film played a significant role.

For Freud (1919j [1918]), the universities had everything to gain by including psychoanalysis in the curriculum, in both medical and academic education. At the same time, he thought that the psychoanalyst could dispense entirely with the university without any loss to himself. Writing in 1918, at about the

time of the Fifth International Congress in Budapest, Freud
(1919j [1918]) felt able to say:

> For what [the psychoanalyst] needs in the matter of theory
> can be obtained from the literature of the subject and,
> going more deeply, at the scientific meetings of the psycho-
> analytic societies as well as by personal contact with their
> more experienced members. As regards practical experi-
> ence, apart from what he gains from his own personal
> analysis, he can acquire it by carrying out treatments,
> providing he can get supervision and guidance from recog-
> nized psycho-analysts. [p. 171]

Later writers have been less sanguine. Sulloway (1986), for
instance, sees it as a short-term gain for psychoanalysis to
have developed outside the universities. It gave a nascent
movement focus and direction, which enabled it to establish
itself coherently and quickly. Heretics could be expelled. On
the other hand, Sulloway considered it a long-term "disaster",
which lead, ultimately, to the narrowness of vision and inertia
that he sees as the hallmark of so much of psychoanalysis,
particularly in the United States. Even Rayner (1987), writing
in the more eccentric and maverick (Kohon, 1986; Rickman,
1951) British context and so "very fond and devoted" to his
Society, bemoans the lack of links with universities. As he put
it in 1987, and the situation is not substantially different
today:

> In fact, one gets the impression that many academics in-
> terested in analysis gravitate to Lacan's work which is
> actually little known in Britain except in the universities.
> Sandler is the only Professor of Psychoanalysis in Britain.
> There are one or two lecturers in other places but there is
> no intellectual climate of interchange. This is a great pity,
> the problem is recognized but the years of neglect will take
> decades to repair. [Rayner, 1987, p. 59]

How, then, are we to ensure that psychoanalytic institutes
do not become insular and inward-looking; that they maintain
breadth and depth in academic scholarship; that systematic
research becomes more well-developed? Anna Freud (1966)

had little doubt. For her father (Freud, 1926e), the ideal psychoanalytic training, in addition to its core in depth psychology, would include introductory study of biology, studies in the sexual life, the symptomatology of psychiatry, together with the history of civilizations, mythology, the psychology of religion, and the science of literature. Anna Freud (1966), seeing this as a piece of "fantastic" wishful thinking, proposes, instead, to ensure that the student body, as a whole, incorporates the disciplines mentioned. She considers that the development of psychoanalysis, in all its aspects, will be enriched, widened, and safeguarded in this way. Every individual member will contribute to psychoanalysis "on the one hand on the basis of his analytic training, on the other hand, on the basis of previous thorough immersion in an allied valuable discipline" (A. Freud, 1966, p. 75).

Freud's (1926e) point had been that unless the analyst is at home in the subjects he mentions, he can make nothing of a large amount of his material in the clinical context. Freeman Sharpe (1930) cast her nets even wider.

> Whatever qualification is necessary in the way of knowledge of pathological states of mind, the future technician will have gained his knowledge of human nature not only in the consulting-room, but in actual living. He will have ranged to some extent through some pathway of literature; biography, history, fiction, poetry or drama. [Freeman Sharpe, 1930, p. 12]

She notes how she would have grasped the unconscious significance of what was being represented in the consulting-room more quickly if, during just one week of work, she had had the necessary knowledge of Peer Gynt, a particular Dutch picture, the duties of a trustee, the makes of motor-cars, and the meaning of football terms, amongst many other things.

Freeman Sharpe was writing in 1930, when cinema was in its relative infancy. By the 1950s cinema had become the major form of mass entertainment. By the 1980s satellite and cable television offered a number of movie channels. Home video had revolutionized the availability of film. For many, it had revolutionized their leisure activity; even, perhaps, their family life. It behoves us to take these developments seriously in the 1990s.

Psychoanalysis and cinema: a review

To this end, I now turn to a review of the major confluences that have taken place between psychoanalysis, cinema, and film studies since the inception of each at the end of the last century (Greenberg & Gabbard, 1990; Kaplan, 1990). In the spirit of the remarks quoted, I pay particular attention to the interrelations between the clinical situation, and between psychoanalysis as researched and taught in the Institutes and in the universities.

Particularly noticeable is the gap between the theoretical studies and the clinical situation. This is, perhaps, the most outstanding single feature of the literature (Charney & Reppen, 1987; Dervin, 1985; Kaplan, 1990; Metz, 1982; Mulvey, 1989; Penley, 1989; Rose, 1986; Silverman, 1988; Smith & Kerrigan, 1987). I address this gap, therefore, with reference to a construction of clinical material in which a film set in pre-war Ireland (The Field, 1990) had a particular resonance for a particular patient and was particularly instructive to the therapist in the psychoanalytic process.

It is instructive to consider the interrelations between psychoanalysis, cinema, and film studies in terms of the study of psychoanalysis IN the cinema; the psychoanalytic study OF the cinema; the role of film in the teaching of psychoanalysis; and the role of film in the psychoanalytic process.

Psychoanalysis IN the cinema

Psychoanalysis features IN the cinema in four main guises. There are the serious and sustained attempts to use psychoanalysis as narrative in film. There is the use—typical of many Hollywood movies—of psychoanalysis and psychoanalytic psychiatry as a sub-text to frame a narrative or "explain" it. There are the serious and sustained attempts to explore the insights of psychoanalysis, particularly the "language" of the unconscious, most notably in the work of surrealist film makers. And there is the use of Freud's theories to legitimate the depicting of the lurid and avowedly erotic.

G. W. Pabst's *Secrets of a Soul* (1926) was the first serious attempt to use psychoanalysis as narrative. Freud, himself, refused to cooperate in the making of the movie, believing that "satisfactory plastic representation of our abstractions" was not possible (Abraham & Freud, 1964). But his disciples— Sachs, a keen moviegoer and film critic, and Karl Abraham— acted as very enthusiastic psychoanalytic consultants. The film was not a major success with either the public or the critics, but it did depict a case study—the origins of a knife phobia and its treatment through analysis—in a serious and authentic fashion, giving full regard to the developments in psychoanalysis at the time. Friedberg gives the flavour:

> *Secrets of a Soul* is a film narrative with the structure of a detective film, the psychoanalyst as sort-of Sherlock Jr. who witnesses each image as the analysand retells the events leading up to his nightmare and his resulting phobia. [It] uses dream analysis as the central hermeneutical tool of its narrative; the dream is a cinematic attempt at direct pictorial transcription of psychic mechanisms, a key to the locked room of the unconscious. [1990, p. 46]

Whatever its alleged weaknesses (Bergstrom, 1990), the film does give a flavour of the analytic process at work, particularly in its focus upon the classical approach to dream analysis as set forth in Freud (1900a).

Gabbard and Gabbard (1987) provide a wide-ranging treatment of the uses made by Hollywood cinema of psychoanalysis and psychoanalytic psychiatry. The regular reincarnations of what Schneider (1985) had christened "Dr Dippy", "Dr Evil", and "Dr Wonderful" are detailed. They document the distortions and trivializations of the realities of the clinical situation, emphasizing the way Hollywood co-opts psychoanalysis in the service of prevalent bourgeois values. Their analysis of *Lady in the Dark* (1944) is typical. This popular Hollywood film features "a faceless psychiatrist", almost without human qualities, who marginalizes painful childhood memories before disposing of them cheerfully wrapped up in "mystifying, pseudo-scientific trappings". The simple cure is based on the recall of childhood memories. For good measure, the psychiatrist duly endorses the ideology of the period, which discouraged women from remaining in the workplace. Women are only "complete" when they surrender to the roles the conventional middle-class ideology assigns to them (Gabbard & Gabbard, 1987, pp. 7–14).

The Hollywood treatments may, indeed, be trivial. But such studies as those by Gabbard and Gabbard (1987) and Schneider (1977, 1985) are worthwhile, nonetheless, for they do sensitize clinicians to the sorts of preconceptions about psychoanalysis that patients so frequently bring in to the analytic process. The Hollywood treatments also provide the starting point for the various forms of ideological analysis so favoured by today's university-based critical film theorists (Kaplan, 1990; Mulvey, 1989; Penley, 1988; Silverman, 1988).

The first serious and sustained attempts to explore the insights of psychoanalysis through the medium of film were those of the "Surrealist school" of the 1920s. Dresden (1985) reviews the links between psychoanalysis and surrealism. Worthy of particular note are the surrealist film makers' concern with irruptions of the id and their frequently extraordinarily sensitive and vivid depictions of the conflict-ridden nature of the human psyche. Bunuel and Dali's early *Un Chien Andalou* (1929) and *L'Age d'Or* (1930) are certainly the most notorious of the surrealist concerns with the visual depiction of the "language" of the unconscious, but the entire corpus of a film-maker such as Bunuel can be seen in terms of its systematic exploration of the fundamentals of classical psychoanalysis. It should be remembered, too, that there were close links between Lacan and early surrealism (Benvenuto & Kennedy, 1986, p. 33). I often think that much of the difficulty of British and American practitioners with Lacanian psychoanalysis might be illuminated if they took cognizance of Lacan's early contact with surrealism and the indelible imprint it left on him.

Finally, in this section on psychoanalysis IN film, the recently re-released *Venus in Furs* (1993) may be taken as illustrative of the widespread use of psychoanalysis, not only to frame and explain a narrative, but also to give it a spurious legitimacy. Within a few minutes of the start of the film, we share the protagonist's blatant voyeurism as he spies through his peep-hole at his "victim", masturbating, dressed only in fur. Simultaneously, the narrator informs us of Freud's explanation for our hero's behaviour. As a young child, he had chanced across a maid and the chauffeur having intercourse and had remained transfixed, both fearful and excited. The chance incident is seen to "explain" what we are observing and sets up the narrative for everything that follows. It is spurious because while the film purports to be a modern version of Leopold von Sacher-Masoch's autobiographically influenced novel *Venus in Furs*—the central characters are named accordingly—in point of fact von Sacher-Masoch's childhood memory was quite different (Sacher-Masoch, 1888). His text did refer to his "Venus in Furs". Moreover, the narrative misleadingly suggests that Freud's thought preceded Sacher-Masoch's, which further confuses the issue.

The psychoanalytic study OF the cinema

It is the psychoanalytic study OF the cinema that has become the major growth area in recent years, particularly in university Film and Media Studies departments. Freud's psychoanalytic studies of creativity and literature (Freud, 1907a, 1908e [1907], 1910c, 1942a [1905–6]) lent themselves well to application and development in the context of film and cinema. We might distinguish studies of creativity, studies in reception, and studies of text.

Andrew (1984, p. 135) points to the natural affinity between the auteur policy in film criticism (Sarris, 1962–63; Truffaut, 1954) and the treatment of "images and entire films as symptoms of the artist who signs his name to them". It is easy to cliché the approach. Hitchcock, for instance, regularly used to trot out the same "explanations" for his work (Hitchcock, 1973). In more sophisticated hands, however, "psycho-biography" can be illuminating (Spoto, 1982), even if currently unfashionable.

To Freud, aesthetic pleasure sprang from the ability of the creative artist to release "tensions in our mind". It was a type of "forepleasure" (Freud, 1908e [1907]). This tack has been taken up by writers—such as Holland (1975)—who consider how and why particular viewers are drawn to particular films. The oral type will prefer the films of Fellini to those of Bergman, and so on (Andrew, 1984, p. 137). Theories of reception have been given particular emphasis in the move to Lacanian psycho-analysis, now the orthodoxy in so many film study pro-grammes. Here the concern becomes the psychoanalytic construction of the viewer. This approach has generated a considerable literature (de Lauretis & Heath, 1980; Metz, 1982; Rosen, 1986). Utilizing, as it does, Lacan's developmental theory structured around the "Imaginary" and the "Symbolic" orders, the study of film centres on the study of how the cinematic apparatus invokes the Imaginary and Symbolic orders of the typical viewer (Greenberg & Gabbard, 1990, p. 101).

The viewer is seen as being "sewn in" ("the system of the suture") within bourgeois, sexist, heterosexist, racist, or what-ever ideologies by the so-called "tutor code of classical cin-ema"—particularly by the shot/reverse-shot formulation, in which each of two characters is viewed alternatively over the other's shoulders (Dayan, 1976; Oudart, 1978; Rothman, 1976).

The question then posed is, how is the spectator to break out of what seems to be an ideological impasse? The favoured methods are through ideological analysis of Hollywood cinema, from the standpoint of variously Marxist, Lacanian, and Femi-nist critical theories, on the one hand, and through various "realist", Marxist, Feminist, and "Altering-Eye" cinemas, on the other (Heath, 1981; Kolker, 1983; Kuhn, 1982; MacCabe, 1985; Mayne, 1990). Typically, the many of these develop-ments that do maintain an allegiance to psychoanalysis do so by co-opting Lacan's Freud in the service of ideology-critique (Althusser, 1971a, 1971b), with, most frequently, no thought whatsoever for the complexities of the clinical situation.

It is important to stress, however, that while Lacanian psy-choanalysis is massively influential in many departments of film study, it by no means holds a monopoly on psychoanalytic approaches to film in the universities. The psychoanalytic study of text and narrative, for instance, takes many forms. Relationships, actions, motives, and text may all be examined from the psychoanalytic point of view. Prominent here are the writings of Wood (1986, 1989), Durgnat (1967), and Cavell and his followers (Smith & Kerrigan, 1987), who lay the emphasis upon more classically inspired psychoanalytic readings of specific films. There are also those writers who explore the relationships between film, theory, and the so-called "dream-screen" (Eberwein, 1984; Kawin, 1978; Kinder, 1980; Lewin, 1963).

In these approaches, the psychoanalytic study of film illuminates both the particular film studied and the particular psychoanalytic approach adopted. Others, like Gabbard and Gabbard (1987), deliberately utilize the range of psychoanalytic paradigms available and choose their conceptual framework in accordance with its usefulness in explaining characters, themes, or the text of particular films. Thus they utilize the Kleinian model of the paranoid–schizoid position to provide a basis for understanding the pervasive anxiety generated by *Alien* (1979), for instance, while using self psychology and object relations theory to illuminate *All That Jazz* (1979) and *Stardust Memories* (1980), in which they see narcissistic themes as paramount, and remaining wedded to a classically Freudian approach in elucidating the Oedipal themes of "Robert Altman's Dream World" of *3 Women* (1977) (Gabbard & Gabbard, 1987, p. 188).

The role of film in the teaching of psychoanalysis

Space does not permit a detailed consideration of particular psychoanalytic studies OF film. However, something of the flavour of adopting a psychoanalytic approach to the study of film can be given in the context of the role of film in the teaching of psychoanalysis.

From the clinician's point of view, many of the difficulties in the teaching of psychoanalysis to students who have neither undergone a psychoanalysis nor have any clinical experience can be overcome by using film to illustrate psychoanalytic

principles. Hitchcock's *Rear Window* (1954) is particularly useful in the illustration of Freud's theory of sexuality (Freud,
1905d), for instance.

In *Rear Window* (following Almansi, 1992, and Monaco et
al., 1992), freelance travelling photographer "Jeff" Jeffries
has a broken leg and is confined to a wheelchair in his
Greenwich Village apartment, where he has nothing to do
but passively sit back and watch the various activities that
take place in the courtyard outside his rear window. He
observes a frustrated drinking bachelor song-writer; a
couple of newly-weds whose blinds have been closed since
they entered their apartment after their marriage; two
women who undress on the roof to sunbathe; a middle-
aged couple who dote on a dog; a lonely middle-aged
woman; a dancer who exercises in her underwear; and—of
particular interest for the development of the plot—a
travelling jewellery salesman with his invalid wife who is
seemingly a hypochondriac. After "playing the voyeur" for
some time, Jeffries begins to suspect that the jewellery
salesman (Thorwald) has murdered his wife.

Meanwhile, in his own apartment, he is visited by a
middle-aged visiting nurse, who comes to massage and
feed him, scolds his voyeurism, and advises him to marry
his beautiful girl-friend (Lisa), who later arrives with an
elegant dinner and pursues the theme of marriage. Faced
with Jeffries' lack of interest in both her and her
proposals—he is taken up with his interests in his "rear
window"—she leaves angrily. When she returns the
following night, Jeffries enlists her aid to expose
Thorwald's murder. Whilst in Thorwald's apartment, and
in full view of the immobile Jeffries, she is confronted by
Thorwald, and a scuffle ensues. Great play is made of
Thorwald's wife's wedding-ring, which Lisa finds and
places upon her own finger, wagging it triumphantly at the
watching Jeffries. Later Thorwell, having realized he is
being spied upon, enters Jeffries' apartment, overpowers
him, and throws him out of the window. The film ends
with the arrest of Thorwell and the return of Jeffries to his
apartment, now with both his legs in a cast! His girl-friend

is looking untypically serene. Maybe they will marry after all.

Almansi (1992) has argued persuasively that the film is grounded in two convergent psychic mechanisms: an intense fear of object loss, echoed again and again in the film, and a sadistically interpreted primal scene. This is, perhaps, open to debate. What is indisputable, however, is the film's voyeuristic theme. Once a viewer is familiar with Freud's basic theory of sexuality—that mature genital sexuality is a developmental achievement in which the various infantile component instincts coalesce, and which is susceptible to fixation and regression— then a psychoanalytic understanding of the film is easily grasped.

Evidently, the injured and infantilized Jeffries (immobile in his wheel-chair, his leg in plaster [castrated], babied by his nurse, and fed by his elegant girl-friend) is in a state of regression. His already suspect abilities for mature object relations (he's on the run from his girl-friend) have fractured, to the point where his libidinal interests are taken up almost entirely with looking and, when not looking, with eating or dozing. It is equally evident that he is watching sexual and aggressive drives, in their different manifestations, in the various scenes he observes. These scenes depict the major alternative "solutions" to the pre-Oedipal and Oedipal difficulties that confront us all. As with so many of Hitchcock's films, viewers can argue about the ending, but it is at least plausible that Jeffries' voyeuristic and investigative activities have enabled him to work through his Oedipal difficulties. Aided by the love of an active helpmate, he is, perhaps, enabled to take the step to mature genital love (Almansi, 1992; Balint, 1947).

The role of film in the psychoanalytic process

I now turn to the role of film in the psychoanalytic process, in order to illustrate how it is possible to introduce psychoanalysis and the study of film in a fashion that does bring together the clinical situation with a tradition of psychoanalysis that might be equally at home both in the training institutes and the universities. In particular, I hope that it might sensitize students, practitioners, and university-based academics to the importance of an understanding of film in making sense of a patient's associations and building upon them.

I have touched on the fact that patients frequently have a distorted view of the psychoanalytic process through being influenced by Hollywood depictions of psychoanalysis. As Gabbard and Gabbard (1987, p. 37) put it: "Many American films conventionally reflect one historical moment in the development of psychoanalysis, when Freud himself was attempting to cure his hysterical patients with (his cathartic) method". It frequently takes time before the patient can be educated out of this belief, or that his wish for a "quick fix", or fear of submission to the analyst, or whatever, can be analysed.

Again, film frequently comes up in many patients' associations and may, like any other association, be used for any number of purposes by analyst and patient alike. One patient, for example, would find Clint Eastwood cowboy movies come up in his thoughts when he was frightened to pursue an interest in a woman. He came to see that by identifying with the lone, self-sufficient cowboy he could save himself the trouble of attempting a relationship that might fail. The same patient was greatly taken with "perfect", idealized female film stars. He came to see that he became frightened by real women when he noticed their flaws and blemishes and felt that these were the marks of untrustworthiness and future betrayal. It will come as no surprise to you that this same patient, when disappointed by his partners, would spend many hours, alone, watching pornographic movies that featured heavily made-up, unblemished, "doll-like" starlets. He preferred his "real" women this way, too, and much of the treatment consisted in looking at the causes and consequences of his thoughts and feelings in this regard.

In contrast, the patient I want to focus on in this presentation rarely went to the cinema and seldom spoke of watching videos. He was, however, greatly affected by one film, which he saw in his third year of five-times-weekly treatment. It was a film I happened to have seen a few days before the patient. This film—The Field (1990)—came to play a major part in my learning from the patient: my learning about his relationship with his past, with me, and with his present. It is this learning that I want to share with you now.

Mr A a man of 35, married with a family of two children, was referred to me with episodes of palpitations, uncontrollable shaking, and fear that he was going to die. His symptoms first appeared shortly after his father's funeral, his father having died from a coronary. The patient was a highly successful businessman, engaging in various property speculations and dealings, in addition to his major business, of which he was managing director. He drove himself hard at work and spoke of wanting to cut down on his work commitments and spend more time with his children.

During the first phase of treatment, which lasted some 18 months, Mr A's symptoms improved dramatically. He was "staggered" when it became apparent that his symptoms mimicked those of his dying father. Once he was able to acknowledge his tremendous hostility to his father, which existed alongside a great love for him, his symptoms began to improve. Gradually, he became able to analyse for himself reoccurrences of his symptoms, particularly when they arose outside the consulting-room. He was able to acknowledge the great good that the treatment had effected, and he was grateful for it.

More puzzling, however, was the apparent lack of a transference neurosis. While I and the treatment were undoubtedly important to him, none of the more obvious signs of the transference neurosis were present. I rarely came up in his associations. He did not seem particularly sensitive to me. This second phase of the treatment came to centre around the gradual unpacking of the transference situation. Now, the emphasis was upon Mr A's relationship with his mother. Here there had remained a "festering family secret", about which Mr A was vague. He knew that he had been brought up by his paternal grandparents from the age of 2, until he was around 5, when he returned to live with his mother. He could not recall ever having seen her during this period, though he was told that she had visited him. His recollections, rather, centred around constant ruminations about why she had gone. Had she left with another man? Had she been suffering from a post-partum depression, following the birth of a younger sibling, as was sometimes hinted at? He felt that he was his mother's favourite, that there was a special bond between them, but that it was a "bond of silence". He knew that he was important to her. She knew that she was important to him. But neither could speak to each other. The family secret festered. He feared to know the truth.

We were at this point when *The Field*—an adaptation by Jim Sheridan of John B. Keane's play—was released in Northern Ireland. As was the case with several of my patients at the time, he made a special point of going to see it and then reported the deep impact it had made on him. I will outline the film's salient features, following Floyd (1991).

Set in West Connemara, Ireland, in 1939, the main plot is simple enough. Bull McCabe is a proud, strong, stubborn, and largely silent old man who has farmed the field his family have rented for years, and in which his own mother died. When it is put up for auction, Bull is outbid by a rich young American, who plans to bring hydro-electric power to the area. The first sale is abandoned when the reserve price is not reached.

The next part of the film then centres on Bull's determination not to lose his field to the young American. Finding out that the American is taking steps to acquire adjoining land, Bull and his son confront him. After a particularly bloody and long-drawn-out fight between the American and Bull's son, Bull intervenes, eventually overpowering the American and drowning him. At the reconvened auction, Bull secures the reserve price. This point marks the revelation of festering family secrets, previously merely hinted at. Bull's wife, who has not spoken to Bull for 18 years, breaks her silence for the first time since their youngest son hanged himself, after hearing his father say that the field would not support the two sons and that, as the youngest, he would have to

emigrate. Bull has not entered his church since his son
was refused a burial on consecrated ground because of his
suicide. Entering the church for the first time since then,
he is denounced, in all but name, by the local priest, who
condemns murder and obsessive hunger for land.

Meanwhile, his elder son (Tadgh), who has fallen for the
spirited tinker's daughter (Redhead), with whose group
Bull is also at odds, has announced that he is leaving with
her. Bull plunges deeper into madness. As his son Tadgh
and Redhead leave the village in their tinker's caravan,
they see Bull driving his cattle and sheep towards the cliff.
When Tadgh tries to head them back, he is himself forced
over the cliff. Wading into the sea, Bull rails against the
incoming waves, reminiscent of King Lear and King
Canute.

Above all else, the film rekindled in my patient a conscious
awareness of the grinding poverty, harshness and brutality of
rural Irish life and his own experiences of it. Brought up for
several years by his grandmother and grandfather in rural Co.
Fermanagh, while his mother was away for reasons he was
never able to fathom, he felt a tremendous tie to the rural life.
As a young boy, during later periods spent with his grandparents, he recalled cutting turf in the bog, the back-breaking
task of removing stones from his grandfather's field, and the
sternness of his grandfather's authority. He felt affection for
him and recalled the pleasure of male camaraderie. But, as in
the film, never far away was cruelty and harshness. At the drop
of a hat, his grandfather might give vent to sudden and unexpected bouts of rage, leaving my patient quite terrified. He had
previously recalled particularly distressing incidents, frequently concerning animals he had befriended on his grandfather's smallholding: how his grandfather would force him to
pull the necks of chickens he had befriended; how upset he was
when the animals were slaughtered, and so on.

However, at the same time he recognized his own similari-
ties to Bull. Here was a man who stuck to his guns. He was
proud of his grandfather. He was proud of his rural roots. His
city "shenanigans", at which he was so successful, were
ephemeral and worthless.

At a conscious level, I felt that our mutual viewing of the film brought me much closer to the realities of his childhood memories and their impact on his psychic life. As a suburban dweller, I could recall once taking a mole that I had found to an elderly, hard-bitten rural gardener. He had unceremoniously squelched it under his hob-nail boot before kicking aside its entrails into a ditch. But I had very few other memories to utilize in building up a child's picture of the "cruelty" of rural life. These were the daily experiences of my patient in many of his childhood years, and the immediacy and impact provided by *The Field* was a revelation to me.

Moreover, as Floyd (1991) points out, the film raises more archetypal themes—note the names: The Bull and The American—and they became useful motifs within which to consider the transference. You will recall that what I have called the second phase of treatment ended with the patient's terror of looking too deeply into the nature of his "bond of silence" with his mother. He had long "done everything himself". He was keeping me very much at a distance. Just as the American was the threatening outsider, so was I. As an Englishman treating him in a part of Northern Ireland far away from his roots, I became the outsider who threatened to divest him of those roots. Yet, at the same time, he could see that I had helped him considerably.

What was he to do? We came to see that while Bull had driven himself mad, by his blind rage and stubbornness, my patient's treatment had alleviated his rages, made him less stubborn. But "no way", just yet, was he going to "give way" to me any more. It was just too dangerous. He could never openly express anger with me in the sessions, of course. That would put at risk the "bond of silence". Rather, he ranted and railed at what seemed to be a never-ending source of outside "enemies". He came to see what he was doing, but he was powerless to stop it.

Then, just as we were reflecting upon the grip of the compulsion to repeat, a new theme began to emerge in his outside life and his associations. He had recently renovated a country house in a large estate not far from his grandfather's former smallholding. Once the immediate tasks of home-building were over, however, he set about various costly and elaborate environmental projects in the neighbouring area. He would return to the Monday sessions having spent busy weekends dredging lakes in preparation for fish stocking. He spoke of the importance of maintaining a proper ecological balance. He realized that the significance of these activities was of a different order to his previous property dealings, where speculation and profit was the major motivation. Now the reverse was the case. He was frightened that he would run out of money to continue his salvage operations. That thought terrified him.

What, then, was the emotional significance of the "repair work"? Once again *The Field* proved revealing. Bull, at the height of his madness, achieves a rare moment of clarity when he roars, "Curse my mother and father for tying me to the famine field". As the third phase of treatment began to crystallize, we came to see how it centred around the patient's enormous guilt about leaving the land, his roots. Part of him was still there. He wanted to make contact with that part again. He was well aware of the "idiocy of rural life"; of how angry he was at the poverty and cruelty of it; but still he felt its call.

He had long recalled the time when, as a schoolboy, he determined to be the one member of the family to achieve success. He set himself the deliberate task to secure for his parents the security, possessions, and comfort that his own mother and father had been unable to provide. He had done precisely this. To the disappointment of his father, he had left his local grammar-school prematurely. We came to see what a hostile act this was. Ignoring advice from his teachers to secure a university place, he had moved to England, where he began to accumulate wealth. He had become increasingly aware that his work held no intrinsic satisfaction for him. For periods at a time he would get "high" on the excitements of wheeling and dealing. This was his "fix"; but he was increasingly seeing it as all "quite worthless". It was "all for mother" and, above all else, "fear-driven". Periodically, there were moments of terror, too, when a particular enterprise looked as though it might fail. In no time, he would rush into another, only to find, again and again, that with each plateau reached his anxieties would return. All this had become well known to us.

However, in this third phase of treatment, a new memory emerged. Mr A was overwhelmed with emotion as he recalled the time when his grandfather had taken him to visit a particular cottage nearby, where his grandfather was born. He recalled the warmth and goodness of the simple rural life, the kindness of his grandfather, the potatoes and bread, the kettle on the stove, and so on. At this point, poverty, cruelties, and fears were as nothing. This was what he wanted more of.

Gradually, as this third phase of treatment progressed, we came to see just how his "house", his "field" which he had abandoned, had come to represent to him those aspects of both his father and mother which he so longed for and which he was trying to recreate in his "repair work". His preoccupations with his grandfather had prepared the ground for these revelations, whilst in part screening their recovery and reconstruction. Now, perhaps for the first time, he was ready to confront the deepest of lacks in his life, his deepest yearnings which centred on his search for what his mother had not provided or enabled; where the "bond of silence" might finally be confronted; where he would no longer need his lifelong defences against betrayal and loss. For the first time, my patient was in a position to build upon the strengths that he shared with Bull—his strength, his drive, his determination—whilst being sufficiently free to jettison his Bull-like self-destructiveness, stubbornness, and fear-driven, defensive fury.

Conclusions and implications

In this chapter I have sought to set forth the various confluences between psychoanalysis, cinema, and film studies from the standpoint of a psychoanalytic tradition that lays particular emphasis upon clinical experience and accessibility. To this end, I have laid particular focus on the role a particular film played in a particular phase of a particular treatment. In one sense, the fact that both film and case featured an Irish dimension calls for no special comment. Insofar as the fundamental truths of psychoanalysis are universal and individual development outcomes unique (A. Freud, 1965a), then it might be wise to refrain from specifically cultural comment.

However, it is sometimes suggested (A. Couch, personal communication 1992) that the convergence of rural, traditional, and religious values, still prevalent in Northern Ireland, might tend to reproduce the same Oedipal conflicts and punishing superegos that marked Freud's practice in turn-of-the-century Vienna. Certainly, the relative prevalence of classic neurotic disorders, like Mr A's, that reach the analytic couch in Northern Ireland—as opposed to the seemingly more prevalent borderline conditions that reach the couch in contemporary Britain and the United States, say (Lasch, 1991)—does warrant further investigation. Again, the peculiar grip of the land in Ireland, as well as the Irishman's sensitivity to the outsider, was thought worthy of special psychoanalytic comment by Ernest Jones back in the early 1920s (Jones, 1923). Maybe Mr A is a contemporary clinical illustration of a prevalent cultural disposition.

I am also mindful of Dervin (1985, p. vii), who remarked of his own study of psychoanalysis and cinema: "Several approaches—diverse as well as overlapping—now appear viable. Yet this field of study is still relatively young, and attempts to consolidate the diversity or redundancy of perspectives would be premature".

This point was brought home to me rather dramatically by a dream I had the night after sketching the major headings for this chapter. The dream led to the generation of an additional heading—namely, "the role of film in the dream process". Certainly, it gave some indication of the possible complexities in the interrelations between psychoanalysis, cinema, and the role of film in the psychoanalytic process that I had previously neglected.

In this dream, *I was standing in Jeffries' apartment-room in Hitchcock's "Rear Window", looking out through his rear window, watching a movie in the apartment blocks opposite. The film ended, and I turned to a man standing next to me. I was shaking my head in wonder, exhilaration, and sheer pleasure as I turned to the man, in awe and admiration. "I don't know how you do it. I just don't understand how you do it. That was just absolutely*

brilliant. Sheer genius". The man turned out to be none
other than Alfred Hitchcock, himself. He gave a typical
Hitchcock chuckle and enigmatic look. Looking me straight
in the eye, he slapped me on the back, saying "Hobson's
Choice, mate! Hobson's Choice!" I was overcome with a
tremendous feeling of warmth and camaraderie with this
man. I awoke, suffused in a glow of pleasure, in the
conviction that his remark was totally intelligible.

The previous day I had been approached by a local general
practitioner with my first referral since being left as the only
psychoanalytic psychotherapist working in Northern Ireland
outside the Belfast area. It was a case of Hobson's Choice, for
the doctor, the patient, and for me. The excitement of the
challenge was both exhilarating and anxiety-provoking. I had,
furthermore just been asked to write a chapter on psychoanalysis and cinema for a book I was preparing. The circumstances
of the request had led to thoughts of yet another "Hobson's
Choice", and the fact that so much of the development of
psychoanalysis in Northern Ireland is a matter of "Hobson's
Choice" (Ekins, 1991; Freeman, 1991).

Other films were not far away. I had watched the film
Hobson's Choice (1954) as a schoolboy, on one of the occasional
moments of particular pleasure when we would venture "up-
town" and take over the local cinema, specially hired for the
occasion. As I reflected upon the particular feeling of camaraderie invoked by Hitchcock's gesture and comment, more personal memories surfaced. Within a day or two of starting my
own analysis, I had dreamed the scene from Richard Burton's
Dr Faustus (1967) where a sixteenth-century scholar, working
at his workbench, conjures up Mephistopheles and offers his
soul in exchange for a life of voluptuousness and knowledge. At
my analytical workbench my analytical father and I were help-
mates, which evoked a number of moving childhood memories
of my working alongside my father, so loved, yet, so frequently,
feared.

It will not have escaped your attention, of course, that my
own name is Richard. I had, in fact, "lost" an early girl-friend to
Burton and Oxford, when she had taken part in the Oxford

University Drama Society production from which the film was made. But, perhaps, I have said enough.

Here was a dream-given example of a film, within a film, within a dream, the interpretation of which led to yet further films. A comprehensive treatment of psychoanalysis, cinema, and the role of film in the psychoanalytic process might do worse than address such issues. In any event, I had certainly been presented with another teaching aid and a convenient way of finishing this chapter.

A note on
Freud's theory of the dream

Freud's *The Interpretation of Dreams* (1900a) is more than a study of the sources of dreams, their purposes, and the mode of their formation. It also presents a psychological theory of the mind based on the phenomena that are to be discerned in the course of dream interpretation.

When dreams are subject to investigation along the lines prescribed by Freud (1900a), it becomes apparent that the dream images (manifest content) are a transformed version of trains of thought no different from those occurring in the waking state. These preconscious thoughts active in sleep (the dream thoughts) are compressed into a compact form (condensation), and their representation is subject to changes of various kinds (displacement). In addition, the abstract (verbal) nature of the thoughts is changed into visual images. The dream is a hallucinatory experience. As Freud (1900a) says, "The dream-thoughts and the dream-content are presented to us like two versions of the same subject matter in two different languages" (p. 277).

Dreams are important in psychoanalytic work, not least because their manifest content, consisting of thoughts, daydreams, and experiences of the previous day, keeps the analyst in touch with the patient's conscious and preconscious preoccupations. This is particularly relevant for transference thoughts (see chapter three) which cannot find access to consciousness but frequently do so through the medium of the dream.

REFERENCES

Abraham, H., & Freud, E. (Eds.). (1964). *A Psychoanalytic Dialogue: The Letters of Sigmund Freud and Karl Abraham, 1907–1926.* New York: Basic Books.

Abraham, K. (1924). A Short Study of the Development of the Libido Viewed in the Light of Mental Disorders. In: *Selected Papers on Psychoanalysis.* London: Hogarth, 1927. [Reprinted London: Karnac Books, 1979.]

Abram, J. (1992). *Individual Psychotherapy Trainings: A Guide.* London: Free Association Books.

Aichhorn, A. (1935). *Wayward Youth.* New York: Viking.

Alexander, F. (1950). *Psychosomatic Medicine.* New York: Norton.

Almansi, R. (1992). Alfred Hitchcock's Disappearing Women: A Study in Scopophilia and Object Loss. *International Review of Psycho-Analysis, 19*: 81–90.

Althusser, L. (1971a). Freud and Lacan. In: *Lenin and Philosophy and Other Essays.* London: New Left Books.

Althusser, L. (1971b). Ideology and Ideological State Apparatuses (Notes Towards an Investigation). In: *Lenin and Philosophy and Other Essays.* London: New Left Books.

Andrew, D. (1984). *Concepts in Film Theory*. Oxford: Oxford University Press.

Aziz, M. (Ed.) (1973). *The Tales of Henry James, Vol. I*. Oxford: Clarendon Press.

Balint, M. (1947). On Genital Love. In: *Primary Love and Psycho-Analytic Technique*. London: Hogarth, 1952. [Reprinted London: Karnac Books, 1985.]

Balint, M. (1949). Changing Therapeutical Aims and Techniques in Psychoanalysis. In: *Primary Love and Psycho-analytic Technique*. London: Hogarth, 1952. [Reprinted London: Karnac Books, 1985.]

Balint, M., & Balint, A. (1939). On Transference and Countertransference. In: *Primary Love and Psycho-analytic Technique*. London: Tavistock, 1965. [Reprinted London: Karnac Books, 1985.]

Basker, R. M., Strudee D. W., & Davenport J. C. (1978). Patients with Burning Mouths. A Clinical Investigation of Causative Factors, Including Climacteric and Diabetes. *British Dental Journal, 145*: 9–16.

Beckford, J. (1985). *Cult Controversies: The Societal Response to the New Religious Movements*. London: Tavistock.

Beckford, J. (Ed.). (1986). *New Religious Movements and Rapid Social Change*. London: Sage Publications.

Benvenuto, B., & Kennedy, R. (1986). *The Works of Jacques Lacan: An Introduction*. London: Free Association Books.

Bergstrom, J. (1990). Psychological Explanation in the Films of Lang and Pabst. In: E. Kaplan (Ed.), *Psychoanalysis and Cinema*. New York & London: Routledge.

Berliner, A. (1983). *Psychoanalysis and Society: The Social Thought of Sigmund Freud*. Washington, DC: University Press of America.

Bion, W. R. (1952). Group Dynamics: A Re-view. In: M. Klein, P. Heimann, & R. E. Money-Kyrle (Eds.), *New Directions in Psycho-Analysis*. London: Tavistock, 1955. [Reprinted London: Karnac Books, 1985.]

Bion, W. R. (1962). *Learning from Experience*. London: Heinemann. [Reprinted London: Karnac Books, 1984.]

Blackmur, R. P. (Ed.) (1934). *The Art of the Novel*. New York: Scribner's.

Bleuler, E. (1911). *Dementia Praecox or the Group of Schizophrenias*. New York: International Universities Press, 1950.

Bleuler, M. (1978). *The Schizophrenic Disorders*. London: Yale University Press.

Brittan, A. (1973). *Meanings and Situations*. London: Routledge & Kegan Paul.

Brooke-Rose, C. (1981). *A Rhetoric of the Unreal*. Cambridge: Cambridge University Press.

Brown, D., & Pedder, J. (1979). *Introduction to Psychotherapy*. London: Tavistock.

Burlingham, D. (1975). Special Problems of Blind Infants: Blind Baby Profile. In: R. S. Eissler, A. Freud, M. Kris, & A. J. Solnit, *Psychoanalytic Assessment: The Diagnostic Profile. An Anthology of the Psychoanalytic Study of the Child*. New Haven, CT: Yale University Press, 1977.

Charney, M., & Reppen, J. (Eds.) (1987). *Psychoanalytic Approaches to Literature and Film*. London & Toronto: Associated University Press.

Chasseguet-Smirgel, J. (1992). Wrestling with the Angel. *International Review of Psycho-Analysis, 19* (Special): 7–9.

Chasseguet-Smirgel, J., & Grunberger, B. (1986). *Freud or Reich? Psychoanalysis and Illusion*. London: Free Association Books.

Coles, R. (1992). *Anna Freud—The Dream of Psychoanalysis*. Reading, MA: Addison-Wesley.

Dayan, D. (1976). The Tutor-Code of Classical Cinema. In: B. Nichols (Ed.), *Movies and Methods: An Anthology*. Berkeley, CA: University of California Press.

de Lauretis, T., & Heath, S. (Eds.) (1980). *The Cinematic Apparatus*. New York: St. Martin's Press.

Dervin, D. (1985). *Through a Freudian Lens Deeply: A Psychoanalysis of Cinema*. Hillsdale, NJ: The Analytic Press.

Dresden, S. (1985). Psychoanalysis and Surrealism. In: P. Horden (Ed.), *Freud and the Humanities*. London: Duckworth.

Dunbar, H. F. (1943). *Psychosomatic Diagnosis*. New York: Hoeber.

Dupee, F. W. (Ed.) (1956). *Henry James: Autobiography*. Princeton, NJ: Princeton University Press.

Durgnat, R. (1967). *Luis Buñuel.* London: Studio Vista.

Dyer, R. (1983). *Her Father's Daughter: The Work of Anna Freud.* New York: Jason Aronson.

Eberwein, R. (1984). *Film and the Dream Scene.* Princeton, NJ: Princeton University Press.

Edel, L. (Ed.) (1974–84). *Henry James Letters* (4 vols.). Cambridge, MA, & London: Macmillan and Belknap.

Edel, L. (1977). *The Life of Henry James* (2 vols., rev. ed.). Harmondsworth: Penguin.

Edgcumbe, R. (1983). Anna Freud—Child Analyst. *International Journal of Psycho-Analysis, 64*: 427–433.

Edgcumbe, R. (1985). Anna Freud's Contribution to Technique and Clinical Understanding in Child Psychoanalysis. *Bulletin of the Anna Freud Centre, 8*: 155–168.

Edgcumbe, R., & Baldwin, J. (1986). The Use of Anna Freud's Developmental Profile in the Differential Diagnosis of a Young Severely Handicapped Child. *Bulletin of the Anna Freud Centre, 9*: 35–49.

Eissler, R. S., Freud, A., Kris, M., & Solnit, A. J. (1977). *Psychoanalytic Assessment: The Diagnostic Profile. An Anthology of the Psychoanalytic Study of the Child.* New Haven, CT: Yale University Press.

Ekins, R. (1991). Psycho-Analysis and Psycho-Analytic Psychotherapy Training in Northern Ireland. *British Journal of Psychotherapy, 8*: 199–201.

Ellenberger, H. (1970). *The Discovery of the Unconscious: The History and Evolution of Dynamic Psychiatry.* New York: Basic Books.

Engel, G. L., & Schmale A. H. (1967). Psychoanalytic Theory of Somatic Disorder: Conversion, Specificity and the Disease Onset Situation. *Journal of the American Psychoanalytic Association, 15*: 344–365.

Fairbairn, W. R. D. (1940). Schizoid Factors in the Personality. In: *Psychoanalytic Studies of the Personality.* London: Routledge & Kegan Paul, 1952.

Fairbairn, W. R. D. (1943). The Repression and Return of Bad Objects. In: *Psychoanalytic Studies of the Personality.* London: Routledge & Kegan Paul, 1952.

Fairbairn, W. R. D. (1944). Endopsychic Structures Considered in

Terms of Object Relations. In: *Psychoanalytic Studies of the Personality*. London: Routledge & Kegan Paul, 1952.

Fairbairn, W. R. D. (1958). On the Nature and Aims of Psychoanalytical Treatment. *International Journal of Psycho-Analysis, 39*: 374–385.

Fenichel, O. (1941). *Problems of Psychoanalytic Technique*. New York: The Psychoanalytic Quarterly, Inc.

Fenichel, O. (1946). *The Psychoanalytic Theory of Neurosis*. London: Routledge & Kegan Paul, 1982.

Fine, B. (Ed.) (1987). *Psychoanalysis Around the World*. New York & London: The Haworth Press.

Floyd, N. (1991). The Field. *Monthly Film Bulletin, 58*: 78–79.

Fox, H. (1935). Burning Tongue. Glossodynia. *New York State Journal of Medicine, 35*: 881–889.

Freeman, R., & Freeman, T. (1992). An Anatomical Commentary on the Concept of Infantile Oral Sadism. *International Journal of Psycho-Analysis, 73*: 343–348.

Freeman, T. (1973). The Metapsychological Profile Schema. In: *A Psychoanalytic Study of the Psychoses*. New York: International Universities Press.

Freeman, T. (1983). Anna Freud—Psychiatrist. *International Journal of Psycho-Analysis, 64*: 441–444.

Freeman, T. (1987). On the Clinical Foundations of Melanie Klein's Developmental Concepts. *Bulletin of the Anna Freud Centre, 10*: 289–305.

Freeman, T. (1988a). The Delusions of the Non-Remitting Schizophrenias: Parallels with Childhood Phantasies. *Bulletin of the Anna Freud Centre, 11*, 217–227.

Freeman, T. (1988b). *The Psychoanalyst in Psychiatry*. London: Karnac.

Freeman, T. (1989). A Sexual Theory of Persecutory Delusions. *International Journal of Psycho-Analysis, 70*: 685–692.

Freeman, T. (1991). Hobson's Choice: Personal Analysis and Supervision in the Training of Psychoanalytic Psychotherapists. *British Journal of Psychotherapy, 8*: 202–205.

Freeman, T., Cameron, I., & McGhie, A. (1958). *Chronic Schizophrenia*. London: Tavistock.

Freud, A. (1922). Beating Fantasies and Daydreams. In: *The Writings of Anna Freud, Vol. 1* (pp. 137–157). New York: International Universities Press. [Hereafter referred to as *Writings*, with volume number from this series.]

Freud, A. (1927). *Four Lectures on Child Analysis. Writings, 1* (pp. 3–69).

Freud, A. (1930). *Four Lectures on Psychoanalysis for Teachers and Parents. Writings, 1* (pp. 73–133).

Freud, A. (1931). *Introduction to Psychoanalysis for Teachers: Four Lectures by Anna Freud.* London: Allen & Unwin.

Freud, A. (1936). *The Ego and the Mechanisms of Defence. Writings, 2.*

Freud, A. (1941). Monthly Report, March 1941. *Writings, 3* (pp. 11–23).

Freud, A. (1946). The Psychoanalytic Study of Infantile Feeding Disturbances. *Writings, 4* (pp. 39–59).

Freud, A. (1951a). An Experiment in Group Upbringing. *Writings, 4* (pp. 163–229).

Freud, A. (1951b). August Aichhorn: July 27, 1878–October 17, 1949. *Writings, 4* (pp. 625–638).

Freud, A. (1955). The Concept of the Rejecting Mother. *Writings, 4* (pp. 586–602).

Freud, A. (1965a). *Normality and Pathology in Childhood: Assessments of Development. Writings, 6.*

Freud, A. (1965b). Preface to *The Hampstead Psychoanalytic Index* (by John Bolland, Joseph Sandler, et al.). *Writings, 5* (pp. 483–485).

Freud, A. (1966). The Ideal Psychoanalytic Institute: A Utopia. *Writings of Anna Freud, 7* (pp. 73–93).

Freud, A. (1967). About Losing and Being Lost. *Writings, 4* (pp. 302–316).

Freud, A. (1968a). *Indications for Child Analysis and Other Papers. Writings, 4.*

Freud, A. (1968b). Indications and Contraindications for Child Analysis. *Writings, 7* (pp. 110–123).

Freud, A. (1969). *Research at the Hampstead Child-Therapy Clinic and Other Papers. Writings, 5.*

Freud, A. (1970). The Symptomatology of Childhood: A Preliminary Attempt at Classification. *Writings, 7* (pp. 157–188).

Freud, A. (1971a). *Problems of Psychoanalytic Training, Diagnosis, and the Technique of Therapy. Writings, 7.*

Freud, A. (1971b). Problems of Termination in Child Analysis. *Writings, 7* (pp. 3–21).

Freud, A. (1974). A Psychoanalytic View of Developmental Psychopathology. *Writings, 8* (pp. 57–74).

Freud, A. (1975). Foreword to *Studies in Child Psychoanalysis: Pure and Applied. The Scientific Proceedings of the Twentieth Anniversary Celebrations of the Hampstead Child-Therapy Course and Clinic.* Monograph No. 5, *Psychoanalytic Study of the Child.* New Haven, CT: Yale University Press.

Freud, A. (1976). Psychopathology Seen against the Background of Normal Development. *Writings, 8* (pp. 82–95).

Freud, A. (1978). The Principal Task of Child Analysis. *Writings, 8* (pp. 96–109).

Freud, A. (1982a). Beyond the Infantile Neurosis. *Writings, 8* (pp. 75–81).

Freud, A. (1982b). *Psychoanalytic Psychology of Normal Development. Writings, 8.*

Freud, A. (1982c). The Widening Scope of Psychoanalytic Child Psychology, Normal and Abnormal. *Writings, 8* (pp. 8–33).

Freud, A., & Burlingham, D. (1944). *Infants Without Families. Writings, 3* (pp. 543–666).

Freud, A., Nagera, H., & Freud, W. E. (1965). Metapsychological Assessment of the Adult Personality: The Adult Profile. *Psychoanalytic Study of the Child, 20*: 10–41.

Freud, S. (1891d). Hypnosis. In: *The Standard Edition of the Complete Psychological Works of Sigmund Freud* (translated by James Strachey & Anna Freud, assisted by Alix Strachey & Alan Tyson), Vol. 1 (pp. 105–114). London: Hogarth. [Hereafter referred to as *S.E.*, with volume number from this series.]

Freud, S. (1895d) (with J. Breuer). *Studies on Hysteria. S.E., 2.*

Freud, S. (1900a). *The Interpretation of Dreams. S.E., 4–5.*

Freud, S. (1905d). *Three Essays on the Theory of Sexuality. S.E., 7* (pp. 130–243).

Freud, S. (1905e [1901]). Fragment of an Analysis of a Case of Hysteria. *S.E., 7* (pp. 7–122).

Freud, S. (1907a). *Delusions and Dreams in Jensen's "Gradiva". S.E., 9* (pp. 7–95).

Freud, S. (1907b). Obsessive Actions and Religious Practices. *S.E., 9* (pp. 117–127).

Freud, S. (1908e [1907]). Creative Writers and Day Dreaming. *S.E., 9* (pp. 143–153).

Freud, S. (1909b). Analysis of a Phobia in a Five-Year-Old Boy. *S.E., 10* (pp. 5–149).

Freud, S. (1910a [1909]). Five Lectures on Psycho-Analysis. *S.E., 11* (pp. 6–55).

Freud, S. (1910c). *Leonardo da Vinci and a Memory of His Childhood. S.E., 11* (pp. 63–137).

Freud, S. (1910d). The Future Prospects of Psycho-Analytic Therapy. *S.E., 11* (pp. 141–151).

Freud, S. (1911c [1910]). Psycho-Analytic Notes on an Autobiographical Account of a Case of Paranoia. *S.E., 12* (pp. 9–82).

Freud, S. (1912–13). *Totem and Taboo. S.E., 13* (pp. 1–161).

Freud, S. (1912b). The Dynamics of the Transference. *S.E., 12* (pp. 99–108).

Freud, S. (1914d). On the History of the Psycho-Analytic Movement. *S.E., 14* (pp. 7–66).

Freud, S. (1914g). Remembering, Repeating and Working Through. *S.E., 12* (pp. 147–156).

Freud, S. (1915c). Instincts and their Vicissitudes. *S.E., 14* (pp. 117–140).

Freud, S. (1915e). The Unconscious. *S.E., 14* (pp. 166–204).

Freud, S. (1916–17). *Introductory Lectures on Psychoanalysis S.E., 15 & 16.*

Freud, S. (1917d [1915]). Metapsychological Supplement to the Theory of Dreams. *S.E., 14* (pp. 222–235).

Freud, S. (1917e [1915]). Mourning and Melancholia. *S.E., 14* (pp. 243–258).

Freud, S. (1919a [1918]). Lines of Advance in Psycho-Analytic Therapy. *S.E., 17* (pp. 159–168).

Freud, S. (1919j [1918]). On the Teaching of Psycho-Analysis in Universities. *S.E., 17* (pp. 171–173).

Freud, S. (1920g). *Beyond the Pleasure Principle. S.E., 18* (pp. 7–64).

Freud, S. (1921c). *Group Psychology and the Analysis of the Ego. S.E., 18* (pp. 69–143).

Freud, S. (1923b). *The Ego and the Id. S.E., 19* (pp. 12–59).

Freud, S. (1923d [1922]). A Seventeenth-Century Demonological Neurosis. *S.E., 19* (pp. 72–105).

Freud, S. (1924f [1923]). A Short Account of Psycho-Analysis. *S.E., 19* (pp. 191–209).

Freud, S. (1925h). Negation. *S.E.*, *19* (pp. 235–239).

Freud, S. (1926d [1925]). *Inhibitions, Symptoms and Anxiety. S.E.,* *20* (pp. 87–172).

Freud, S. (1926e). *The Question of Lay Analysis. S.E., 20* (pp. 183–258).

Freud, S. (1927c). *The Future of an Illusion. S.E., 21* (pp. 5–56).

Freud, S. (1928a). A Religious Experience. *S.E., 21* (pp. 167–172).

Freud, S. (1930a). *Civilization and its Discontents. S.E., 21* (pp. 64–145).

Freud, S. (1933a). *New Introductory Lectures on Psycho-Analysis. S.E., 22* (pp. 5–182).

Freud, S. (1939a). *Moses and Monotheism. S.E., 23* (pp. 7–137).

Freud, S. (1940a [1938]). *An Outline of Psycho-Analysis. S.E., 23* (pp. 144–207).

Freud, S. (1941f [1938]). Findings, Ideas, Problems. *S.E., 23* (pp. 299–300).

Freud, S. (1942a [1905–6]). Psychopathic Characters on the Stage. *S.E., 7* (p. 305).

Freud, S. (1950 [1892–1899]). Extracts from the Fleiss Papers. *S.E., 1* (pp. 177–280).

Freud, S. (1950 [1895]). A Project for a Scientific Psychology. *S.E., 1* (pp. 259–343).

Freud, S. (1974). Indexes and Bibliographies. *S.E. 24.*

Freud, W. E. (1967). The Baby Profile. In: R. S. Eissler, A. Freud, M. Kris, & A. J. Solnit, *Psychoanalytic Assessment: The Diagnostic Profile. An Anthology of the Psychoanalytic Study of the Child.* New Haven, CT: Yale University Press, 1977.

Friedberg, A. (1990). An *Unheimlich* Maneuver between Psychoanalysis and the Cinema: Secrets of a Soul (1926). In: E. Rentschler (Ed.), *The Films of G. W. Pabst: An Extraterritorial Cinema.* New Brunswick, NJ, & London: Rutgers University Press.

Frosh, S. (1991). *Identity Crisis: Modernity, Psychoanalysis and the Self.* London: Macmillan.

Gabbard, K., & Gabbard, G. (1987). *Psychiatry and the Cinema.* Chicago, IL: The University of Chicago Press.

Gaddini, E. (1982). Early Defensive Fantasies and the Psychoanalytic Process. *International Journal of Psycho-Analysis, 63*: 379–388.

Gaddini, E. (1987). Notes on the Mind–Body Question. *International Journal of Psycho-Analysis, 68*: 315–329.

Gehrie, M. (1992). Freud's Vision: Key Issues in the Methodology of Applied Psychoanalysis, Report. *Journal of the American Psychoanalytic Association, 40*: 239–244.

Glover, E. (1949). *Psychoanalysis.* London: Staples Press.

Glover, E. (1955). *The Technique of Psychoanalysis.* London: Balliere.

Goldstein, J., Freud, A., & Solnit, A. J. (1973). *Beyond the Best Interests of the Child.* New York: Free Press.

Goldstein, J., Freud, A., & Solnit, A. J. (1979). *Before the Best Interests of the Child.* New York: Free Press.

Goldstein, J., Freud, A., & Solnit, A. J. (1986). *In the Best Interests of the Child.* New York: Free Press.

Greenberg, H., & Gabbard, K. (1990). Reel Significations: An Anatomy of Psychoanalytic Film Criticism. *The Psychoanalytic Review, 77*: 89–110. [Revised version in: H. Greenberg, *Screen Memories: Hollywood Cinema on the Psychoanalytic Couch.* New York: Columbia University Press, 1993.]

Greenberg, J. R., & Mitchell, S. A. (1983). *Object Relations in Psychoanalytic Theory.* Cambridge, MA: Harvard University Press.

Greenson, R. R. (1967). *The Technique and Practice of Psychoanalysis.* New York: International Universities Press.

Grosskurth, P. (1985). *Melanie Klein: Her World and Her Work.* London: Karnac Books, 1986.

Grushka, M. (1983). Burning Mouth : Review and Update. *Ontario Dentist, 60*: 56–61.

Grushka, M. (1987). Clinical Features of Burning Mouth Syndrome. *Oral Surgery, Oral Medicine, Oral Patholology, 63*: 30–36.

Habermas, J. (1970). Systematically Distorted Communication. *Inquiry, 13*: 205–218.

Hammaren, M., & Hugoson, A. (1989). Clinical Psychiatric Assessment of Patients with Burning Mouth Syndrome Resisting Oral Treatment. *Swedish Dental Journal, 13*: 77–88.

Heath, S. (1981). *Questions of Cinema.* Bloomington, IN: Indiana University Press.

Heimann, P. (1950). On Counter-transference. *International Journal of Psycho-Analysis, 31*: 81–84.

Heimann, P. (1960). Counter-transference. *British Journal of Medical Psychology, 33*: 9–15.

Hill, J. (1993). Am I a Kleinian? Is Anyone? *British Journal of Psychotherapy, 9*: 463–475.

Hitchcock, A. (1973). *Hollywood Legends.* London: Virgin Archive, Video.

Holland, N. (1975). *Five Readers Reading.* New Haven, CT: Yale University Press.

Hug-Hellmuth, H. (1921). On the Technique of Child Analysis. *International Journal of Psycho-Analysis, 2*: 287–305.

Hugoson, A. (1986). Results Obtained from Patients Referred for Investigation of Complaints Related to Oral Galvanism. *Swedish Dental Journal, 10*: 15–28.

Hugoson, A., & Thorstensson, B. (1990). Patients with Burning Mouth Syndrome, Their Vitamin B Status and Response to Replacement Therapy. (Unpublished mimeo.)

Isaacs, S. (1952). The Nature and Function of Phantasy. In: M. Klein, P. Heimann, S. Isaacs, & J. Riviere, *Developments in Psychoanalysis.* London: Hogarth, 1952. [Reprinted London: Karnac Books & The Institute of Psychoanalysis, 1989.]

Jackson, M., & Cawley, R. H. (1992). Psychodynamics and Psychotherapy on an Acute Psychiatric Ward: The Story of an Experimental Unit. *British Journal of Psychiatry, 160*: 44–50.

James, H. (1879). *Society the Redeemed Form of Man.* Boston, MA: Osgood.

James, H. (1901). *The Sacred Fount.* New York: Scribner's.

James, H. (Ed.) (1920). *The Letters of William James* (2 vols.). London: Longmans, Green.

James, W. (Ed.) (1884). *The Literary Remains of the Late Henry James.* Boston, MA: Osgood.

Jones, E. (1923). The Island of Ireland: A Psycho-Analytic Contribution to Political Psychology. In: *Essays in Applied Psycho-Analysis.* London: The International Psycho-Analytical Press.

Kaplan, E. (Ed.) (1990). *Psychoanalysis and Cinema.* New York & London: Routledge

Katan, M. (1962). A Causerie on Henry James's "The Turn of the Screw". *Psychoanalytic Study of the Child, 17*: 473–493.

Katan, M. (1966). The Origin of "The Turn of the Screw". *Psychoanalytic Study of the Child, 21*: 583–635.

Katan, M. (1975). Childhood Memories as Contents of Schizophrenic Hallucinations and Delusions. *Psychoanalytic Study of the Child, 30*: 357–375.

Kaufmann, W. (1980). *Discovering the Mind, Vol. 3: Freud versus Adler and Jung.* New York: McGraw-Hill.

Kawin, B. (1978). *Mindscreen: Bergman, Godard, and First Person Film.* Princeton, NJ: Princeton University Press.

Kernberg, O. F. (1965). Notes on Counter-Transference. *Journal of the American Psychoanalytic Association, 13*: 38–56.

Kernberg, O. F. (1975). *Borderline Conditions and Pathological Narcissism.* North Vale, NJ: Jason Aronson.

Kimbrough, R. (Ed.) (1966). *Henry James: The Turn of the Screw* [1898]. New York: Norton.

Kinder, M. (1980). The Adaptation of Cinematic Dreams. *Dreamworks, 1*: 54–68.

King, P., & Steiner, R. (Eds.) (1991). *The Freud–Klein Controversies, 1941–45.* London: Tavistock/Routledge.

Klein, M. (1932). *The Psychoanalysis of Children.* In: *The Writings of Melanie Klein, 1.* London: Hogarth, 1975. [Reprinted London: Karnac Books, 1992.]

Klein, M. (1935). A Contribution to the Psychogenesis of Manic-Depressive States. In: *The Writings of Melanie Klein, 1.* London: Hogarth, 1975. [Reprinted London: Karnac Books, 1992.]

Klein, M. (1946). Notes on Some Schizoid Mechanisms. In: *The Writings of Melanie Klein, 3.* London: Hogarth, 1975. [Reprinted London: Karnac Books, 1993.]

Klein, M. (1952). The Origins of the Transference. In: *The Writings of Melanie Klein, 3.* London: Hogarth, 1975. [Reprinted London: Karnac Books, 1993.]

Klein, M. (1957). Envy and Gratitude. In: *The Writings of Melanie Klein, 3.* London: Hogarth, 1975. [Reprinted London: Karnac Books, 1993.]

Kohon, G. (1986). Notes on the History of the Psychoanalytic Movement in Great Britain. In: G. Kohon (Ed.), *The British School of Psychoanalysis: The Independent Tradition.* London: Free Association Books.

Kolker, R. (1983). *The Altering Eye: Contemporary International Cinema.* Oxford: Oxford University Press.

Kris, E. (1951). Opening Remarks on Psychoanalytic Child Psychology. *Psychoanalytic Study of the Child, 6*: 9–17.

Kuhn, A. (1982). *Women's Pictures: Feminism and Cinema.* New York & London: Routledge.

Lamey, P. J., & Lamb, A. B. (1988). Prospective Study of Aetiological Factors in Burning Mouth Syndrome. *British Medical Journal, 296*: 1243–1246.

Lasch, C. (1991). *The Culture of Narcissism: American Life in an Age of Diminishing Expectations*. New York: W.W. Norton.

Laufer, M. (1965). Assessment of Adolescent Disturbances: The Application of Anna Freud's Diagnostic Profile. *Psychoanalytic Study of the Child, 20*: 99–123.

Lewin, B. (1963). *Dreams and the Uses of Regression*. New York: International Universities Press.

Limentani, A. (1983). Anna Freud's Contribution to the Work of the International Psychoanalytical Association. *International Journal of Psycho-Analysis, 64*: 375–377.

Little, M. (1960). Countertransference. *International Journal of Psycho-Analysis, 33*: 29–31.

MacCabe, C. (1985). *Tracking the Signifier, Theoretical Essays: Film, Linguistics, Literature*. Minneapolis, MN: University of Minnesota Press.

MacLean, G., & Rappen, U. (1991). *Hermine Hug-Hellmuth: Her Life and Work*. New York: Routledge.

Main, T. F. (1957). The Ailment. *British Journal of Medical Psychology, 30*: 129–145. [Also in: *The Ailment and Other Psychoanalytic Essays*. London: Free Association Books.]

Mayne, J. (1990). *The Woman at the Keyhole: Feminism and Women's Cinema*. Bloomington, IN: Indiana University Press.

Metz, C. (1982). *The Imaginary Signifier: Psychoanalysis and Cinema*. Houndmills, Basingstoke: Macmillan.

Minkowski, E. (1927). La schizophrenie. Quoted in: R. Dalbiez, *Psychoanalytic Method and Doctrine of Freud, Vol. 1*. London: Longman, 1941.

Monaco, J., et al. (Eds.) (1992). *The Virgin Film Guide*. London: Virgin.

Montgomery Hyde, H. (1969). *Henry James at Home*. London: Methuen.

Mulvey, L. (1989). *Visual and Other Pleasures*. London: Macmillan.

Niederland, W. (1980). Schreber: Father and Son. In: M. Kanzer & J. Glenn (Eds.), *Freud and His Patients*. New York: Jason Aronson.

Niederland, W. (1984). *The Schreber Case: Psychoanalytic Profile of a Paranoid Personality*. Hillsdale, NJ: The Analytic Press.

Nunberg, H., & Federn, E. (Eds.) (1962–75). *Minutes of the Vienna Psychoanalytic Society* (4 vols.). New York: International Universities Press.

Oudart, J.-P. (1978). Cinema and Suture. *Screen, 18*: 35–47.

Paul, R. (1991). Freud's Anthropology: A Reading of the Cultural Books. In: J. Neu (Ed.), *The Cambridge Companion to Freud*. Cambridge: Cambridge University Press.

Penley, C. (Ed.) (1988). *Feminism and Film Theory*. New York & London: Routledge.

Penley, C. (1989). *The Future of an Illusion: Film, Feminism and Psychoanalysis*. New York & London: Routledge.

Persaud, R. (1993). Talking Your Way Out of Trouble. *Sunday Times*, 26 September, Section 8, p. 8.

Porter, R. (1989). *A Social History of Madness*. London: Weidenfeld & Nicolson.

Rayner, E. (1987). Psychoanalysis in Britain. In: R. Fine (Ed.), *Psychoanalysis Around the World*. New York & London: The Haworth Press.

Reich, A. (1951). On Counter-Transference. *International Journal of Psycho-Analysis, 32*: 25–31.

Reich, A. (1960). Further Remarks on Counter-Transference. *International Journal of Psycho-Analysis, 41*: 389–395.

Reisenberg-Malcolm, R. (1981). Technical Problems in the Analysis of a Pseudo-Compliant Patient. *International Journal of Psycho-Analysis, 62*: 477–484.

Richards, B. (1989). *Images of Freud: Cultural Responses to Psychoanalysis*. London: J. M. Dent.

Richardson, J. T. (Ed.) (1978). *Conversion Careers: In and Out of the New Religious Movements*. London: Sage Publications.

Rickman, J. (1951). Reflections on the Function and Organization of a Psychoanalytic Society. *International Journal of Psycho-Analysis, 32*: 218–237.

Ricoeur, P. (1970). *Freud and Philosophy: An Essay in Interpretation*. London: Yale University Press.

Rieff, P. (1966). *The Triumph of the Therapeutic*. Harmondsworth, Middlesex: Penguin.

Roazen, P. (1976). *Freud and His Followers*. Harmondsworth, Middlesex: Allen Lane.

Rose, J. (1986). *Sexuality in the Field of Vision*. London: Verso.

Rose, N. (1990). *Governing the Soul: The Shaping of the Private Self.* London: Routledge.

Rosen, P. (Ed.) (1986). *Narrative, Apparatus, Ideology: A Film Theory Reader.* New York: Columbia University Press.

Rothman, W. (1976). Against "The System of the Suture". In: B. Nichols (Ed.), *Movies and Methods: An Anthology.* Berkeley, CA: University of California Press.

Sacher-Masoch, L. von (1888). A Childhood Memory and Reflections on the Novel. In: G. Deleuze & L. von Sacher-Masoch, *Masochism.* New York: Zone Books, 1991.

Sandler, J. (1976). Counter-transference and Role-responsiveness. *International Review of Psycho-Analysis, 3*: 43–47.

Sandler, J. (1988). Psychoanalysis and Psychoanalytic Psychotherapy: Problems of Differentiation. *British Journal of Psychotherapy, 5*: 172–177.

Sandler, J., Dare, C., & Holder, A. (1992). *The Patient and the Analyst* (2nd ed.). London: Karnac Books.

Sandler, J., Holder, A., Kawenoka, M., et al. (1969). Notes on Some Theoretical and Clinical Aspects of Transference. *International Journal of Psycho-Analysis, 50*: 633–645.

Santayana, G. (1905). *Life of Reason, Vol. 1* (Chapter 12). [Quotation in text taken from *The Oxford Dictionary of Quotations* (p. 414). Oxford: Oxford University Press, 1979.]

Sarris, A. (1962–63). Notes on the Auteur Theory. *Film Culture, 27* (Winter).

Schneider, I. (1977). Images of the Mind: Psychiatry in the Commercial Film. *American Journal of Psychiatry, 134*: 613–620.

Schneider, I. (1985). The Psychiatrist in the Movies: The First Fifty Years. In: J. Reppen & M. Charney (Eds.), *Psychoanalytic Study of Literature.* Hillsdale, NJ: The Analytic Press.

Schoenberg, B. (1967). Psychogenic Aspects of Burning Mouth. *New York State Dental Journal, 33*: 467–473.

Schoenberg, B., Carr, A. C., Kutscher, A. H., & Zegarelli, E. V. (1971). Chronic Idiopathic Orolingual Pain. Psychogenesis of Burning Mouth. *New York State Journal of Medicine* (August): 1832–1837.

Schreber, D. G. M. (1858). *Kallipädie oder Erziehung zur Schönheit* [Callipedics or Education for Beauty]. Leipzig: Fleischer.

Schreber, D. P. (1988). *Memoirs of My Nervous Illness* (translated & edited by Ida Macalpine & Richard Hunter, with a new introduction by Samuel Weber). London: Harvard University Press.

Schroff, J. (1935). Burning Tongue. *Review of Gastroenterology, 2*: 347–350.

Schwartz, M. (1992). Reviewing the Review. *International Review of Psycho-Analysis, 19* (Special): 11–14.

Sennett, R. (1977). *The Fall of Public Man*. Cambridge: Cambridge University Press.

Sharpe, E. Freeman (1930). The Technique of Psycho-Analysis. Seven Lectures. In: *Collected Papers on Psycho-Analysis*. London: Hogarth, 1950.

Silverman, K. (1988). *The Acoustic Mirror: The Female Voice in Psychoanalysis and Cinema*. Bloomington/Indianapolis, IN: Indiana University Press.

Smith, J., & Kerrigan, W. (Eds.) (1987). *Images in Our Souls: Cavell, Psychoanalysis and Cinema*. Baltimore, MD, & London: The Johns Hopkins University Press.

Solnit, A. (1983). Anna Freud's Contribution to Child and Applied Analysis. *International Journal of Psycho-Analysis, 64*: 379–390

Solnit, A. J., & Newman, L. M. (1984). Anna Freud: The Child Expert. *Psychoanalytic Study of the Child, 39*: 45–63.

Spitz, R. (1956). Counter-Transference: Comments on Its Varying Role in the Analytic Situation. *Journal of the American Psychoanalytic Association, 4*: 256–265.

Spoto, D. (1982). *The Dark Side of Genius: The Life of Alfred Hitchcock*. Boston & Toronto: Little Brown.

Strouse, J. (1980). *Alice James*. New York: Houghton Mifflin.

Sulloway, F. (1986). *Freud under Analysis*. Equinox Television Film.

Sutherland, J. D. (1989). *Fairbairn's Journey into the Interior*. London: Free Association Books.

Tanner, T. (1967). *Hawthorne: Henry James*. London: Macmillan.

Taylor, G. J. (1989). *Psychosomatic Medicine and Contemporary Psychoanalysis*. New Haven, CT: International Universities Press.

THERIP (1993). Psychoanalysis at the University. *The Psychoanalysis Newsletter, Issue 12*.

THERIP (1994). *The T.H.E.R.I.P. Register.* London.

Thomä, H., & Kächele, H. (1987). *Psychoanalytic Practice, Vol. 1.* New York: Springer Verlag.

Thomas, R., Edgcumbe, R., Kennedy, H., Kawenoka, M., & Weitzner, L. (1966). Comments on Some Aspects of Self and Object Representation in a Group of Psychotic Children: An Application of Anna Freud's Diagnostic Profile. *Psychoanalytic Study of the Child, 21:* 527–580.

Truffaut, F. (1954). A Certain Tendency of the French Cinema. In: B. Nichols (Ed.), *Movies and Methods: An Anthology.* Berkeley, CA: University of California Press, 1976.

Tyson, P., & Tyson, R. L. (1990). *Psychoanalytic Theories of Development.* New Haven, CT: Yale University Press.

Varendonck, J. (1921). *The Psychology of Daydreams.* London: Allen & Unwin.

Wallace, E. (1983). *Freud and Anthropology: A History and Reappraisal.* New York: International Universities Press.

Wallerstein, R. (1984). Anna Freud: Radical Innovator and Staunch Conservative. *Psychoanalytic Study of the Child, 39:* 65–80.

Wallerstein, R. (1990). Foreword. In: P. Tyson & R. Tyson, *Psychoanalytic Theories of Development.* New Haven, CT: Yale University Press.

Wallerstein, R. (1992). Comments on Psychoanalysis, Pure and Applied. *International Review of Psycho-Analysis, 19* (Special): 1–6.

Wallis, R. (1979). Varieties of Psycho-salvation. *New Society, 50* (897–898): 649–651.

Wallis, R. (1984). *The Elementary Forms of the New Religious Life.* London: Routledge & Kegan Paul.

Wallis, R. (1985). Betwixt Therapy and Salvation: The Changing Form of the Human Potential Movement. In: R. K. Jones (Ed.), *Sickness and Sectarianism.* London: Gower.

Wharton, E. (1934). *A Backward Glance.* London: Century, 1987.

Wilson, B. (1976). *Contemporary Transformations of Religion.* London: Oxford University Press.

Wilson, E. (1952). *The Triple Thinkers.* New York: John Lehmann.

Wood, R. (1986). *Hollywood from Vietnam to Reagan.* New York: Columbia University Press.

Wood, R. (1989). *Hitchcock's Films Revisited.* London: Faber & Faber.

Wright, E. (1986). Modern Psychoanalytic Criticism. In: A. Jefferson & D. Robey (Eds.), *Modern Literary Theory: A Comparative Introduction*. London: Batsford.

Yorke, C. (1983). Anna Freud and the Psychoanalytic Study and Treatment of Adults. *International Journal of Psycho-Analysis*, *64*: 391–400.

Yorke, C., Wiseberg, S., & Freeman, T. (1989). *Development and Psychopathology: Studies in Psychoanalytic Psychiatry*. New Haven, CT: Yale University Press.

Young-Bruehl, E. (1988). *Anna Freud: A Biography*. New York: Summit Books.

Ziskin, D. E., & Moulton, R. (1946). Glossodynia. A Study of Idiopathic Orolingual Pain. *Journal of the American Dental Association*, *33*: 1422–1432.

INDEX

Abraham, H., 197, 217
Abraham, K., 55–57, 197, 217
Abram, J., 8, 217
abreactive therapy, 72
Adler, A., 54
adolescent genitality, 46
adolescent period of
    development, 28
aggression, child's, analysis of,
    30
aggressive wish, repressed, 130
aggressor, identification with,
    35, 82
Aichhorn, A., 19, 21, 22, 42, 51,
    217
Alexander, F., 131, 217
Alien, 201
All That Jazz, 201
Almansi, R., 202, 203, 217
"Altering-Eye" cinema, 200
Althusser, L., 200, 217
anality, 54, 147
anal phase, 45

analysis:
    "good-enough", 110
    training, 16, 95, 110
analyst:
    as idealized figure, 58
    and patient, relation between,
        64
Andreas-Salomé, L., 20, 21
Andrew, D., 199, 200, 218
Anna Freud Centre, 40
anti-libidinal ego, 67
anxiety, 23, 58, 69, 82, 104,
        123, 124, 139, 181, 201
    attacks emanating from, 35
    castration, 188
    children's, 57
    depressive, 61, 62, 73
        and manic-depressive
            states, 62
    hysteria, 64
    infantile, 62
    instinctual, defences against,
        34

anxiety *(continued)*
Klein's emphasis on, 37
objective, defences against, 34
persecutory, 61, 62, 73
psychotic, 61, 62, 63
separation, 57
state, 50, 130
superego, defences against,
34
appersonation, 116
applied psychoanalysis, 1, 9–13
Aziz, M., 176, 218

Bailie, R., xiv, 9, 10, 169–192
Baldwin, J., 48, 220
Balint, A., 96, 203, 218
Balint, M., 218
Basker, R. M., 129, 218
Baumgarten Children's Home,
18, 23
Beckford, J., 197, 218
Benvenuto, B., 218, 234
Bergman, I., 200
Bergstrom, J., 197, 218
Berliner, A., 10, 218
Bernfeld, S., 18, 21, 23
Bion, W. R., 96, 97, 103, 218
Blackmur, R. P., 171, 199, 218
Bleuler, E., 123, 124, 132, 219
Blind Study Group, 40
BMS: *see* burning mouth
syndrome
body–mind–body circuit, 131
borderline personality, 7, 40, 47,
50, 101, 103, 211
Bornstein, B., 29
breast–mother, oral–sadistic
attack on, 56
Breuer, J., 72, 75, 223
British object relations school,
3
British Psychoanalytical Society,
5, 41
Brittan, A., 176, 219
Brooke-Rose, C., 176, 219
Brown, D., 151, 219

Bunuel, L., 198
Burlingham, B., 20
Burlingham, D., 20, 21, 37, 38,
39, 40, 41, 43, 48, 52,
219
Burlingham, M., 20
burning mouth syndrome
(BMS), psychotherapeutic
approach to, 9, 129–141
Burton, R., 212

Cameron, I., 127, 221
Carr, A. C., 130, 231
castration anxiety, 188
catatonic sign, 115, 116
cathartic therapy, 72, 204
Cawley, R. H., 125, 227
character neurosis, 58, 62, 119,
120
Charney, M., 196, 219
Chasseguet-Smirgel, J., 9, 144,
193, 219
chemotherapeutic agents, 115
in treatment of schizophrenia,
8
chemotherapy, 115, 116, 117,
126, 127
Chien Andalou, Un, 198
child:
analysis, 5, 16, 17, 19, 21,
30, 45, 52
indications and
contraindications for, 50
termination in, 50
training in, 49
development of:
assessment of, 5, 45–48
and early experiences, 152
environmental influences
on, 25
and external world, 16
mental, effect of mother on,
54, 56
stages in, 28
education, vs. child care, 25
law, 51

play of, and free association, 30

psychoanalytic study of, 5

removal of from parents, 51

childhood:

pathology, assessment of, 41

symptomatology, classification of, 50

Cihlarz, J., 18

cinema, and psychoanalysis, 10, 193–215

clinical examples:

acting out in transference, 88–89

aggressiveness, roots of in childhood pathology, 35–36

burning mouth syndrome, 132–139

causes of children's behaviour, 24–25

childhood sexual experience, and defence mechanisms, 31

countertransference:

in clinical setting, and complexes in therapist, 98–101

reactions, in psychiatric ward, 105–108

as tool in analysis, 101–103

endopsychic object relations, 65–66

floating transference, 82–85

identification, and delusional ideas, 120–121

id transference, 90–91

loss and mourning, 44

masturbatory phantasies, 124

negative transference as resistance, 87–89

power of defensive operations in child, 31–33

regression, 47

religious delusions, 154–159

reverse transference, 91–93

schizophrenia, end state in, 117–118

sexual drives in puberty, 27–28

significance of dreams, 68–69

superego transference, 89–90

transference dream, 80–81

unconscious homosexual wishes, and psychic dissolution, 121–123

unresolved conflict between patient's projection, and therapist's inner reality, 100–101

use of The Field in psychoanalysis, 205–210

closed system, 71, 131

intrapsychic, 71

Coles, R., 18, 22, 42, 53, 219

consolation, 152, 168

search for, 144, 145

containment, 103

of projection, 97

Contemporary Freudian group, in British Psychoanalytical Society, 5

Controversial Discussions, 41

conversion hysteria, 64

Couch, A., 211

couch technique, 70

countertransference, 6, 7

clinical aspects of, 94–113

in clinical setting, 98–104

and empathy, 110

managing, 109–234

permanent, 104

phenomena, 109

in psychiatric ward, 105–109

reaction:

acute, 104

permanent, 104

as tool, 101–104

Dali, S., 198

Dare, C., 231

Davenport J. C., 185, 218
Dayan, D., 200, 219
day-dream, 23, 215
death instinct, 37, 49, 58, 61,
  73
death wish, 26, 89, 123, 126,
  139
deep interpretation, 21, 22
defence, analysis of, 29–37
de Lauretis, T., 200, 219
delusion, 10, 98, 115, 116, 117,
  120, 126, 148
  persecutory, 35, 60, 124, 125,
  156
  religious, childhood origin of,
  154–159
  wish, 119
Deming, J., 37
demonological neurosis, 161
depressive position, 61, 148
depth psychology, 11
Dervin, D., 196, 211, 219
detrimental alternative, 51
development, assessment of, 5,
  45–48
  mental, effect of mother on, 54
developmental lines, 40, 45, 46
developmental principle [Freud],
  5
developmental processes,
  somatic, 59
developmental psychoanalysis,
  49–52
developmental psychopathology,
  and infantile neurosis, 49
Dewey, J., 18
diagnostic interview, 48
Dora, 76
dream, 43, 44, 63, 72, 73, 76,
  80, 92, 93, 120, 131,
  187, 188, 213
  analysis, 6, 57, 197
  manifest content of, and
  endopsychic situation, 69
  process, role of film in, 211
  -screen, 201

significance of, 68
theory of, Freud's, 215
Dresden, S., 198, 219
drive:
  instinctual, 26, 29, 46
  regression, 47
  structural model, 15, 16
  theory, 16
Dunbar, H. F., 131, 219
Dupee, F. W., 176, 180, 187,
  188, 219
Durgnat, R., 201, 220
Dyer, R., 38, 41, 220

Eastwood, C., 204
eating disturbance, rooted in
  mother–child
  relationship, 39
Eberwein, R., 201, 220
Edel, L., 183, 184, 185, 220
Edgcumbe, R., 45, 48, 52, 220,
  233
ego, 3, 6, 16, 28, 29, 34, 35, 36,
  39, 60, 63, 81, 82, 89,
  150, 162, 166, 170
  analysis of, 30
  anti-libidinal, 67
  central, 67, 68, 71
  defensive function of, 23
  development, 45, 47, 48
  functions of, 30, 46, 184
  and id, interactions between,
  46
  -ideal, 151, 152
  infantile, 30, 61
  splitting of, 67
  introjecting parents, 149
  libidinal, 67, 68, 69, 71
  and object structures, 73
  psychology, 4
  regression, 47
  split in, 65
  in schizophrenias, 60
  structure, 67, 68
  -syntonicity, 33
Eissler, R. S., 219, 220, 225

Eitingon, M., 19, 20, 21
Ekins, R., xiii, xv, 1–13, 9, 10,
        193–215, 212, 220
Ellenberger, H., 3, 220
Emerson, E., 180
end state, 119, 126
    types of, 117
Engel, G. L., 131, 140, 220
English School (Kleinians), 34
envy:
    analyst as object of, 62
    and death instinct, 61
evil, representation of, 162–165

Fairbairn, W. R. D., xiv, 5, 6, 54,
        64–73, 74, 116, 220, 221
father
    child's identification with,
        150–151
    child's relation to, 26, 160
    influence of, on child's
        development, 56, 149–
        151
    transference, 28
Federn, E., 175, 230
Fellini, F., 200
Feminist cinema, 200
Fenichel, O., 42, 72, 81, 131,
        140, 221
Ferenczi, S., 18
Field, The, 196, 204–210
film, role of, in psychoanalytic
        process, 193–215
Fine, B., 5, 221
"fine weather", 77
Floyd, N., 206, 208, 221
Fox, H., 129, 221
free association, 22, 70, 76
    and child's play, 30
free-floating responsiveness, 97
Freeman, R., xiv, 6, 8, 9, 56, 59,
        74–93, 129–141, 221
Freeman, T., xiv, xv, 6, 7, 8, 17,
        48, 52, 54–73, 115–128,
        212, 221, 234
Freud, A., xiii–xiv, 5, 15–53, 78,

82, 193–195, 210, 219–
        221
    and M. Klein, theoretical
        dispute between, 21–23,
        37, 41
Freud, E., 197, 217
Freud, Martha, 18
Freud, Minna, 18
Freud, Sigmund, xiii, 2–11, 15–
        21, 43, 49, 62, 72–73,
        120, 175, 196–204, 211,
        223–225
    cultural writings of, 10
    on the death instint, 61
    and concept of
        countertransference, 94
    and concept of transference,
        74–81, 89, 117
    and content of dreams, 69,
        215–216
    on defences, and type of
        illness, 33–34
    developmental theory of, 29
    metapsychology of, 3
    on normal and abnormal
        mental life, 54, 55, 58
    on psychoanalysis and
        academic education, 193–
        195
    on religion, and Oedipus
        complex, 143–168
    and training analyses, 110
    and unconscious phantasies,
        176
Freud, Sophie, 18
Freud, W. E., 48, 223
Friedberg, A., 197, 225
Friedlander, K., 40
Friedmann, M., 40
Frosh, S., 144, 225

Gabbard, G., 197, 198, 201,
        204, 225
Gabbard, K., 196, 197, 198,
        200, 201, 204, 225, 226
Gaddini, E., 131, 139, 140, 225

Gehrie, M., 193, 226
Glover, E., 79, 80, 82, 131, 140, 226
Goldberger, A., 39
Goldstein, J., 51, 52, 226
Greenberg, H., 15, 16, 196, 200, 226
Greenson, R. R., 77, 226
Grosskurth, P., 22, 37, 226
Grunberger, B., 144, 219
Grushka, M., 129, 130, 226
guilt, and manic-depressive depressions, 55

Habermas, J., 168, 226
Haitzmann, C., 160, 161, 162
hallucination, 116, 117, 120, 148, 156, 161
Hammaren, M., 130, 226
Hampstead:
   Child Therapy Clinic, 40, 41, 42, 48, 49
   Group, 41
   Index, 38, 41
   Training Course, 49
   War Nurseries, 38, 39, 40
Hartmann, H., 20
Heath, S., 200, 219, 226
Heimann, P., 96, 104, 226
Hellman, I., 40
Hill, J. C., 16, 38, 227
Hitchcock, A., 199, 202, 203, 211, 212, 227
Hoffer, W., 19, 21
Holder, A., 74, 79, 231
Holland, N., 200, 227
homosexual wishes, unconscious, 85
hospital practice, treatment of schizophrenias in, psychoanalytic approach to, 115–128
Hug-Hellmuth, H., 19, 227
Hugoson, A., 129, 130, 226, 227
human potential movement, 144

hypnotherapy, 75, 130
hysteria, 34, 66, 77, 79
   anxiety, 64
   conversion, 64, 140
hysterical amnesic state, 65

id, 6, 28–30, 33, 34, 36, 39, 81, 89
   development, 45
   and ego, interactions between, 46
   impulse, repressed, 82
   transference, 90–91
idealization, 58, 63
Identical Twins Study Group, 40
Independent group, in British Psychoanalytical Society, 5
infant, experiences of, effect of, 146–151
infantile neurosis, 17, 47, 49, 50
infantile origins of religious experience, 143–168
infantile psychopathology, classification of, 50
infantilism, 47
instinctual drive, 26, 29, 46
internal saboteur, 67, 68, 69, 71
International Psychoanalytical Association (IPA), 8, 19, 49, 52
interpretation, deep, 21, 22
introjection, 34, 35, 55, 59, 61
Isaacs, S., 58, 227
isolation, 33

Jackson, E., 37
Jackson, M., 125, 227
Jackson Nursery, 37–38, 39, 41
Jacobson, E., 16
James, H., xiv–xv, 10, 227
   The Turn of the Screw, psychoanalytic analysis of, 169–192
James, H., Sr., 184, 190, 192
James, M., 190

James, W., 179, 180, 184, 191, 227
Jaws, 162
Jones, E., 211, 227
Jung, C. G., 54
Jurassic Park, 162

Kächele, H., 72, 233
Kaplan, E., 196, 198, 227
Katan, M., 120, 169, 227
Kaufmann, W., 3, 228
Kawenoka, M., 74, 79, 231, 233
Kawin, B., 201, 228
Keane, J. B., 206
Kennedy, H., 233, 234
Kennedy, R., 198, 218
Kernberg, O. F., 16, 97, 103, 228
Kerrigan, W., 196, 201, 232
Kimbrough, R., 171, 182, 228
Kinder, M., 201, 228
King, P., 5, 228
Klein, M, xiv, 5, 6, 16, 17, 36, 50, 54–64, 72–73, 80, 116, 228
and A. Freud, theoretical dispute between, 21–23, 37, 41
Kleinian group, in British Psychoanalytical Society, 5
Kleinian metapsychology, 3
Kohon, G., 194, 228
Kohut, H., 4, 16
Kolker, R., 200, 228
Kris, E., 41, 42, 49, 50, 228
Kris, M., 220
Kuhn, A., 200, 228
Kut-Rosenfeld, S., 40
Kutscher, A. H., 130, 231

Lacan, J., 194, 198, 200
Lady in the Dark, 197
L'Age d'Or, 198
Lamb, A. B., 130, 228
Lamey, P. J., 130, 228

Landauer, E., 20
Lantos, B., 40
Lasch, C., 144, 211, 229
latency period, 28, 45
    characteristics of, 26
Laufer, M., 48, 229
Lewin, B., 201, 229
libidinal ego, 67, 68, 69, 71
libido, 26, 29, 43
life instinct, 58
Limentani, A., 52, 229
literature, and psychoanalysis, 169–192
Little, M., 110, 229
LITTLE HANS, 19, 23
loss:
    dynamic interpretations of, 43
    and mourning, 44
    traumas of, 167

MacCabe, C., 200, 229
Mack Brunswick, R., 42
MacLean, G., 19, 229
Mahler, M., 16
Main, T. F., 105, 229
manic defence, 60, 61, 62, 63, 73
manic-depressive depressions, and guilt, 55
manic-depressive state, depressive anxieties in, 62
Marx, K., 168
Marxist cinema, 200
Mayne, J., 200, 229
McGhie, A., 127, 221
memories, forgotten, and role of transference, 75
mental activity, nature of, 72
Metapsychological or Diagnostic Profile, 48
Metz, C., 196, 200, 229
Middle Group, 3, 41
mind–body continuum, 131
Minkowski, E., 120, 229
Mitchell, S. A., 15, 16, 226

Monaco, J., 202, 229
Montgomery Hyde, H., 180, 182,
    183, 229
mother:
  –child relationship, 44
  child's desire for possession
    of, 26
  child's identification with,
    149–150
  relationship with, 70
  rejecting, 43, 44
  role of:
    in child's development, 56
    during infancy, 149–151
  splitting of, 57, 66
  as whole object
    representation, 56
Motherless Children Project, 40
Moulton, R., 130, 234
mourning, and loss, 44
Mulvey, L., 196, 198, 229
Murray, J., xiii, 5, 15–53
mysticism, 165, 167

Nagera, H., 48, 223
neurosis, 3, 7, 23, 34, 49, 58,
    62, 64, 65, 78, 103, 124,
    176
  character, 58, 62, 119, 120
  demonological, 161
  infantile, 17, 47, 49, 50
  obsessional, 34, 56, 64, 77,
    160
  organ, 131
  vs. psychosis, 20
  speech, 182
  transference, 3, 21, 62, 78,
    79, 80, 81, 82, 125, 205
  traumatic theory of, 72
  and unacceptable wishes, 72
Newman, L. M., 52, 232
Niederland, W., 156, 157, 158,
    229
Nietzsche, F., 168
normality, nature of, 25
Nunberg, H., 175, 230

object:
  constancy, 148
  good, introjected whole, 60
  internal, anal expulsion of, 55
  lost, introjection of, 55
  part, 55, 59, 60, 61, 62
    breast as, 56, 59
    concept of, 56
  relations, 67
    endopsychic, 54, 65, 69,
      70, 71
    theory, 5, 64, 116, 201
obsessional neurosis, 34, 56,
    64, 77, 160
obsessive–compulsive symptom,
    57
"oceanic" feeling, 165, 166
O'Connor, S., xiv, 94–113
Oedipus complex:
  and depressive position, 61
  Freud's theory of, 2
  and girl's relation to father, 60
  and infantile religious
    experience, 10, 143–168
  timing of, 21, 37, 54
omnipotence, 60, 63, 73, 119,
    159
  phantasies of, 64
  of thoughts, 151
oral incorporation, 55, 147
orality, 147
oral phase, 45, 56
oral-sadism, 55
oral–sadistic attack, on breast–
    mother, 56
organ neurosis, 131
Oudart, J.-P., 200, 230
Oxford University Drama
    Society, 212

Pabst, G. W., 10, 197
paranoia, 154
paranoid–schizoid position, 60,
    61, 147, 201
parasuicidal behaviour, 105,
    108

pathology:
  assessment of, 48
  mental, effect of mother on, 54
  and normality, difference
    between, 23
patient:
  deluded, 98–100
  difficult, 104, 105
Paul, R., 10, 230
Paul, St., 163
Payer-Thurn, R., 160
pedagogy, and psychoanalysis,
  28
Pedder, J., 151, 219
Penley, C., 196, 198, 230
Persaud, R., 144, 230
persecutory anxiety, 62
persecutory delusion, 35, 60,
  124, 125, 156
personality:
  developmental defects in, 50
  multiple, 65, 67
  tripartite division of, 28
phallic phase, 45
phantasies, 19, 23, 52
  of body, 131
  destructive, 58, 60, 61, 62
  of omnipotence, 64
  oral-sadistic, 55
  sexual, 65, 124, 130
  unconscious, 56–60, 62, 63,
    73, 176
  as innate, 58
phantasy play, 23
phobia, 23, 57, 162, 197
Piaget, J., 17
play:
  as child's free association, 22
  symbolic content of, 22
    interpretation of, 57
  technique, therapeutic, 57
pleasure principle, 49, 73
Porter, R., 158, 159, 230
positive transference, 22
pre-latency period of
  development, 28

pre-Oedipal attachment, 147
pre-Oedipal distortion, 148
pre-Oedipal stage, 147
primary process, 120
projection, 34, 35, 43, 57–59,
    95, 97, 100, 104, 109,
    153, 158, 161, 163, 168
  mechanism of, 36
projective identification, 36, 60–
    63, 96, 127
psychiatric ward,
    countertransference in,
    105–109
psychic regression, 124
psychoanalysis:
  vs. analytical psychotherapy,
    8
  applied, 1, 9–13, 193
    vs. pure, 9
  and literature, 169–192
  and pedagogy, 28
  vs. psychoanalytic
    psychotherapy, 8
  pure, 9, 193
  teaching of, role of film in,
    201–203
  theory of, factors comprising,
    2
psychoanalytic approach to
    treatment of
    schizophrenias, 115–
    128
psychoanalytic process, role of
    film in, 203–210
psycho-biography, 199
psychological parent, 51
psychology, depth, 11
psycho-salvation, 143, 144
psychosexual history, 95
psychosexual stages, 26
psychosis, 7, 61, 116, 120,
    158
  manic-depressive, 55, 60
  vs. neurosis, 20
  schizophrenic, 115, 116, 125
  transference, 125

psychosomatic disorder, 9, 50
psychotherapeutic approach
    to, 129–141
psychotherapist, sex of,
    relevance of, 81
psychotic state, 148
psychotrophic drug, 130
puberty:
    anxieties of, 37
    ego and id in, 36

Rappen, U., 19, 229
Rayner, E., 5, 194, 230
reaction formation, 26, 33
"realist" cinema, 200
reality, psychic, 60, 68, 99, 116
reality principle, 166
Rear Window, 202–203
regression, 33, 45, 166, 203
    drive, 47
    ego, 47
    in normal development, 46
    permanent, 47
    psychic, 124
    in schizophrenias, 124
    on side of ego, 47
    superego, 47
    temporary, 46
Reich, A., 104, 109, 230
Reik, T., 20
Reisenberg-Malcolm, R., 63, 64,
    230
religious experience, infantile
    origins of, 10, 143–168
religious genocide, 163
repetition compulsion, 49, 72,
    78
Reppen, J., 196, 219
repression, 33, 72, 73, 158
    of bad object, 67
    pathogenic nature of, 2
resistance, 63, 67, 72, 75–79,
    81–83, 90, 92, 94, 96,
    104, 110, 119, 123–
    124
    analysis of, 6
    internal, 7

negative transference as, 6,
    87–89
positive transference as, 6,
    85–87
unconscious, 70, 75
responsiveness, free-floating, 97
reversal, 34, 187
reverse transference, 91–93
Richards, B., 144, 230
Richardson, J. T., 165, 230
Rickman, J., 194, 230
Ricoeur, P., 168, 230
Rieff, P., 144, 230
Roazen, P., 3, 7, 230
role-responsiveness, 97
Rolland, R., 165, 166
Rose, J., 196, 230
Rose, N., 144, 231
Rosen, P., 200, 231
Rosenfeld, E., 21, 40
Rothman, W., 200, 231
Royal Society of Medicine,
    Psychiatry Section, 41

Sacher-Masoch, L. von, 199,
    231
Sachs, H., 197
sadism, infantile, 59
Sandler, J., xiii–xv, 7, 8, 74, 79,
    97, 194, 231
Santayana, G., 168, 231
Sarris, A., 199, 231
Schilder, P., 20
schizoid mechanism, 60–62
schizoid personality, 64
schizophrenia, 56, 59–62, 65
    ego split in, 60
    and psychoanalysis, 8
    psychoanalytic approach to
        treatment of, in hospital
        practice, 115–128
    treatment of, 8
schizophrenic psychosis, 115,
    116, 125
Schmale A. H., 131, 140, 220
Schneider, I., 197, 198, 231
Schoenberg, B., 130, 231

Schreber, D. G. M., 157, 231
Schreber, D. P., 154–159, 161,
    232
Schroff, J., 129, 232
Schwartz, M., 9, 193, 232
Secrets of a Soul, 10, 197
self:
    -analysis, 43, 103, 110
    psychology [Kohut], 4, 201
    turning against, 34
Sennett, R., 144, 232
separation anxiety, 57
Sharpe, E. Freeman, 193, 195,
    232
Sheridan, Jim, 206
sign, and signified, split
    between, 116
Silverman, K., 196, 198, 232
Smith, J., 196, 201, 232
Solnit, A. J., 51, 52, 220, 226,
    232
somatization, 131
Spanish Inquisition, 163
speech neurosis, 182
Spielberg, S., 162
Spitz, R., 110, 232
splitting, 58–63, 65–67, 70, 73
    of ego, 60, 66, 69
    infantile, 67
    systematic, 116
Spoto, D., 199, 232
Stardust Memories, 201
Steiner, R., 5, 228
Sterba, E., 23
Stross, J., 38, 40
Strouse, J., 191, 192, 232
structural model, 16, 81
Strudee D. W., 159, 218
sublimation, 19, 26, 34, 154
suicide, 109, 122
Sulloway, F., 194, 232
superego, 6, 28–30, 36, 46, 69,
    81, 82, 152, 162
    anxiety, defences against, 34
    child's, 21
    development of, 34, 37, 48
    and morality, 35

emergence of, 151
regression, 47
severity of, 35, 151, 211
as successor of parents, 28
transference, 81, 89–90
surrealism, 198
Surrealist school, 198
Sutherland, J. D., 5, 232
Sweetzer, A., 20
Sweetzer, H., 20

Tanner, T., 183, 232
Taylor, G. J., 140, 232
technologies of self, 143
Thomä, H., 72, 233
Thomas, R., 48, 233
Thorstensson, B., 129, 227
Three Women, 201
topographical model of mind, 6
Torney, P., xiv, 9, 10, 143–168
transference, 3, 26, 29, 35, 71,
    94–97, 103, 104, 117,
    120, 124, 208, 216
    acting in, 33, 79
    acting out in, 87, 88
    analysis of, 6, 82
    concept:
        development of theory of,
            75–82
        and role of, 74–93
    of defence, 82, 91–93
    dream, 80, 81
    ego, 81
    father, 28, 81, 96
    floating, 6, 72, 79, 80, 82–85,
        86, 89
    hate, 62
        unconscious, 72
    id, 81, 90–91
    interpretation, 64, 71
        here-and-now, 63, 72
    of libidinal impulses, 33
    negative, 22, 30, 77, 79, 82,
        87, 88
        interpretation of, 58
        vs. positive, 77
    as resistance, 6, 87–89

transference (continued)
  neurosis, 3, 17, 21, 62, 78–
    82, 125, 205
  of patient's defences, 33
  phantasies, 63, 64
  phenomena, types of, 33
  positive, 22, 85, 86
    vs. negative, 77
    as resistance, 6, 85–87
  as resistance, 94
  reverse, 82, 91–93
  superego, 81, 89–90
  in terms of psychic structures,
    6
  working, 119
Truffaut, F., 199, 233
Turn of the Screw, The [Henry
  James], 10, xiv–xv
  psychoanalytic analysis of,
    169–192
Tyson, P., 16, 233
Tyson, R. L., 16, 233

unconscious, the, 25, 29, 94,
    150–153, 170, 171, 173,
    175, 177, 196–198
unconscious envy, 60, 63
unconscious mental process, 2,
    58, 153
unconscious phantasies:
  destructive, 58, 62
  transference, 63
undoing, 33
university:
  curriculum, inclusion of
    psychoanalysis in, 11,
    193, 194, 196
  Film and Media Studies
    departments, 199
  psychoanalytic approaches to
    film in, 200, 204

Varendonck, J., 18, 233
Venus in Furs, 198, 199
Vienna Psychoanalytical Society,
    18, 19, 20, 23, 40

Training Institute of, 21
Vienna school of child analysis,
    22
Viereck, G. S., 164

Wagner-Jauregg, J. von, 20
Wallace, E., 167, 233
Wallerstein, R., 3, 4, 9, 52, 193,
    233
Wallis, R., 143, 144, 233
Wednesday seminar [A. Klein],
    40
Weitzner, L., 233
Wharton, E., 179, 233
whole object representation,
    mother as, 56
Wilson, B., 143, 233
Wilson, E., 169, 233
Wiseberg, S., 7, 234
wish, 54, 73, 82
  aggressive, 130
  death, 26, 89, 123, 126, 139
  delusion, defensive, 119
  fulfilment, delusions of, 119
  homosexual, 85, 121
  incestuous, 126
    father/daughter, 19
  intolerable, 159
  nature of, 72
  phantasies, 119, 125
  repressed, 131
  sexual, 85, 91, 121, 123, 140
  unacceptable, 23, 65, 72, 82,
    125
  unconscious, 97
witch trials, 163
Wood, R., 201, 233
Wright, E., 10, 234

Yale Child Study Centre, 51
Yorke, C., 7, 52, 234
Young-Bruehl, E., 5, 18, 19, 20,
    234

Zegarelli, E. V., 130, 231
Ziskin, D. E., 130, 234